A
SCOTT
Reading
STREET

Author's Purpose

Cause and Effect

Classify and Categorize

Compare and Contrast

Details and Facts

Draw Conclusions

Graphic Sources

Main Idea and Details

Sequence

Steps in a Process

Literary Elements

A Comprehension Handbook

Author's Purpose

Authors write to inform or entertain

To Inform

To Entertain

Cause and Effect

Classify and Categorize

Which toys belong together?

Space ships

Action figures

Compare and Contrast

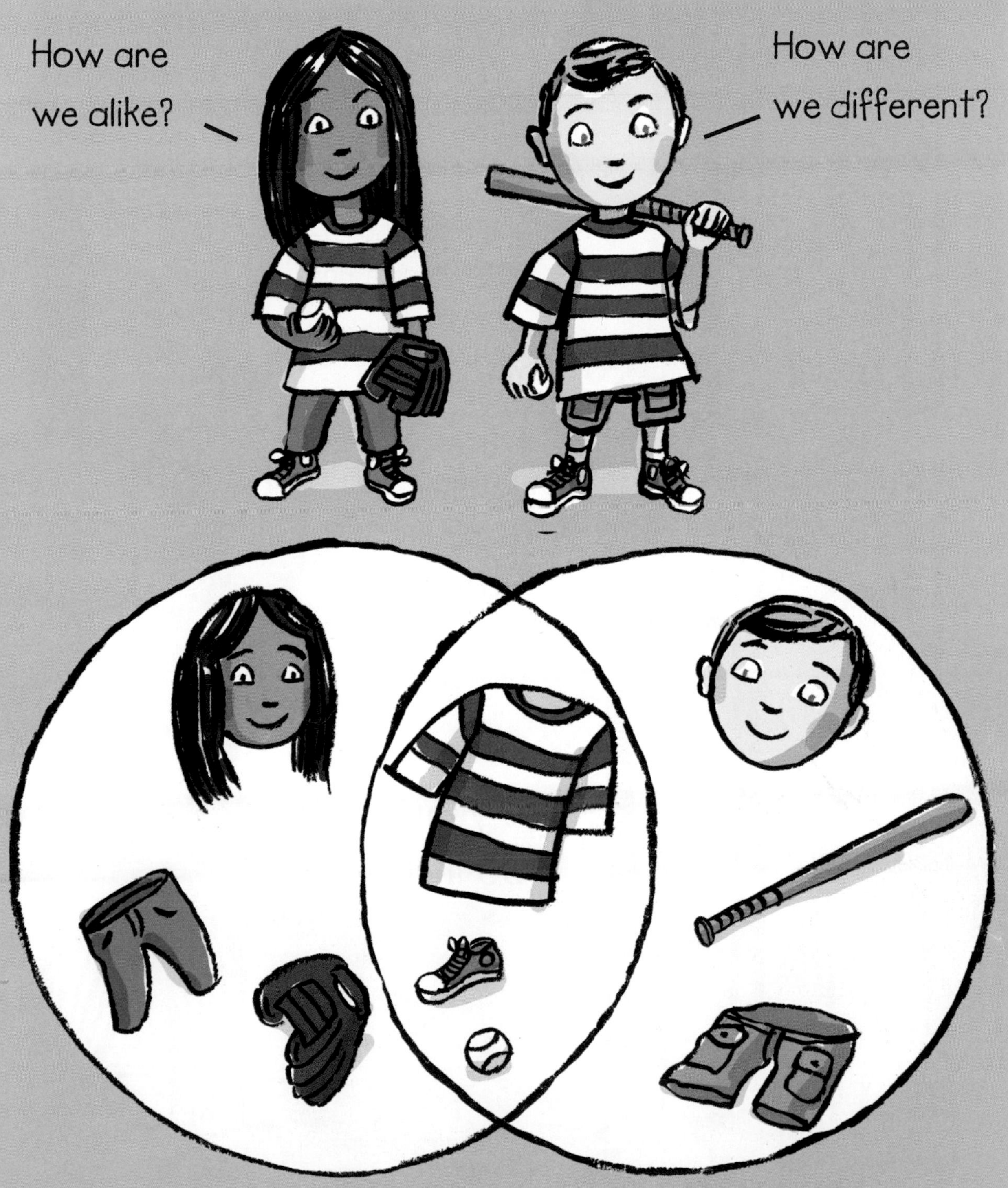

Details and Facts

Draw Conclusions

Use what you already know to help you understand what is happening.

Graphic Sources

Time Line

Circle Graph

How We All Get There

20%

40%

10%

30%

SCHOOL

Main Idea and Details

Main Idea

What is the selection all about?

Details

Sequence

What happens first, next, and last?

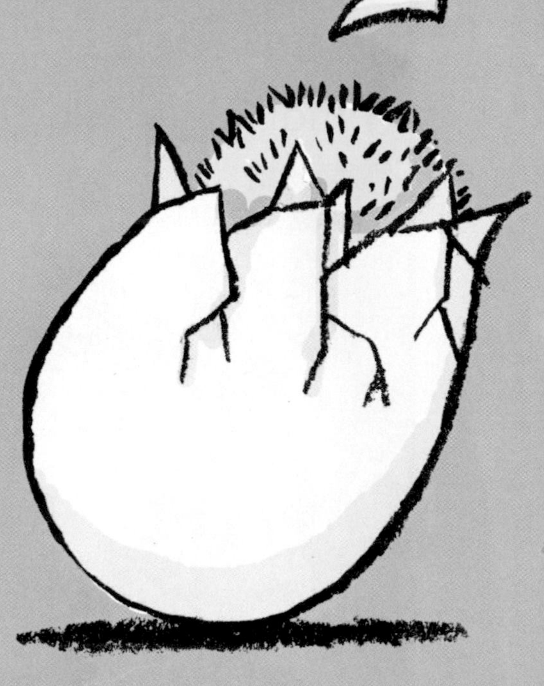

Steps in a Process

1

2

3

4

Literary Elements

Characters

Plot

Beginning

Middle

End

What happens in the beginning, middle, and end of the story?

Problem/Solution
Problem
Solution
Setting
Where and when does the story take place?
Theme
What is the big idea in the story?

ISBN-13: 978-0-328-36589-0
ISBN-10: 0-328-36589-0

1 2 3 4 5 6 7 8 9 10 V063 17 16 15 14 13 12 11 10 09 08

Program Authors

Peter Afflerbach
Camille Blachowicz
Candy Dawson Boyd
Wendy Cheyney
Connie Juel
Edward Kame'enui
Donald Leu
Jeanne Paratore
Sam Sebesta
Deborah Simmons
Alfred Tatum
Sharon Vaughn
Susan Watts Taffe
Karen Kring Wixson

Glenview, Illinois • Boston, Massachusetts • Mesa, Arizona
Shoreview, Minnesota • Upper Saddle River, New Jersey

Exploration

What can we learn from exploring new places and things?

Unit Opener 22

Build Language 24
High Frequency Words 26

realistic fiction/social studies
The Twin Club 28
by Ina Cumpiano; illustrated by Jana Christy

poetry/social studies
1st Day of School, 179th Day of School 48
by Jenny Whitehead

Writing and Conventions TRAIT Conventions 50
Grammar: Sentences 51

Build Language 52
High Frequency Words 54

expository nonfiction/science
Exploring Space with an Astronaut 56
by Patricia J. Murphy

expository nonfiction/science
A Trip to Space Camp 72
by Ann Weil

Writing and Conventions TRAIT Sentences 76
Grammar: Subject 77

Build Language 78
High Frequency Words 80

realistic fiction/science
Henry and Mudge and the Starry Night 82
by Cynthia Rylant; illustrated by Suçie Stevenson

riddles/social studies
Where Can We Camp? 100
by Joan Holub; illustrated by Rob McClurcan

Writing and Conventions TRAIT Organization 104
Grammar: Predicates 105

Build Language 106
High Frequency Words 108

narrative nonfiction/social studies
Sailing in the Wind 110
by Tina Fakhrid-Deen; illustrated by Paule Trudel

New Literacies online reference sources/social studies
Magnets 126
by Jo Knowl

Writing and Conventions TRAIT Word Choice 130
Grammar: Statements and Questions 131

Build Language 132
High Frequency Words 134

play/social studies
The Strongest One 136
from *Pushing Up the Sky* by Joseph Bruchac; illustrated by David Diàz

expository nonfiction/science
Anteaters 156
by John Jacobs

Writing and Conventions TRAIT Organization 160
Grammar: Commands and Exclamations 161

Picture It! A Comprehension Handbook **PI•1– PI•13**

Working Together

THE BIG ? How can we work together?

Unit Opener 162

Build Language 164
High Frequency Words 166

narrative nonfiction/social studies
Tara and Tiree, Fearless Friends 168
by Andrew Clements; illustrated by Scott Gustafson

photo essay/social studies
Rescue Dogs 186
by Rena Moran

Writing and Conventions TRAIT Voice 190
Grammar: Nouns 191

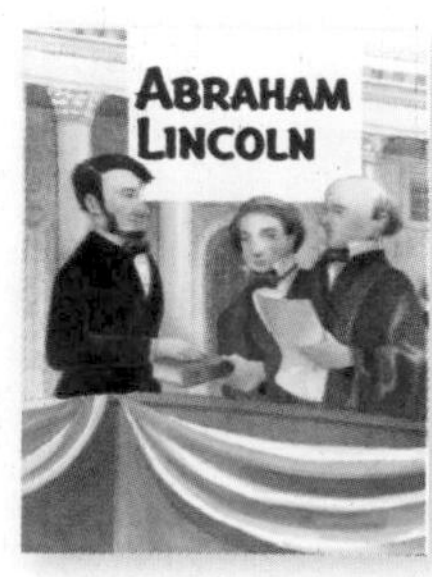

Build Language 192
High Frequency Words 194

biography/social studies
Abraham Lincoln 196
by Delores Malone; illustrated by Stephen Costanza

poetry/social studies
Lincoln 214
by Nancy Byrd Turner

Writing and Conventions TRAIT Focus/Ideas 216
Grammar: Proper Nouns 217

Build Language 218

High Frequency Words 220

expository nonfiction/science

Scarcity 222
by Janeen R. Adil

New Literacies **web site/social studies**

Goods and Services 238

Writing and Conventions TRAIT Word Choice 242

Grammar: Singular and Plural Nouns 243

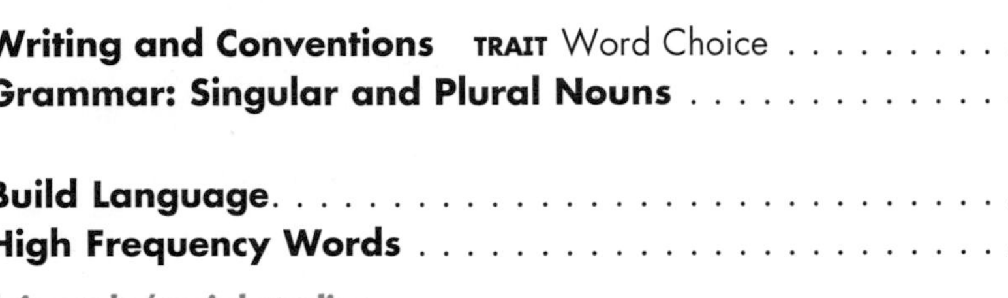

Build Language 244

High Frequency Words 246

fairy tale/social studies

The Bremen Town Musicians 248
from *Easy-to-Read Folk and Fairy Tale Plays*
by Carol Puglianos Martin; illustrated by Jon Goodell

New Literacies **web site/social studies**

Animals Helping Animals 268

Writing and Conventions TRAIT Focus/Ideas 272

Grammar: Plural Nouns That Change Spelling 273

Build Language 274

High Frequency Words 276

fable/social studies

One Good Turn Deserves Another 278
told by Judy Sierra; illustrated by Will Terry

fable/social studies

The Lion and the Mouse 296
retold by Claire Daniels; illustrated by Dan Andreasen

Writing and Conventions TRAIT Sentences 300

Grammar: Possessive Nouns 301

Picture It! A Comprehension Handbook **PI•1– PI•13**

Creative Ideas

What does it mean to be creative?

Unit Opener 302

Build Language 304
High Frequency Words 306

animal fantasy/science
Pearl and Wagner: Two Good Friends 308
by Kate McMullan; illustrated by R.W. Alley

expository nonfiction/science
Robots at Home 328
from *Robots* by Clive Gifford

Writing and Conventions TRAIT Voice 330
Grammar: Verbs 331

Build Language 332
High Frequency Words 334

realistic fiction/social studies
Dear Juno 336
by Soyung Pak; illustrated by Susan Kathleen Hartung

expository nonfiction/social studies
Saying It Without Words: Signs and Symbols 356
by Arnulf K. Esterer and Louise A. Esterer

Writing and Conventions TRAIT Focus/Ideas 358
Grammar: Verbs with Singular and Plural Nouns 359

Build Language 360
High Frequency Words 362

folk tale/social studies
Anansi Goes Fishing 364
retold by Eric A. Kimmel; illustrated by Janet Stevens

poetry
Do spiders stick to their own webs? 386
by Amy Goldman Koss

Writing and Conventions TRAIT Conventions 388
Grammar: Verbs for Present, Past, and Future 389

Build Language 390
High Frequency Words 392

realistic fiction/social studies
Rosa and Blanca 394
by Joe Hayes; illustrated by José Ortega

fable/social studies
The Crow and the Pitcher 408
retold by Eric Blair

Writing and Conventions TRAIT Word Choice 412
Grammar: More About Verbs 413

Build Language 414
High Frequency Words 416

biography/science
A Weed Is a Flower 418
by Aliki

New Literacies **search engines/science**
What's Made from Corn 442

Writing and Conventions TRAIT Organization 446
Grammar: Verbs—*Am, Is, Are, Was,* and *Were* 447

Glossary 448
Tested Word List 456
California English/Language Arts Standards 460

Picture It! A Comprehension Handbook **PI•1– PI•13**

Unit 1

Get Online!

PearsonSuccessNet.com

See It!

- Concept Talk Video
- Background Building Audio Slide Show
- *Picture It!* Animation
- e-Books

Hear It!

- Amazing Words *Sing with Me*
- Selection Snapshot and Response
- Paired Selection e-Text
- Grammar Jammer
- e-Books

Do It!

- Online Journal
- Story Sort
- New Literacies Activity
- Success Tracker

Exploration

THE BIG ?

What can we learn from exploring new places and things?

The Twin Club REALISTIC FICTION

How are the places the boys live and visit the same and different?

Paired Selection
1st Day of School, 179th Day of School POETRY

Exploring Space with an Astronaut EXPOSITORY NONFICTION

What will you find out about space from an astronaut?

Paired Selection
A Trip to Space Camp EXPOSITORY NONFICTION

Henry and Mudge and the Starry Night REALISTIC FICTION

What will Henry and Mudge find on a starry night?

Paired Selection
Where Can We Camp? RIDDLES

Sailing in the Wind NARRATIVE NONFICTION

How did it feel to cross an ocean alone in a boat?

Paired Selection
Magnets ONLINE REFERENCE SOURCE

The Strongest One PLAY

What does Little Red Ant learn about being strong?

Paired Selection
Anteaters EXPOSITORY NONFICTION

Let's Talk About
Exploration

LS1.0 Students listen critically and respond appropriately to oral communication. They speak in a manner that guides the listener to understand important ideas by using proper phrasing, pitch, and modulation.

Sí se puede!

Words to Read

friends
beautiful
front
someone
somewhere
country

G1R1.11 Read common, irregular sight words (e.g., *the, have, said, come, give, of*).

Read the Words

My friends moved to a beautiful home in the woods. Little animals come right up to their front door. Someone, somewhere, might like a different place in the country better, but I don't see why they would.

Genre: Realistic Fiction
Realistic fiction is a made-up story that could happen in real life. Now read about two boys who start a club.

The Twin Club

Written by Ina Cumpiano
Illustrated by Jana Christy

How are the places the boys live and visit the same and different?

One day last summer, a lady said to us, "Twins! How cute!"

Jorge put a silly look on his face and I tried very hard not to roll my eyes.

Jorge and I are not twins. We are not even brothers. We're cousins. We are best friends.

But the lady called us twins. We could start a club. It would be the Twin Club!

Even before we were the Twin Club, we stayed all summer with Grandma Inés. We did everything together.

Now we were the Twin Club. We had a secret handshake. We built a clubhouse. It was big. But it was hard for both of us to fit.

And, as Twins, we made a promise. "We'll always, always be friends," we told each other.

Together, we walked around Grandma's beautiful small town. We did tricks in front of stores.

Someone, somewhere might have a better club than ours. But I don't think so!

Then one day, Grandma said, "I have news. The summer is almost over, *chicos,*" she said. "It's time for you to go home to your parents."

It was too soon for the summer to end!

"Jorge and I won't live here again until next summer, Grandma. We won't be the Twin Club anymore. Will we?"

"Juan Ramón, your parents miss you very much. They are looking forward to having you back on the farm. And soon you will start second grade. School will be fun!" Grandma Inés said.

Oh, no, it won't, I thought.

We knew it really was both good news and bad news. We would be with our families and friends again, which was good. But Jorge and I would not be together, which was bad. Very, very bad.

Grandma was right. Being back home on our farm was great. The first day back, I went for a walk to our neighbor's barn.

I climbed a ladder in the barn and jumped into the soft hay. I said hello to the goat. The old goose chased me!

That night, I watched fireflies in the meadow.

I thought about the Twin Club when Papi drove me to the bus stop in the morning. I thought about the Twin Club during the bus ride to school. It was a really long ride.

I thought about the Twin Club when I picked fruit off our trees and when I watched fireflies. I thought about the Twin Club all the time.

Then, one day, I got an e-mail message. It was from Jorge.

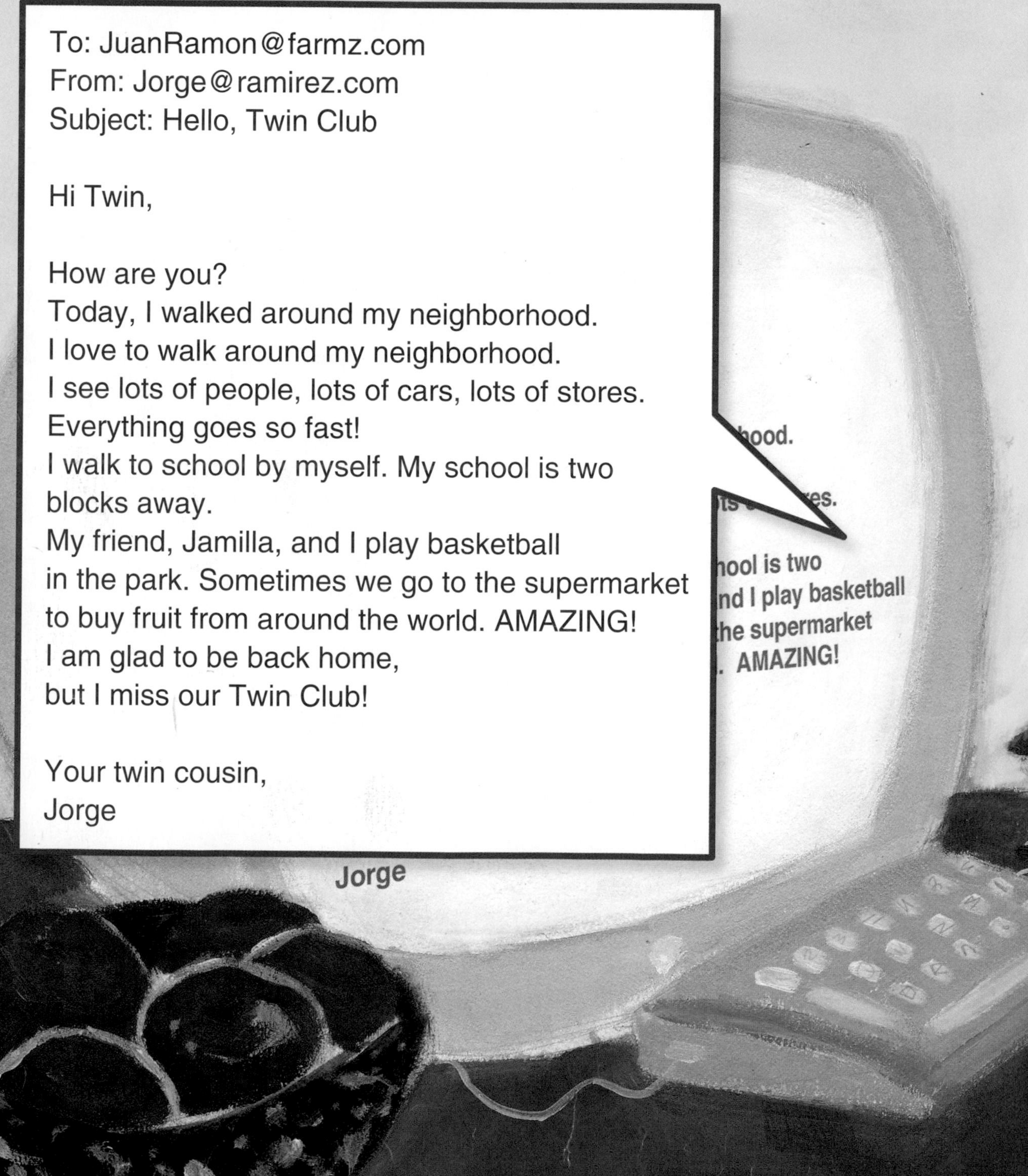

To: JuanRamon@farmz.com
From: Jorge@ramirez.com
Subject: Hello, Twin Club

Hi Twin,

How are you?
Today, I walked around my neighborhood.
I love to walk around my neighborhood.
I see lots of people, lots of cars, lots of stores.
Everything goes so fast!
I walk to school by myself. My school is two blocks away.
My friend, Jamilla, and I play basketball in the park. Sometimes we go to the supermarket to buy fruit from around the world. AMAZING!
I am glad to be back home,
but I miss our Twin Club!

Your twin cousin,
Jorge

I still missed Jorge. But I remembered what I liked about my home in the country.

Jorge remembered he liked walking in his neighborhood.

And do you know what was even more fun? Changing our club name to "The AMAZING E-mail Twins"!

Now we write to each other about everything. And we are making plans for next summer at Grandma's!

Talk About It Stories can go past the ending you read. What do you think the Twin Club will do next summer?

1. Use the pictures below to retell the story. Retell
2. Who are the characters in the story? How are they alike and different? Where does the story take place? Character and Setting
3. Did anything in this story confuse you? What did you do about it? Monitor and Clarify

TEST PRACTICE **Look Back and Write** Look back at page 35. What is the news the twins receive? How do they feel about it? Use details from the story to help you.

Retell

LR3.2 Generate alternative endings to plots and identify the reason or reasons for, and the impact of, the alternatives. **LS1.8** Retell stories, including characters, setting, and plot.

Meet the Author and the Illustrator

Ina Cumpiano

Ina Cumpiano is a Puerto Rican poet and translator. She lives in a busy San Francisco neighborhood and has written nearly twenty books for children.

Ms. Cumpiano has had many different jobs, but so far her favorite has been being a grandmother to her ten grandchildren.

Read another book illustrated by Jana Christy

Jana Christy

Jana Christy once wrote a comic book, but her usual work is illustrating books for children. Ms. Christy lives in Massachusetts with her husband and two sons.

The 1st Day of School

By Jenny Whitehead

Brand-new crayons and
  unchipped chalk.
Brand-new haircut,
  spotless smock.
Brand-new rules—
  "No running, please."
Brand-new pair of
  nervous knees.
Brand-new faces,
  unclogged glue.
Brand-new hamster,
  shiny shoes.
Brand-new teacher,
  classroom fun.
Brand-new school year's
  just begun.

The 179th Day of School

By Jenny Whitehead

Broken crayons and
  mop-head hair.
Scuffed-up shoes and
  squeaky chair.
Dried-up paste,
  chewed, leaky pens.
Dusty chalkboard,
  lifelong friends.
One inch taller,
  bigger brain.
Well-worn books,
  old grape-juice stain.
Paper airplanes,
  classroom cheer.
School is done and
  summer's here!

Writing Realistic Fiction

Prompt In *The Twin Club,* we read about two cousins who spend the summer with their grandmother in a small town. Think about what we could learn by exploring a new place. Now write a realistic story about someone visiting to a new place.

Writing Trait

Conventions are rules for writing.

Student Model

A Walk in the Woods

Writer follows conventions for writing.

Marley went for a walk in the woods. There were birds in the trees. She saw many squirrels and chipmunks.

Each sentence tells a complete idea.

She turned over a log. There were insects and worms under the log.

A realistic story has events that could happen in real life.

It was wonderful to spend time in the woods.

W2.1 Write brief narratives based on their personal experience. **LC1.2** Recognize and use the correct word order in written sentences. **LC1.6** Capitalize all proper nouns, words at the beginning of sentences and greetings, months and days of the week, and titles and initials of people.

Writer's Checklist

- Could my story really happen?
- Do I begin each sentence with a capital letter and end it with a period?
- Does each sentence tell a complete idea?

Grammar Sentences

A **sentence** is a group of words that tells a complete idea. The words are in an order that makes sense. A sentence begins with a capital letter. Many sentences end with a **period(.)**.

The Twin Club went swimming.

This is a sentence. It tells a complete idea.

Practice Look at the sentences in the model. How do you know they are sentences?

Let's Talk About Exploration

LS1.0 Students listen critically and respond appropriately to oral communication. They speak in a manner that guides the listener to understand important ideas by using proper phrasing, pitch, and modulation.

USA
NASA
Challenger
United States

Words to Read

live
work
woman
machines
move
everywhere
world

G1R1.11 Read common, irregular sight words (e.g., *the, have, said, come, give, of*).

Read the Words

Astronauts live and work in space.
A woman can be an astronaut.

Machines in space can move large things.

Stars are everywhere.
Can you see our world?

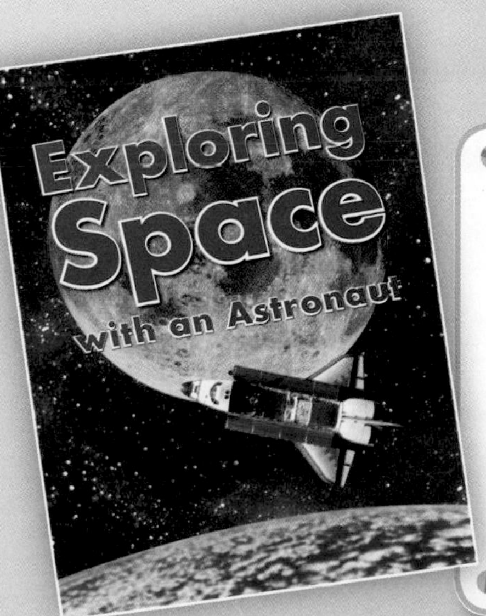

Genre: Expository Nonfiction
Expository nonfiction tells facts about a topic. Next you will read facts about the crew of a real space shuttle.

Exploring Space with an Astronaut

by Patricia J. Murphy

What will you find out about space from an astronaut?

Lift-off!

3 . . . 2 . . . 1 . . . Lift-off!

A space shuttle climbs high into the sky. Inside the shuttle, astronauts are on their way to learn more about space.

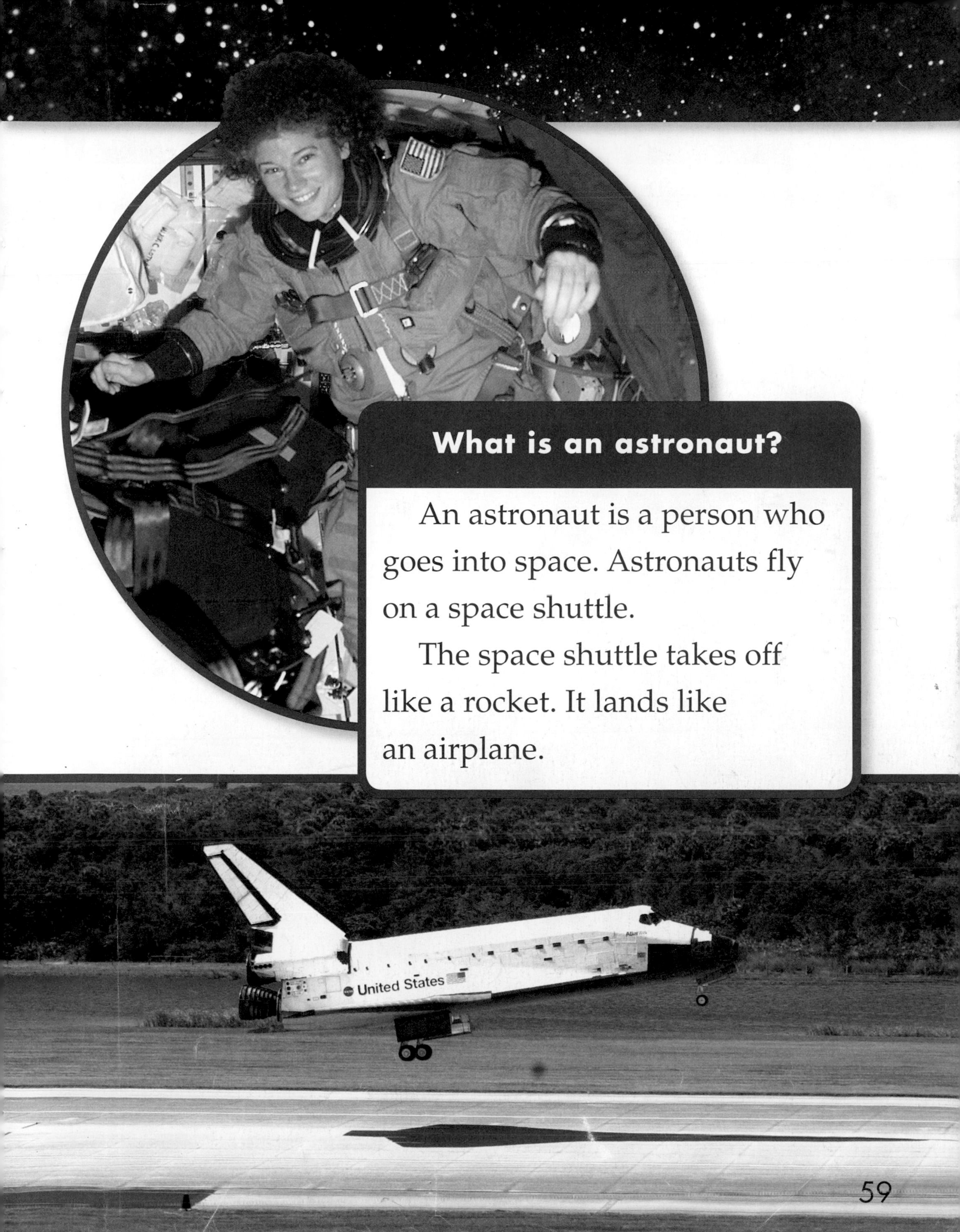

What is an astronaut?

An astronaut is a person who goes into space. Astronauts fly on a space shuttle.

The space shuttle takes off like a rocket. It lands like an airplane.

Meet Eileen Collins.

Eileen Collins is an astronaut. She was the first woman to be a space shuttle pilot. She was also the first woman to be the leader of a space shuttle trip.

She and four other astronauts worked as a team. Some astronauts flew the space shuttle. Others did experiments.

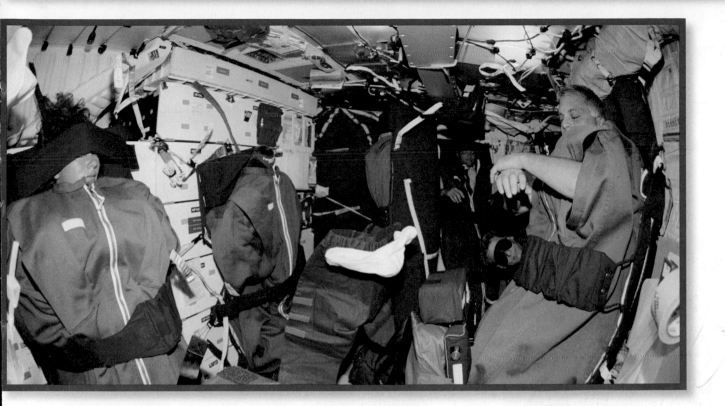

How do astronauts live in space?

In the space shuttle, astronauts float everywhere. Sleeping bags are tied to walls. Toilets have a type of seat belt.

Astronauts exercise to stay strong. They take sponge baths to keep clean.

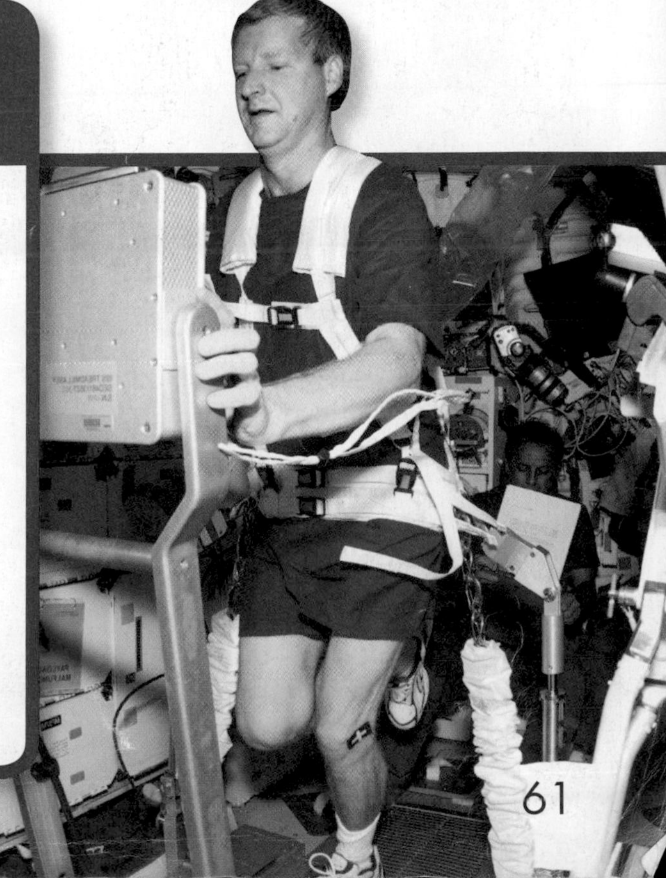

Why do astronauts go into space?

Astronauts test ways to live and work in a world that is very different from Earth. In space, there is no up and down, no air, and the sun always shines.

Astronauts do experiments. They look for problems and fix them. This will make space travel safer.

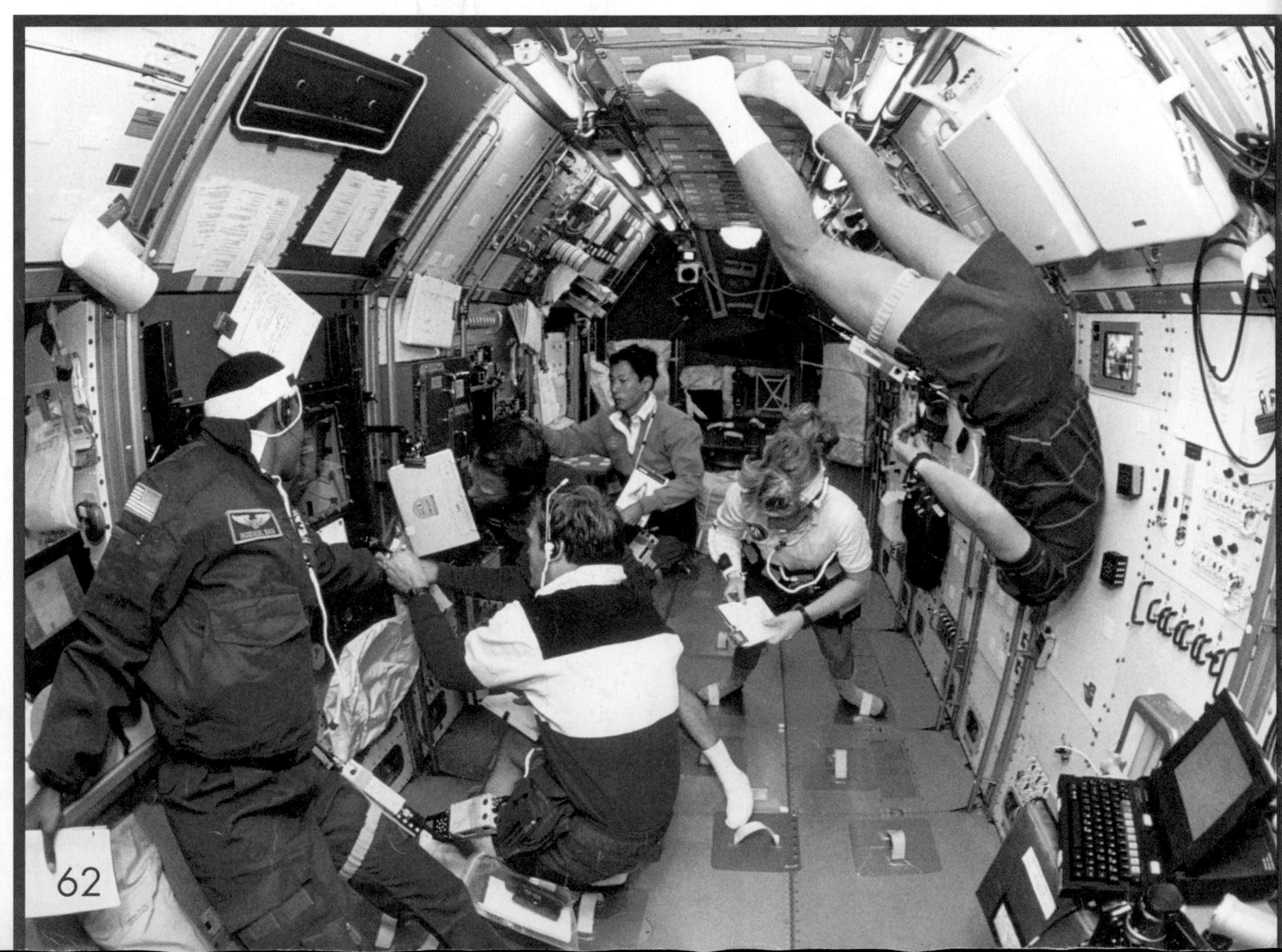

OCA
STS1
OCA Router

robot arm

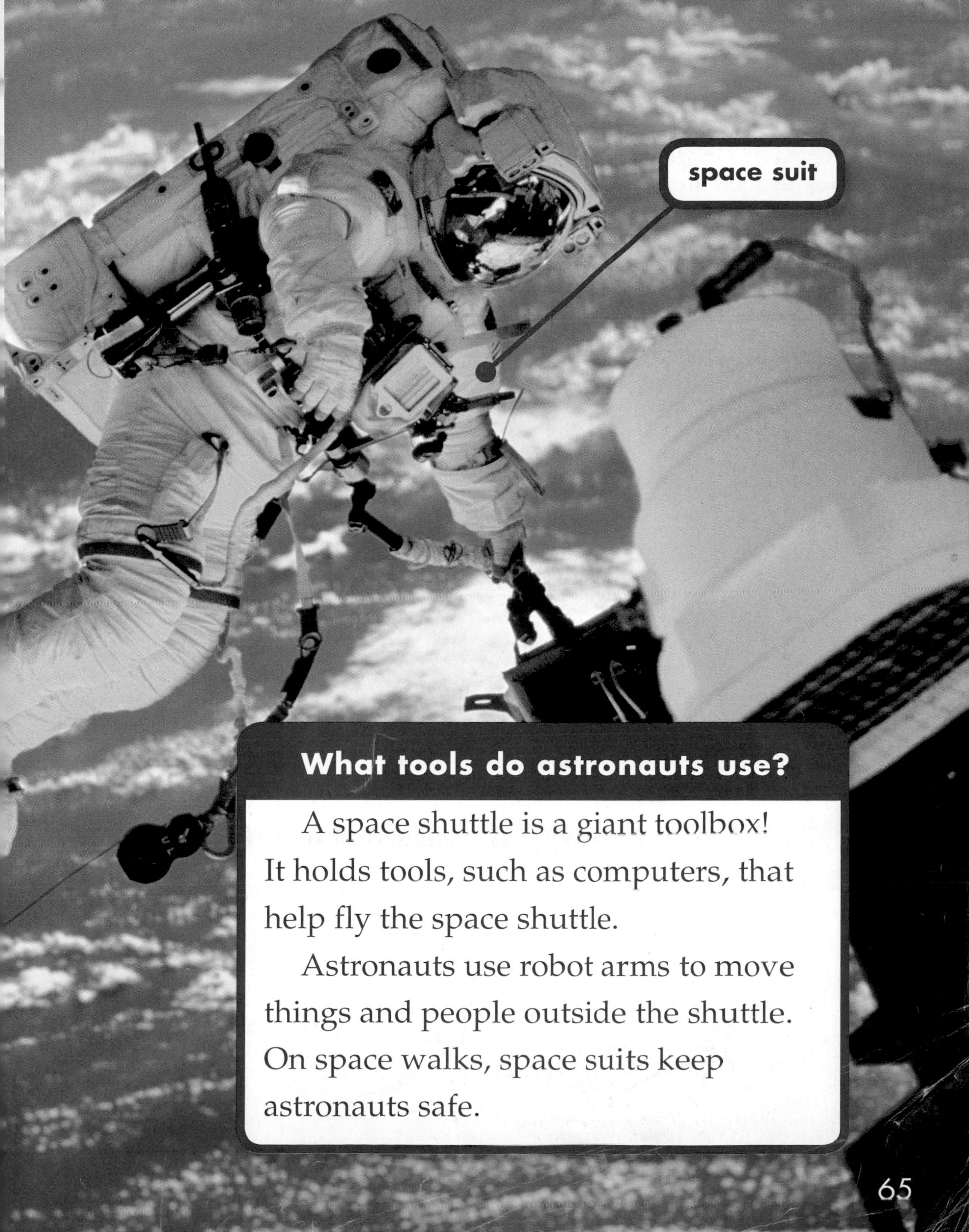

What tools do astronauts use?

A space shuttle is a giant toolbox! It holds tools, such as computers, that help fly the space shuttle.

Astronauts use robot arms to move things and people outside the shuttle. On space walks, space suits keep astronauts safe.

space shuttle

The crew's special job.

Eileen Collins and her crew had a special job to do. They took an X-ray telescope into space with them.

First, they tested the telescope. Next, they flipped some switches and let the telescope go into space. Then, the telescope used its rockets to fly higher into space.

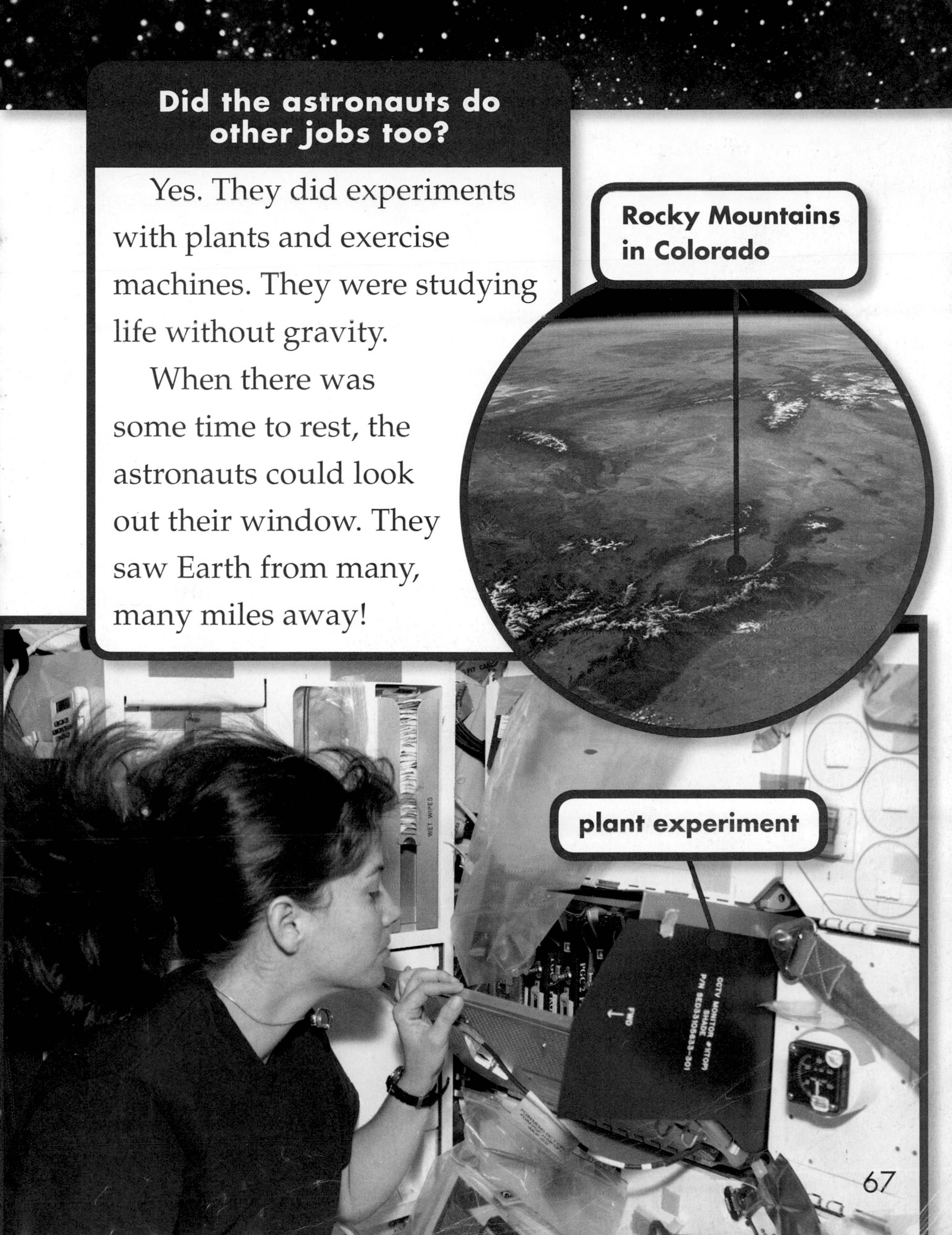

Did the astronauts do other jobs too?

Yes. They did experiments with plants and exercise machines. They were studying life without gravity.

When there was some time to rest, the astronauts could look out their window. They saw Earth from many, many miles away!

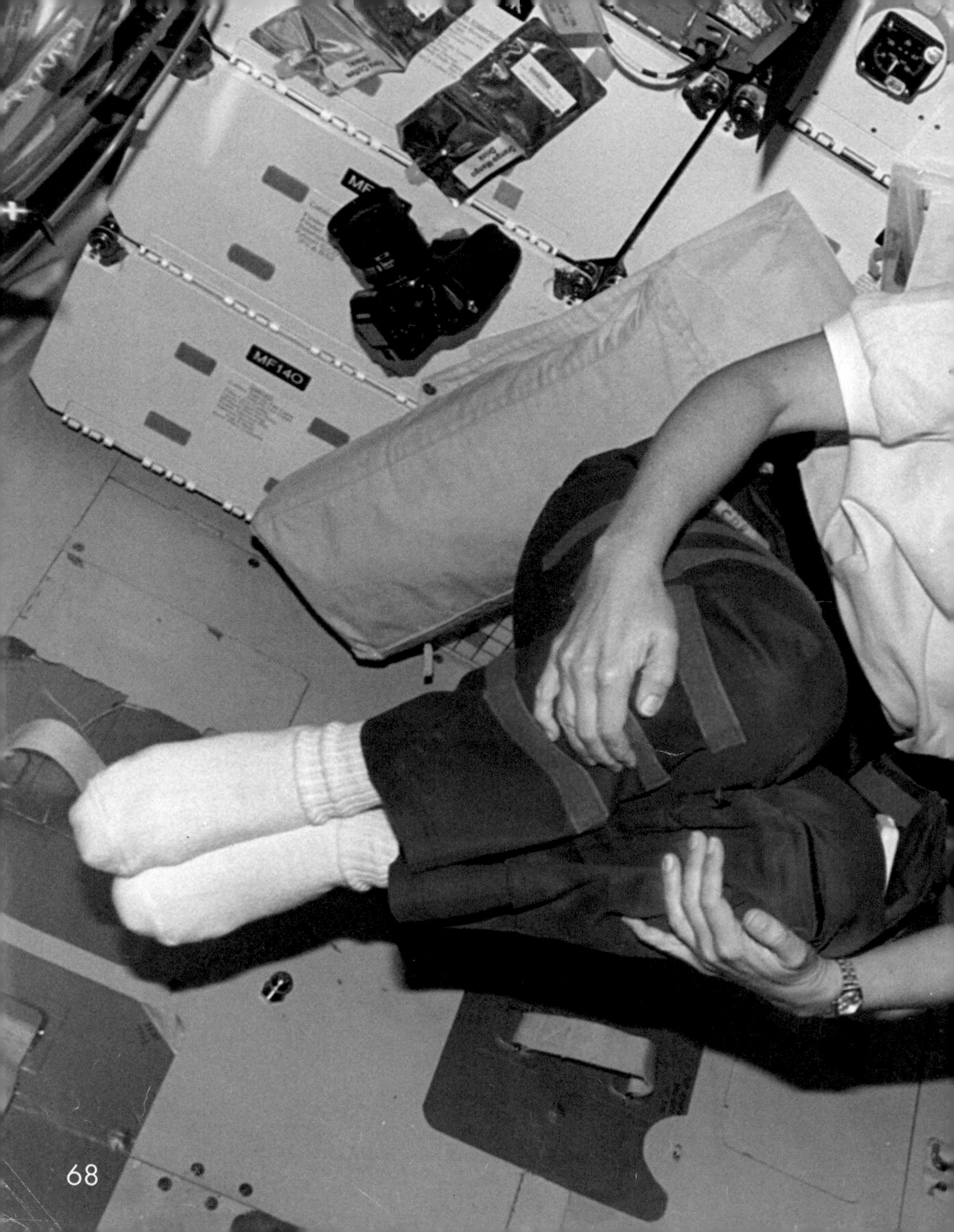
MF140

Would you like to fly into space?

Do you like math and science? Do you like to visit new places? Do you like fast roller coasters? Astronauts do too! Maybe someday you will become an astronaut, just like Eileen Collins.

Talk About It You are an astronaut. Send a one-minute message to Earth. Tell about your trip.

1. Use the pictures below to summarize what you read. **Summarize**
2. What do you think is the most important thing the author wanted you to know? **Main Idea and Details**
3. Look at page 61. Read the words. How did you know what *exercise* means? **Context Clues**

TEST PRACTICE

Look Back and Write What can you find out about space from an astronaut? Look back through the selection for help in answering.

Summarize

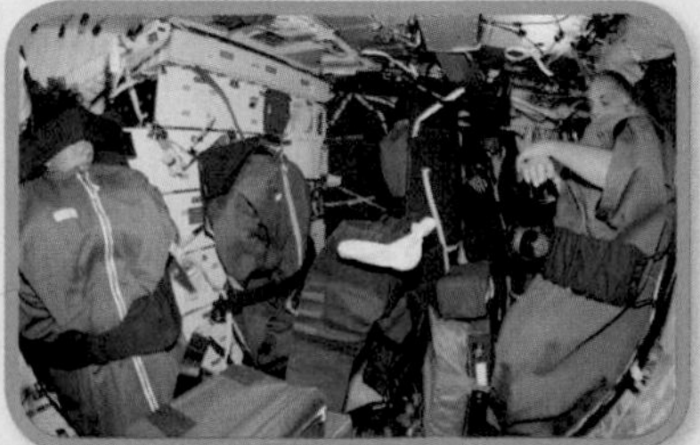

R2.3 Use knowledge of the author's purpose(s) to comprehend informational text.
R2.5 Restate facts and details in the text to clarify and organize ideas.
G3R1.6 Use sentence and word context to find the meanings of unknown words.

Meet the Author

Patricia J. Murphy

Patricia Murphy likes everything about writing a book. When she starts a new book, she says, it's "fun and scary." When she's in the middle, her days are filled with "unexpected adventure and surprises—and a lot of mess and hard work." In the end, when the book is written, she feels excited and a little sad that it's all over. Then it's on to the next book!

Ms. Murphy is a writer and a photographer. She lives in Illinois.

Read more books by Patricia Murphy.

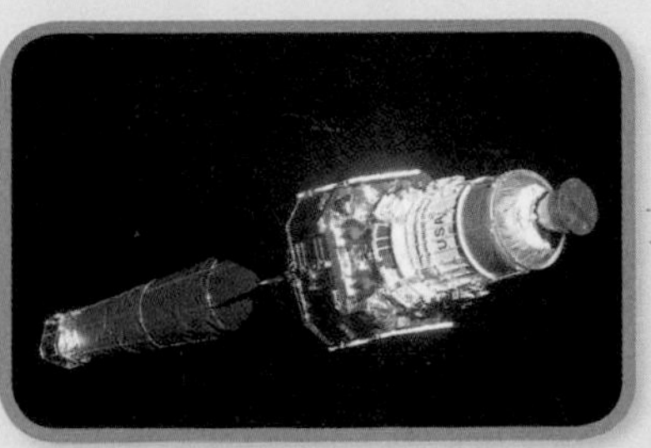

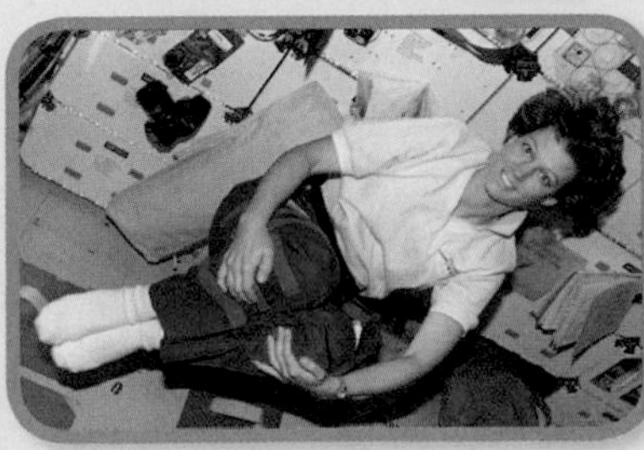

A Trip to Space Camp

by Ann Weil

What does it feel like to go into space? Would you like to find out? Then maybe Space Camp is for you!

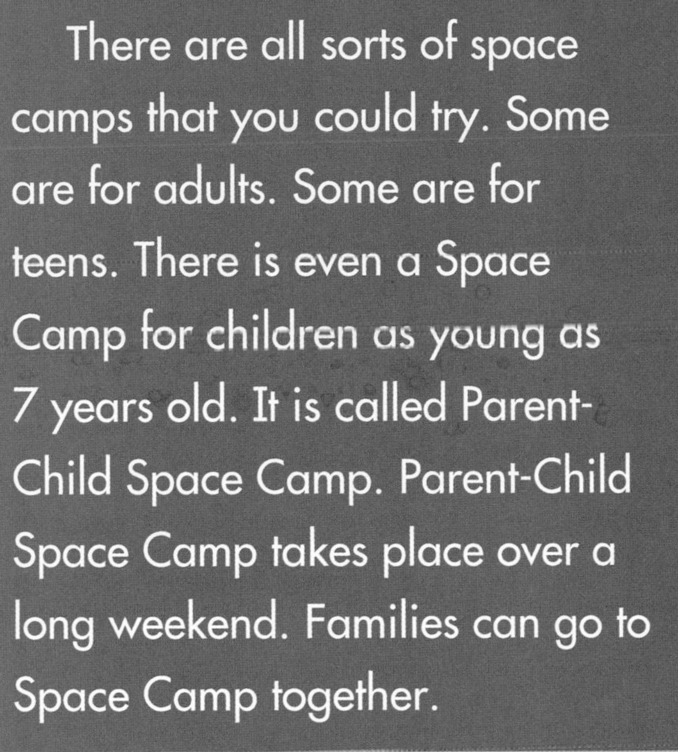

There are all sorts of space camps that you could try. Some are for adults. Some are for teens. There is even a Space Camp for children as young as 7 years old. It is called Parent-Child Space Camp. Parent-Child Space Camp takes place over a long weekend. Families can go to Space Camp together.

Space Camp uses some of the same machines used to train real astronauts. There's a special chair that makes you feel like you are walking on the moon. Another chair is like the kind that astronauts use when they go outside their rocket ship to fix something. A third kind of chair makes you feel like you're floating in space. Still another machine spins you in circles and flips you head over heels. Then there's the Space Shot. The Space Shot shoots you straight into the air at about 45 to 50 miles per hour. You fall back down just as fast. Then you bump up and down a few times before it's over.

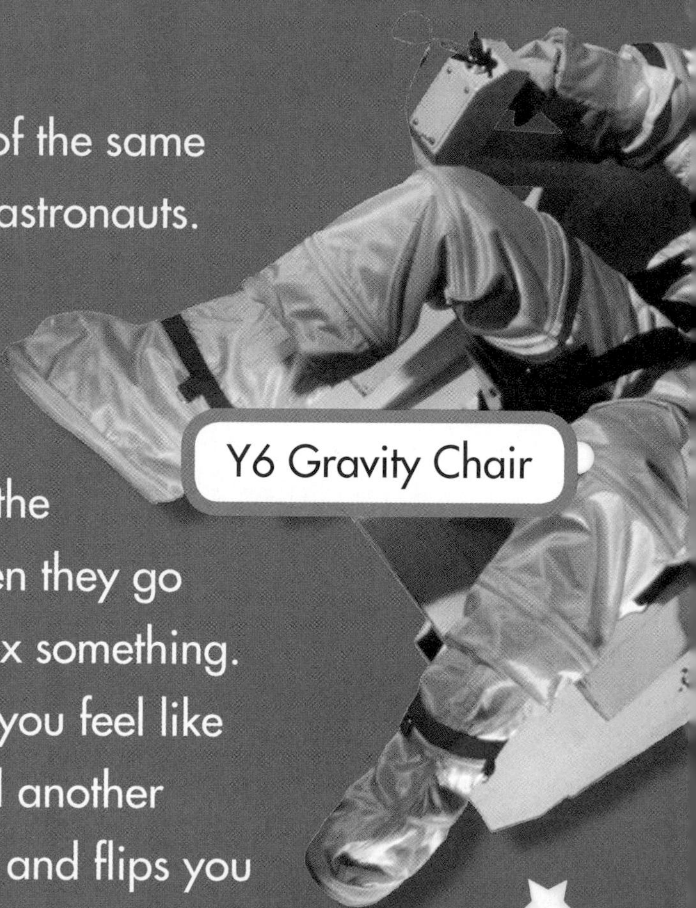

Y6 Gravity Chair

Working in Space

A Multi-Axis Giro

Everyone at space camp works together on special missions. On these missions you'll do work like real astronauts do in space. You might get to fly a rocket ship. It's only pretend, of course. You won't really fly into space. But it looks and feels like the real thing. And that's really fun!

Moon Gravity Chair

Writing Expository Nonfiction

Prompt In *Exploring Space with an Astronaut,* we find out about daily life on a space shuttle. Think about what scientists have learned from exploring space. Now write a paragraph telling something you have learned.

Writing Trait

Different kinds of **sentences** make writing smoother.

Student Model

Each sentence has a subject.

Expository nonfiction tells about real people, places, or events.

Writer uses different kinds of sentences.

Astronauts in Space

The astronauts on the space shuttle have different jobs. Some fly the shuttle and others do experiments. They have to fix problems. They study life without gravity. Being an astronaut is hard work! Would you like to be an astronaut?

LC1.1 Distinguish between complete and incomplete sentences. **LC.1.3** Identify and correctly use various parts of speech, including nouns and verbs, in writing and speaking.

Writer's Checklist

- ✓ Does my writing tell about real people, places, or events?
- ✓ Do I use different kinds of sentences in my writing?
- ✓ Is each of my sentences complete, including a subject?

Grammar Subject

The **subject** of a sentence tells who or what does something.

An astronaut goes into space.

An astronaut is the subject of this sentence.

Practice Look at the sentences in the paragraph. Write the subject of each sentence.

Let's Talk About
Exploration

LS1.0 Students listen critically and respond appropriately to oral communication. They speak in a manner that guides the listener to understand important ideas by using proper phrasing, pitch, and modulation.

Words to Read

love
mother
father
straight
bear
couldn't
build

 G1R1.11 Read common, irregular sight words (e.g., *the, have, said, come, give, of*).

Read the Words

We all love camping. My mother and father take us camping every year. We go straight to the woods when we get there. Something new always happens on these trips. Last year, we saw a bear! I couldn't believe it. This year, my dad promised to teach us how to build a campfire. I can't wait!

Genre: Realistic Fiction
Realistic fiction means that a story could happen. Next read about Henry and his dog, Mudge, and their camping trip.

Henry and Mudge and the Starry Night

by Cynthia Rylant
illustrated by Suçie Stevenson

What will Henry and Mudge find on a starry night?

Contents

Big Bear Lake	85
A Good Smelly Hike	90
Green Dreams	95

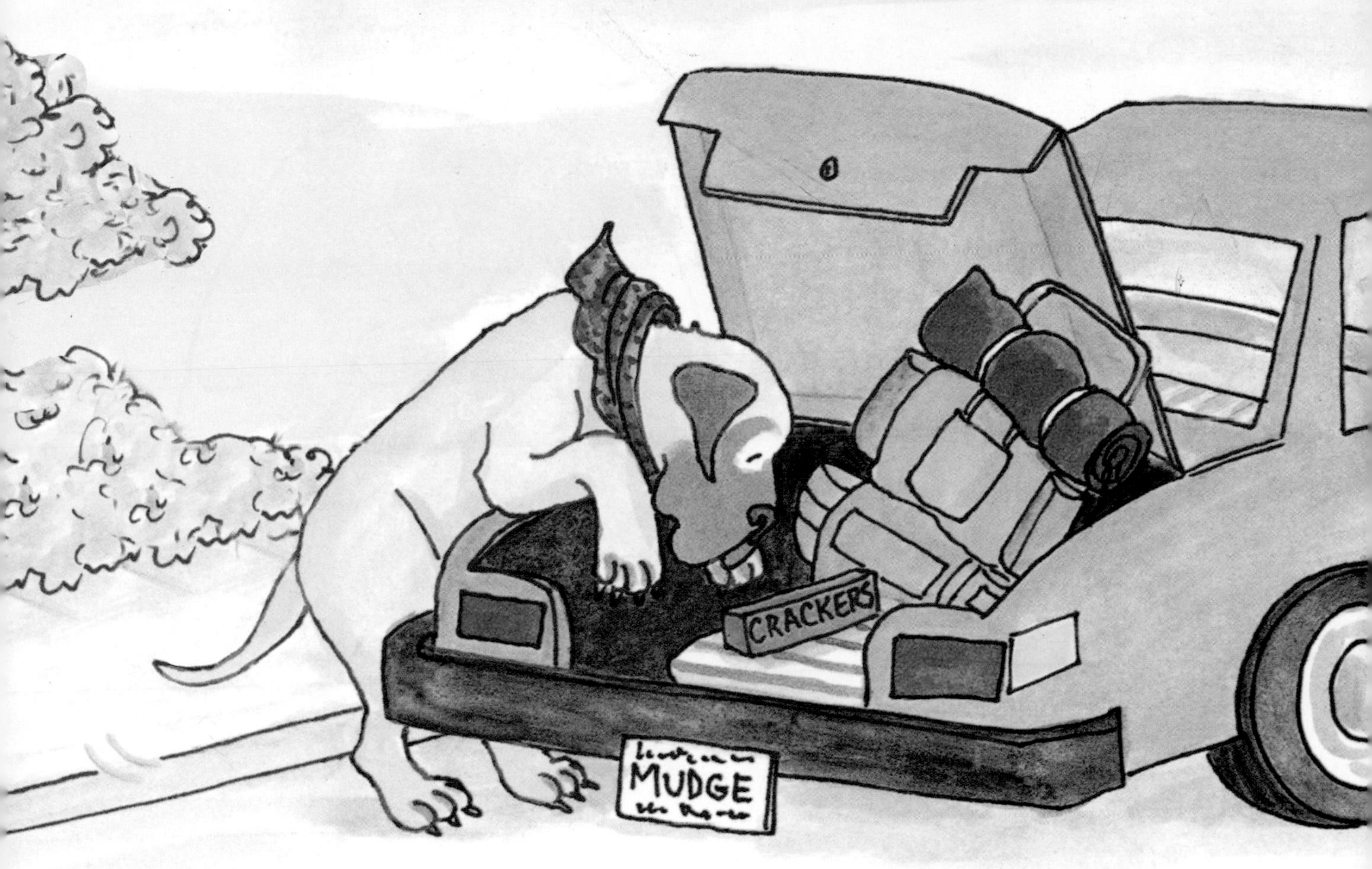

Big Bear Lake

In August Henry and Henry's big dog Mudge always went camping. They went with Henry's parents.

Henry's mother had been a Camp Fire Girl, so she knew all about camping.

She knew how to set up a tent.

She knew how to build a campfire. She knew how to cook camp food.

Henry's dad didn't know anything about camping. He just came with a guitar and a smile.

Henry and Mudge loved camping. This year they were going to Big Bear Lake, and Henry couldn't wait.

"We'll see deer, Mudge," Henry said. Mudge wagged.

"We'll see raccoons," said Henry. Mudge shook Henry's hand.

"We might even see a *bear*," Henry said. Henry was not so sure he wanted to see a bear. He shivered and put an arm around Mudge.

Mudge gave a big, slow, *loud* yawn. He drooled on Henry's foot.

Henry giggled. "No bear will get *us*, Mudge," Henry said. "We're too *slippery!*"

A Good Smelly Hike

Henry and Mudge and Henry's parents drove to Big Bear Lake. They parked the car and got ready to hike.

Everyone had a backpack, even Mudge. (His had lots of crackers.) Henry's mother said, "Let's go!" And off they went.

They walked and walked and climbed and climbed. It was beautiful.

Henry saw a fish jump straight out of a stream. He saw a doe and her fawn. He saw waterfalls and a rainbow.

Mudge didn't see much of anything. He was smelling. Mudge loved to hike and smell. He smelled a raccoon from yesterday. He smelled a deer from last night.

He smelled an oatmeal cookie from Henry's back pocket. "Mudge!" Henry laughed, giving Mudge the cookie.

Finally Henry's mother picked a good place to camp.

Henry's parents set up the tent. Henry unpacked the food and pans and lanterns. Mudge unpacked a ham sandwich. Finally the camp was almost ready. It needed just one more thing: "Who knows the words to 'Love Me Tender'?" said Henry's father with a smile, pulling out his guitar. Henry looked at Mudge and groaned.

Green Dreams

It was a beautiful night.

Henry and Henry's parents lay on their backs by the fire and looked at the sky. Henry didn't know there were so many stars in the sky.

"There's the Big Dipper," said Henry's mother.

"There's the Little Dipper," said Henry.

"There's E. T.," said Henry's dad.

Mudge wasn't looking at stars. He was chewing on a log. He couldn't get logs this good at home. Mudge loved camping.

Henry's father sang one more sappy love song, then everyone went inside the tent to sleep. Henry's father and mother snuggled. Henry and Mudge snuggled.

It was as quiet as quiet could be. Everyone slept safe and sound, and there were no bears, no scares. Just the clean smell of trees . . . and wonderful green dreams.

Talk About It Pretend you are Mudge. What were the best sights and smells on the camping trip?

1. Use the pictures below to retell the story. **Retell**
2. Who are the characters in the story? Describe the setting. What do the characters do? **Character, Setting, and Plot**
3. Look at page 89. Read the words. How did you know what *shivered* means? **Context Clues**

TEST PRACTICE

Look Back and Write What did Henry and Mudge learn on a starry night? Use details from the story in your answer.

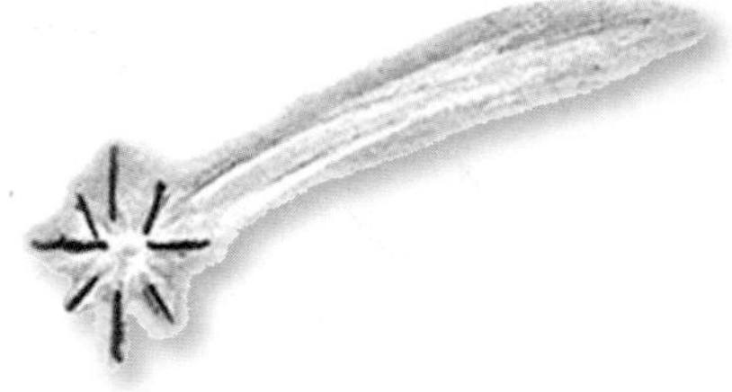

Retell

LS1.8 Retell stories, including characters, setting, and plot.
G3R1.6 Use sentence and word context to find the meanings of unknown words.

Meet the Author and the Illustrator

Cynthia Rylant

Cynthia Rylant never read many books when she was young. There was no library in her town.

After college, Ms. Rylant worked in a library. "Within a few weeks, I fell in love with children's books," she says. She has written over 60 books!

Read more books by Cynthia Rylant.

Suçie Stevenson

Suçie Stevenson has drawn pictures for most of the Henry and Mudge books. Her brother's Great Dane, Jake, was her inspiration for Mudge.

Where Can We Camp?

Riddles by Joan Holub
Illustrated by Rob McClurcan

Look at the map. Where would you like to go camping? Maybe some riddles will help.

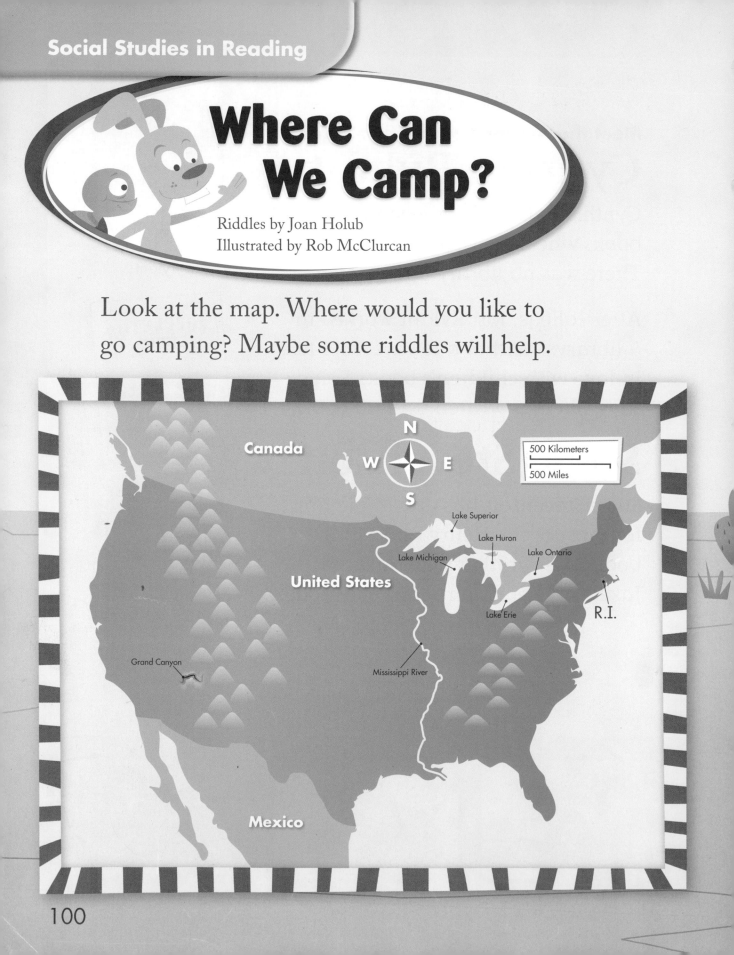

N
W
E
S
500 Kilometers
500 Miles
Canada
United States
Mexico
Lake Superior
Lake Huron
Lake Michigan
Lake Ontario
Lake Erie
R.I.
Grand Canyon
Mississippi River

Great States

The United States of America
was once land undivided.
It's first state was Delaware.
(I wonder who decided?)
More states joined, one by one,
to stand in strength beside it.
Hawaii was the last of all.
(I'm glad it was invited.)
How many states are there now
in this land, united?

Answer: Fifty

Name the U.S.A.'s Neighbors

South is a country that starts with **M.**
North is a country that starts with **C.**
East is an ocean that starts with **A.**
West is an ocean that starts with **P.**

Answers: Mexico, Canada, Atlantic Ocean, Pacific Ocean

We're All Wet

There are five of us.
Our pools connect.
In our fresh waters,
ships have wrecked.
We touch Canada
and eight states, too.
We're smaller than the oceans,
but every bit as blue.

What are we?

Answers: The Great Lakes
(Erie, Huron, Michigan,
Ontario, Superior

Gorge-ous

The Colorado River
eroded the land
in Arizona state
and carved something grand.
The Colorado River
roared along its way
to dig this giant chasm
that remains today.

What is it?

Answer: The Grand Canyon

Mighty

I'm mighty long.
I'm mighty strong.
I'm sailed by barges and ships.
From Minnesota I flow
to the Gulf of Mexico
on countless river trips.

What am I?

Answer: The Mississippi River

The Smallest State

I'm very small, and that's why
mapmakers draw me and sigh.
There's no room for my name.
So although it's a shame,
on maps I get labeled R.I.

What state am I?

Answer: Rhode Island (1,231 square miles)

Writing Realistic Fiction

Prompt *Henry and Mudge and the Starry Night* is about a family camping experience. Think about things that can be discovered in nature. Now write a realistic story about a child who discovers something outdoors.

Writing Trait

Organize your sentences so your story is clear.

Student Model

Realistic fiction happens in a setting that seems real.

Each sentence has a predicate.

Sentences are in an order that makes sense.

A Day at the Beach

Luke went to the beach on a hot summer day. He splashed in the cool water. He dug in the warm sand.

Luke discovered a small tide pool full of starfish. He found a smooth rock. He took the rock home to remind him of his day at the beach.

W1.1 Write brief narratives based on their experiences.
LC1.2 Recognize and use the correct word order in written sentences.

Writer's Checklist

- ☑ Does my writing tell about events that could happen in real life?
- ☑ Are my sentences in an order that makes sense?
- ☑ Is each of my sentences complete, including a predicate?

Grammar Predicates

The **predicate** tells what the subject of the sentence does or is.

Henry and Mudge **walked down the trail.**

The words **walked down the trail** tell what Henry and Mudge did.

Practice Look at the sentences in the beach story. Write the predicates of the first three sentences.

Let's Talk About
Exploration

LS1.0 Students listen critically and respond appropriately to oral communication. They speak in a manner that guides the listener to understand important ideas by using proper phrasing, pitch, and modulation.

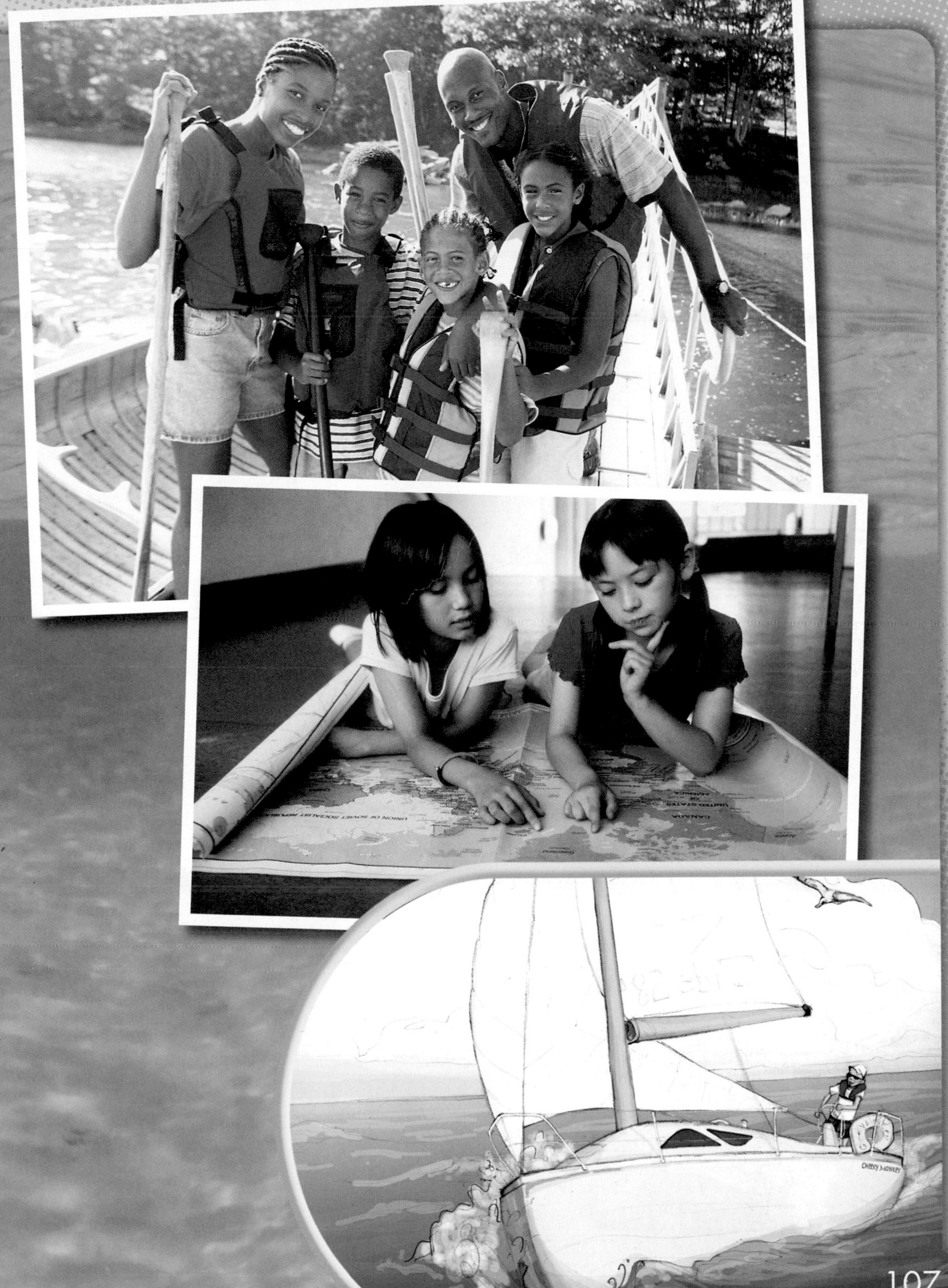
UNION OF SOVIET SOCIALIST REPUBLICS
UNITED STATES OF AMERICA
CANADA
CHEEKY MONKEY

Words to Read

early
warm
full
water
eyes
animals

Read the Words

Early one warm evening, Dad and I sat at the edge of the lake and watched the full moon on the water. We were sitting very still. But we could hardly believe our eyes when small animals came so close to us to drink.

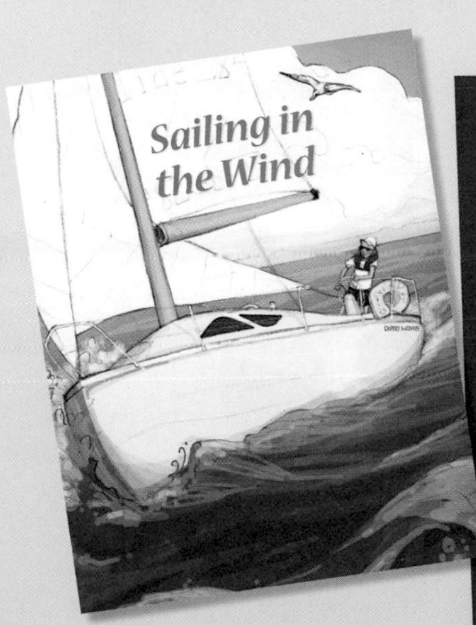

Genre: Narrative Nonfiction

Narrative nonfiction is true events told like a story. Now read about a brave boy who sailed across the Atlantic Ocean.

Sailing in the Wind

Written by Tina Fakhrid-Deen
Illustrated by Paule Trudel

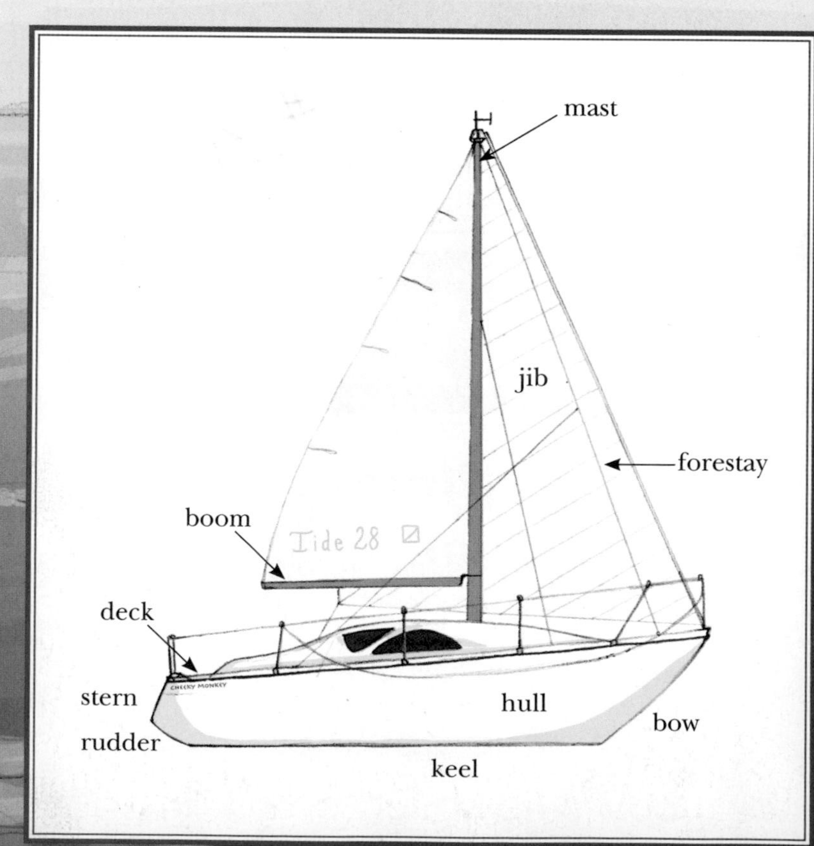

How did it feel to cross an ocean alone in a boat?

Michael Perham started sailing when he was just seven years old. His father taught him how to use the force of wind to make his boat move.

When Michael was fourteen, he wanted to sail across an ocean. No one that young had ever sailed alone across the Atlantic. Michael wanted to be first.

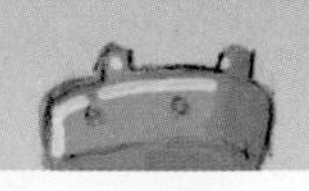

Michael packed his boat, the *Cheeky Monkey.* He packed food and water. He packed compasses, a life vest, and a telephone.

Early on November 18, 2006, Michael set sail. Michael's father sailed behind him in another boat. They started at Gibraltar.

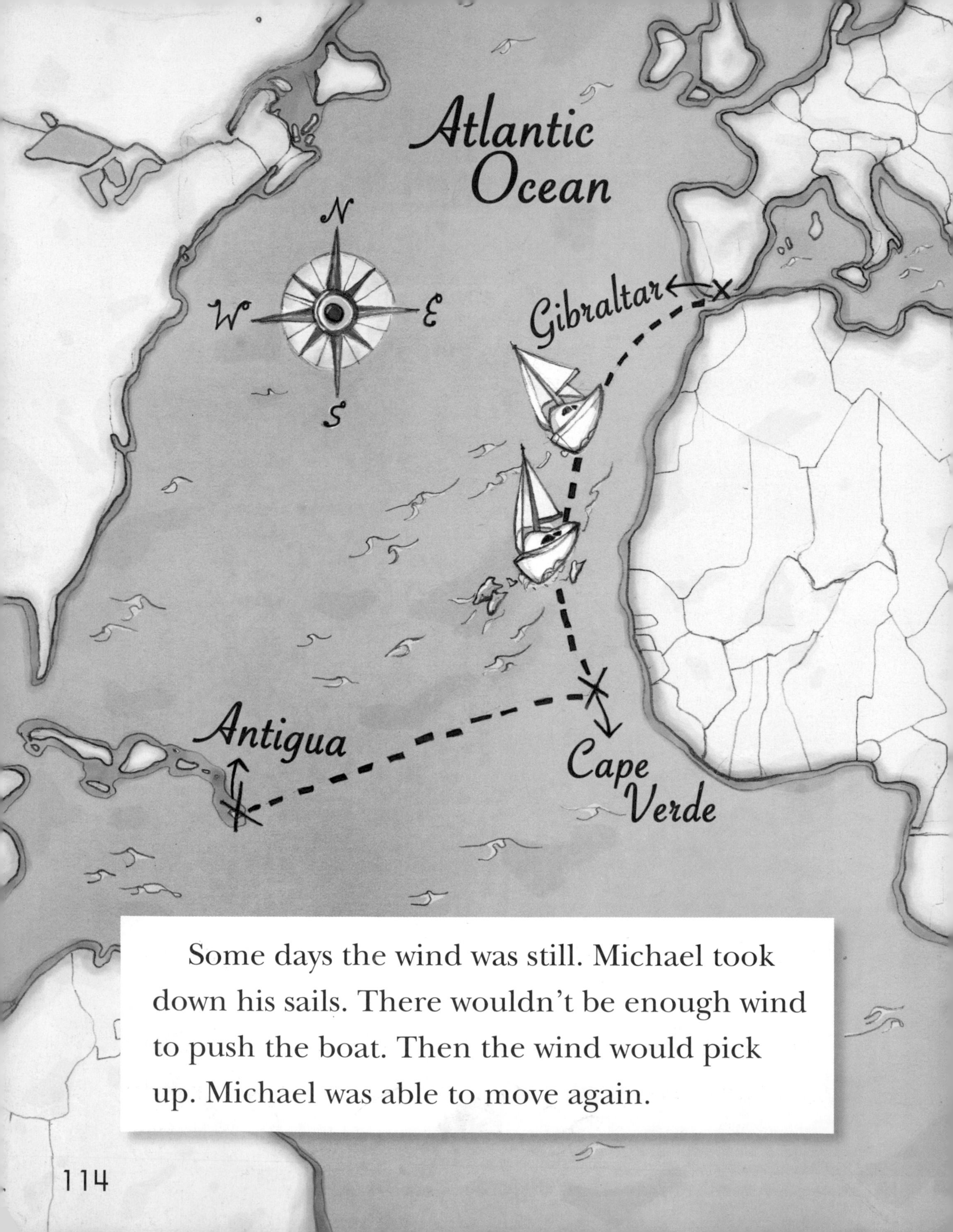

Some days the wind was still. Michael took down his sails. There wouldn't be enough wind to push the boat. Then the wind would pick up. Michael was able to move again.

When it was time to sleep, Michael let his boat drift. He had to wake up during the night to check on things. He looked at the compass to make sure that his boat was going the right direction. Michael made sure that his father's boat was not too far away.

When he was not busy with the sails, Michael did his school work. He also sang songs and played the guitar. Michael liked watching the animals around him. The sky was full of birds, and there were friendly dolphins in the water.

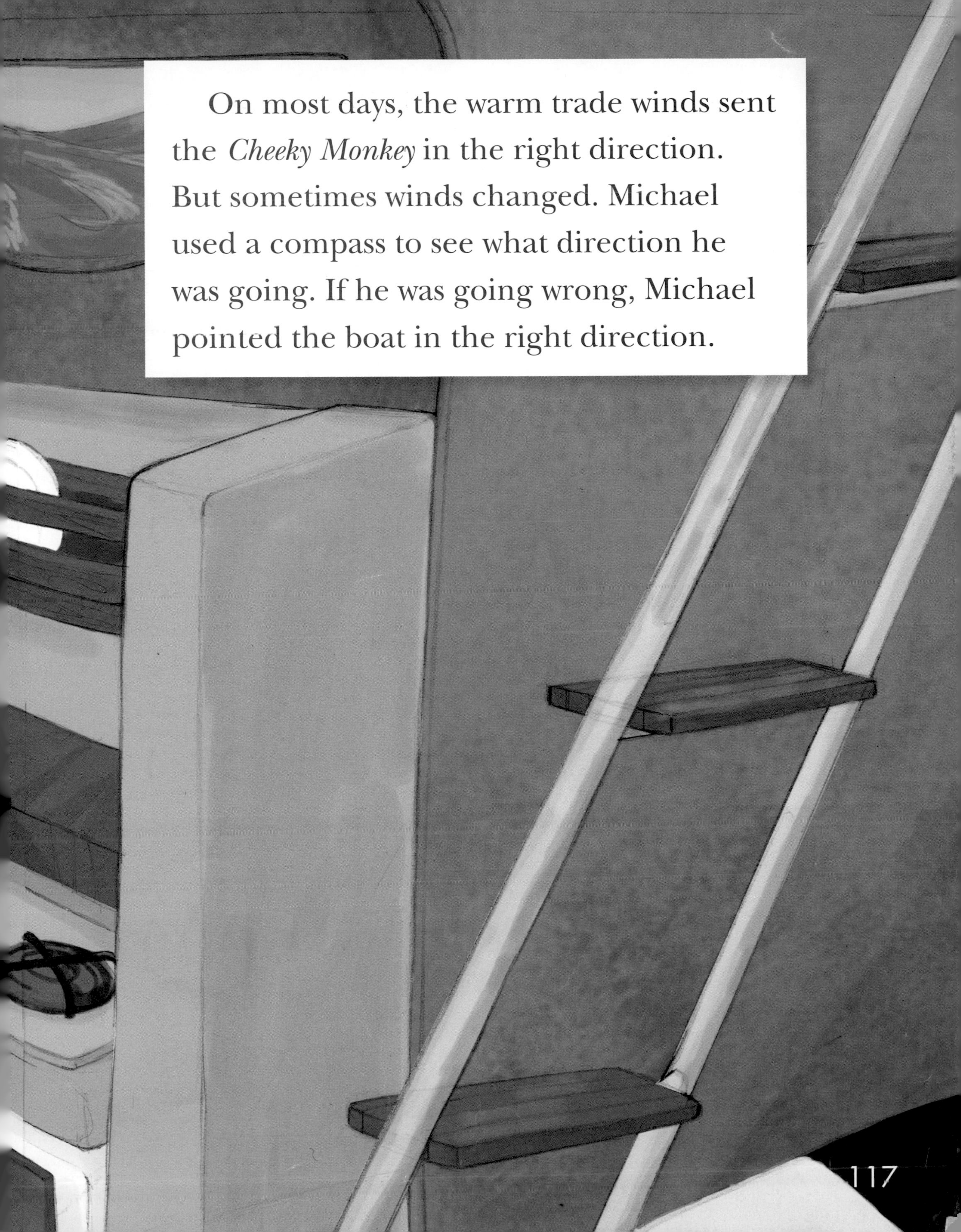

On most days, the warm trade winds sent the *Cheeky Monkey* in the right direction. But sometimes winds changed. Michael used a compass to see what direction he was going. If he was going wrong, Michael pointed the boat in the right direction.

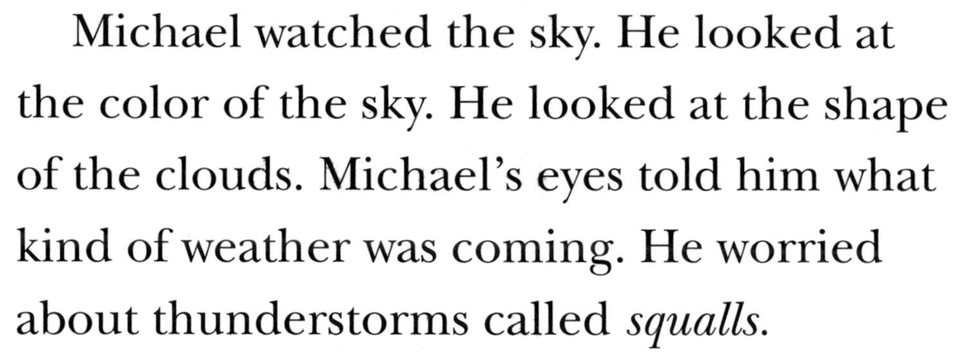

Michael watched the sky. He looked at the color of the sky. He looked at the shape of the clouds. Michael's eyes told him what kind of weather was coming. He worried about thunderstorms called *squalls*.

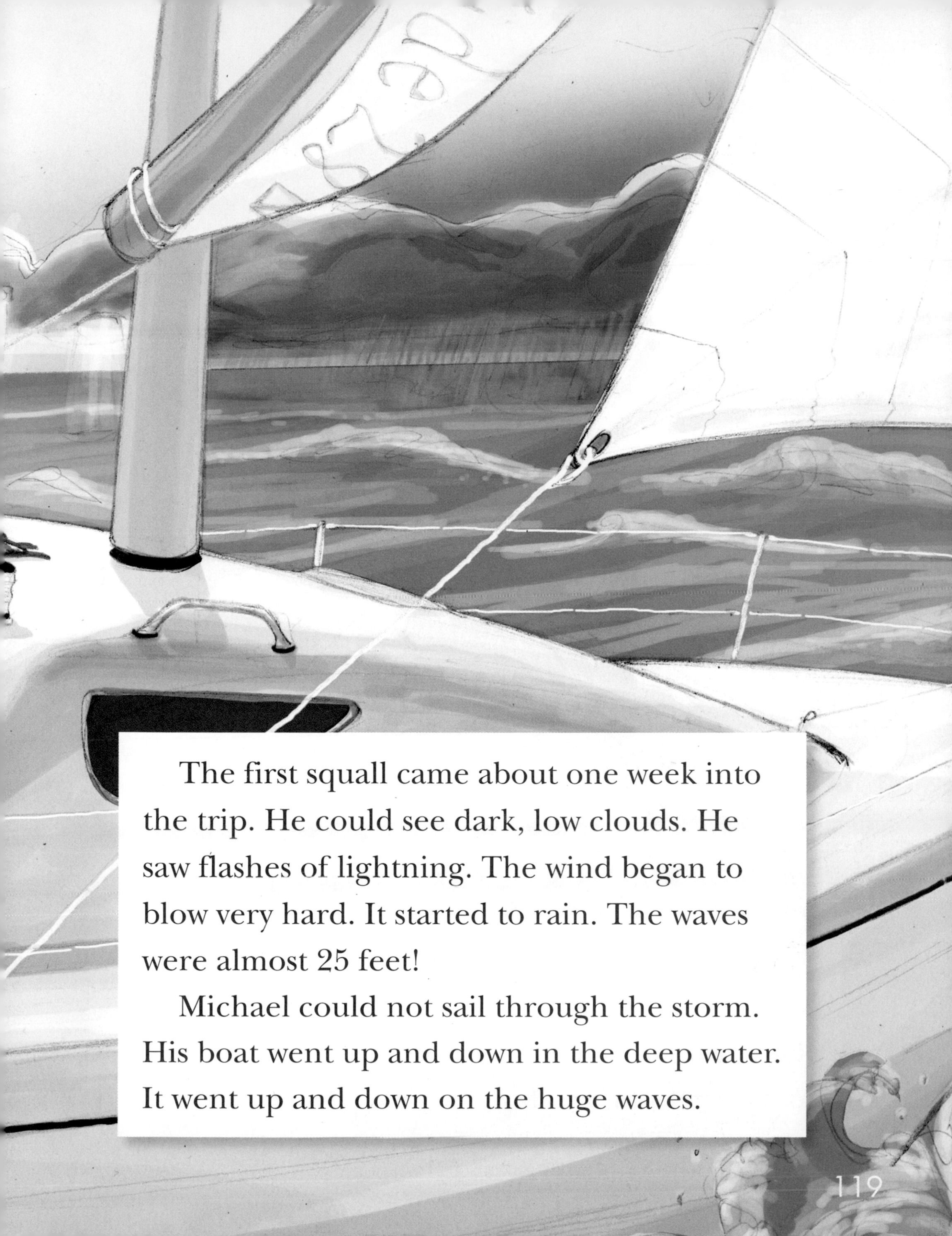

The first squall came about one week into the trip. He could see dark, low clouds. He saw flashes of lightning. The wind began to blow very hard. It started to rain. The waves were almost 25 feet!

Michael could not sail through the storm. His boat went up and down in the deep water. It went up and down on the huge waves.

The clouds were full and dark. The sky was gray. Michael could hear thunder and see lightning. Rain poured. The boat was very wet. Michael had to be careful not to fall.

He rolled up one of the sails and let the other sail flap. Michael did not want the wind to tear his sails. But there was nothing else he could do. He had to go inside the cabin. It would be a safer place for him until the bad weather passed.

At last the bad weather passed. Michael sailed and sailed.

After six weeks at sea, Michael sailed into Antigua. He had sailed 3,500 miles. His family was very proud of him. Michael was now the youngest person to ever sail alone across the Atlantic.

Talk About It Imagine you and some friends are on a boat, sailing across the ocean. Tell your friends what to look at and listen for.

1. Use the pictures below to summarize the selection. **Summarize**
2. Look back at the story to find details about sailing on a boat. **Main Idea and Details**
3. Did anything in the story confuse you? What questions did you ask yourself as you read? **Ask Questions**

TEST PRACTICE

Look Back and Write Look back at page 113. What other things would you bring on a trip across the ocean?

Summarize

R2.4 Ask clarifying questions about essential textual elements of exposition (e.g., *why, what if, how*). **R2.5** Restate facts and details in the text to clarify and organize ideas.

Meet the Author

Tina Fakhrid-Deen

Tina Fakrid-Deen is a freelance writer and high school teacher. She is currently at work on her first young adult novel.

Ms. Fakhrid-Deen lives in Chicago with her daughter and husband and is very active in her community. She loves to travel to countries where English is not spoken.

Read more books about sailing.

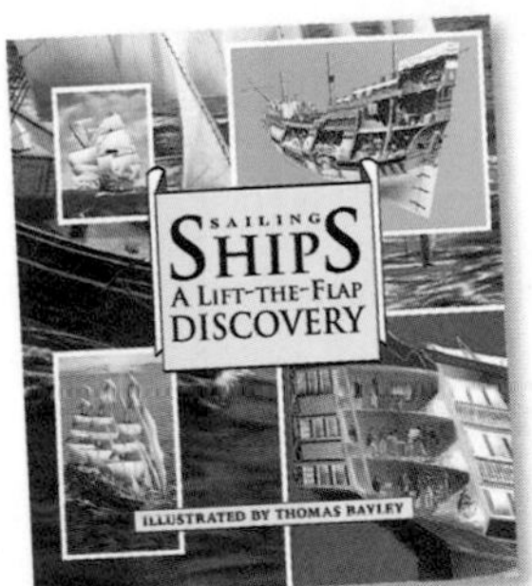

Meet the Illustrator

Paule Trudel

Paule Trudel says that drawing has always been a huge part of her life and she has always loved the sea. In fact when she was asked to illustrate *Sailing in the Wind* she was on a holiday at sea. Ms. Trudel lives in Canada.

Magnets

Written by Jo Knowl

Sailing in the Wind made Sammy wonder how a compass works. To find answers, Sammy goes to a Web site.

Here Sammy finds four different sources: an atlas, an almanac, a dictionary, and an encyclopedia.

Sammy clicks on Encyclopedia. Then he types the keyword *compass* into the search engine and clicks on "go." He gets a list of results that begins like this:

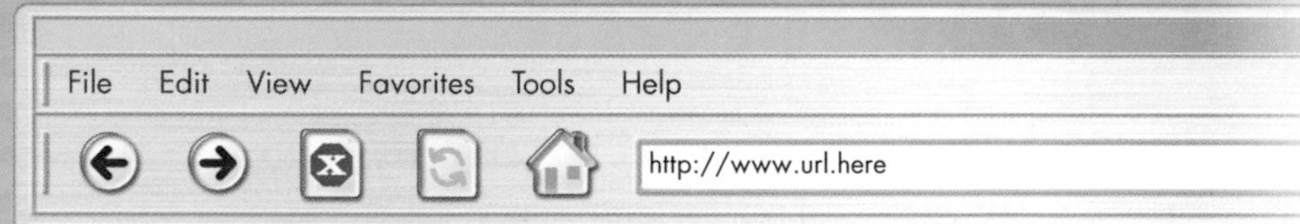

Search Results: compass

compass (encyclopedia)

compass: a device for showing directions, with a magnetic needle that always points to the Magnetic North Pole.

Sammy clicks on the compass link and finds an encyclopedia article. As he reads it, he finds a link to How a Compass Works. This makes him curious. He clicks on How a Compass Works and finds this information.

http://www.url.here

How a Compass Works

The needle in a compass is a magnet. The North Pole of the Earth has a force that pulls on magnets. This makes the needle point north.

Now Sammy knows that magnets make a compass work. Sammy wants to know more about magnets. He wonders what other ways magnets are used.

So far, Sammy has read part of an encyclopedia article and looked at a diagram. Sammy now goes back to the reference Web site. He wants to find more information about magnets. Sammy follows the steps and does another search. He finds these diagrams and photos on the Web site of a large university.

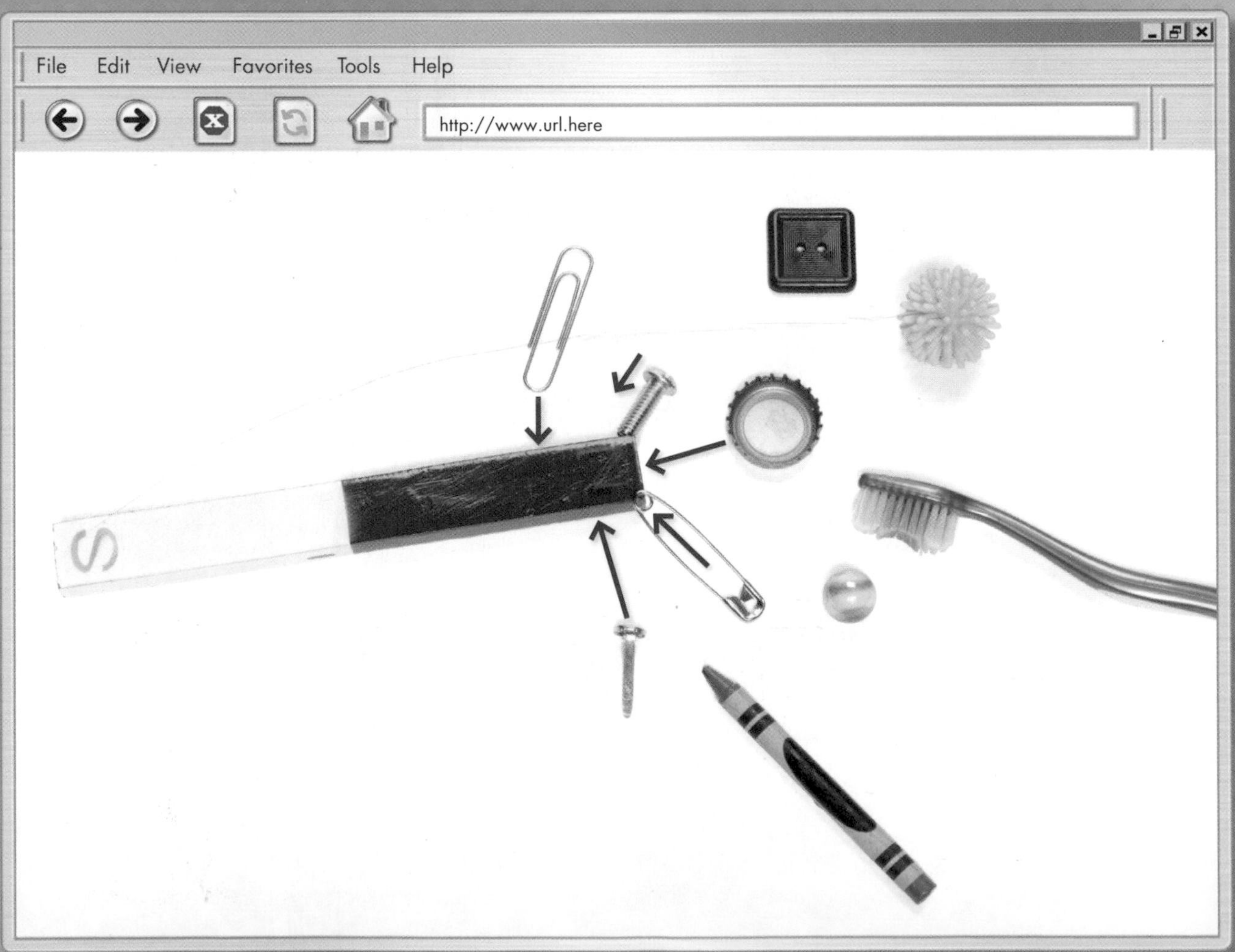

Sammy is so interested that he continues searching until he finds out all he needs to know about magnets.

How do magnets work?

Magnets are made of special metals. These metals have magnetic power. They are pulled to other metals. Magnets can also pull on metal things, like paper clips.

Magnets are strong!

The magnet in a compass is small. But magnets can do a lot of work! Magnets help run things we use every day, like radios and computers. Machines use big magnets to lift heavy things. Magnets also help run trains and keep them on their tracks.

Writing Narrative Nonfiction

Prompt In *Sailing in the Wind,* we learned about a boy who was the youngest to sail across the Atlantic Ocean alone. Think about all of the ways he prepared for that trip. Now write a paragraph explaining how you prepare to come to school every day.

Writing Trait

Choose words that make your meaning clear.

Student Model

Getting Ready for School

How do I get ready for school? I do the same thing every day. Each morning I wake up at 7:30 a.m. I get dressed and then I eat breakfast. Next, I brush my teeth. I pack my school bag. Then I walk to school.

A question ends with a question mark.

Writer chooses words that tell when things happen.

Narrative nonfiction is told in time order.

W1.1 Write brief narratives based on their experiences.
LC1.2 Recognize and use the correct word order in written sentences.

Writer's Checklist

- Does my writing tell about events in time order?
- Did I choose words that make my meaning clear?
- Do my statements end with periods and questions end with question marks?

Grammar Statements and Questions

A **statement** is a sentence that tells something. A statement ends with **a period(.)**.

A squall is dangerous**.**

A **question** is a sentence that asks something. A question ends with a **question mark (?)**.

Would you like to sail alone**?**

Practice Write a statement and a question from the model. Circle the period and the question mark.

Let's Talk About
Exploration

LS1.0 Students listen critically and respond appropriately to oral communication. They speak in a manner that guides the listener to understand important ideas by using proper phrasing, pitch, and modulation.

Words to Read

pieces
often
very
together
though
gone
learn

G1R1.11 Read common, irregular sight words (e.g., *the, have, said, come, give, of*).

Read the Words

Chip looked at the pieces of the puzzle. He often did these things with his very best friend Mike. He and Mike couldn't work together today, though. Mike had gone to visit his uncle. Chip knew he would have to learn to do things on his own.

Genre: Play
A play is a story written to be acted out for others. Next you will read a play about an ant who sets out to learn who is the strongest one.

The Strongest One

retold as a play by Joseph Bruchac
illustrated by David Diaz
from *Pushing Up the Sky*

What does Little Red Ant learn about being strong?

Characters:

NARRATOR
LITTLE RED ANT
SECOND ANT
THIRD ANT
FOURTH ANT
SNOW
SUN
WIND
HOUSE
MOUSE
CAT
STICK
FIRE
WATER
DEER
ARROW
BIG ROCK

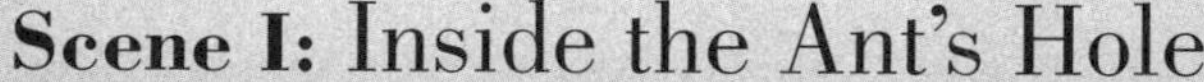

Scene I: Inside the Ant's Hole

(On a darkened stage, the ants crouch together.)

NARRATOR: Little Red Ant lived in a hole under the Big Rock with all of its relatives. It often wondered about the world outside: Who in the world was the strongest one of all? One day in late spring Little Red Ant decided to find out.

LITTLE RED ANT: I am going to find out who is strongest. I am going to go outside and walk around.

SECOND ANT: Be careful! We ants are very small. Something might step on you.

THIRD ANT: Yes, we are the smallest and weakest ones of all.

FOURTH ANT: Be careful, it is dangerous out there!

LITTLE RED ANT: I will be careful. I will find out who is strongest. Maybe the strongest one can teach us how to be stronger.

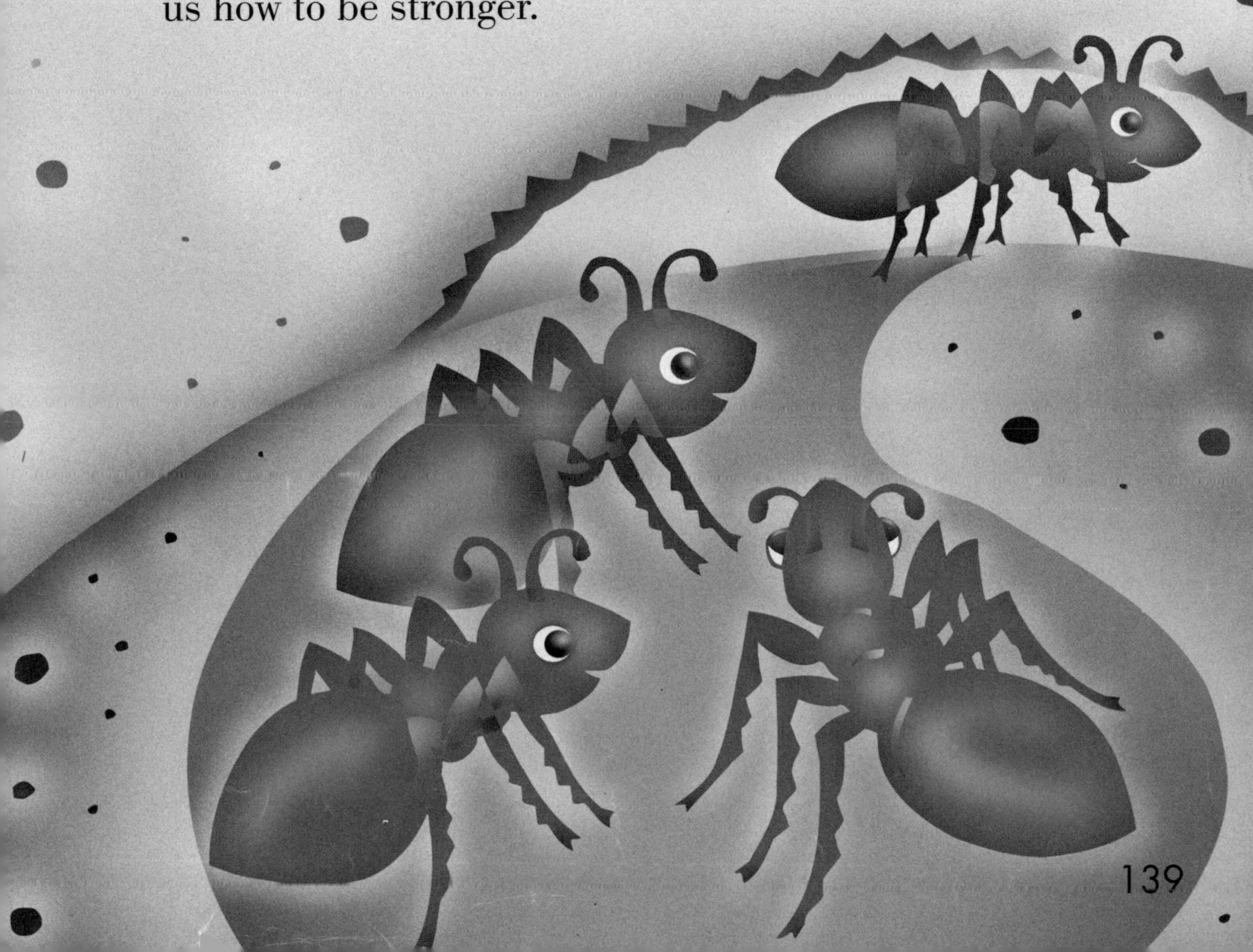

Scene II: The Mesa

(Ant walks back and forth onstage.)

NARRATOR: So Little Red Ant went outside and began to walk around. But as Little Red Ant walked, the snow began to fall.

(Snow walks onstage.)

LITTLE RED ANT: Ah, my feet are cold. This snow makes everything freeze. Snow must be the strongest. I will ask. Snow, are you the strongest of all?

SNOW: No, I am not the strongest.

LITTLE RED ANT: Who is stronger than you?

SNOW: Sun is stronger. When Sun shines on me, I melt away. Here it comes!

(As Sun walks onstage, Snow hurries offstage.)

LITTLE RED ANT: Ah, Sun must be the strongest. I will ask. Sun, are you the strongest of all?

SUN: No, I am not the strongest.

LITTLE RED ANT: Who is stronger than you?

SUN: Wind is stronger. Wind blows the clouds across the sky and covers my face. Here it comes!

(As Wind comes onstage, Sun hurries offstage with face covered in hands.)

LITTLE RED ANT: Wind must be the strongest. I will ask. Wind, are you the strongest of all?

WIND: No, I am not the strongest.

LITTLE RED ANT: Who is stronger than you?

WIND: House is stronger. When I come to House, I cannot move it. I must go elsewhere. Here it comes!

(As House walks onstage, Wind hurries offstage.)

LITTLE RED ANT: House must be the strongest. I will ask. House, are you the strongest of all?

HOUSE: No, I am not the strongest.

LITTLE RED ANT: Who is stronger than you?

HOUSE: Mouse is stronger. Mouse comes and gnaws holes in me. Here it comes!

(As Mouse walks onstage, House hurries offstage.)

LITTLE RED ANT: Mouse must be the strongest. I will ask. Mouse, are you the strongest of all?

MOUSE: No, I am not the strongest.

LITTLE RED ANT: Who is stronger than you?

MOUSE: Cat is stronger. Cat chases me, and if Cat catches me, Cat will eat me. Here it comes!

(As Cat walks onstage, Mouse hurries offstage, squeaking.)

LITTLE RED ANT: Cat must be the strongest. I will ask. Cat, are you the strongest of all?

CAT: No, I am not the strongest.

LITTLE RED ANT: Who is stronger than you?

CAT: Stick is stronger. When Stick hits me, I run away. Here it comes!

(As Stick walks onstage, Cat hurries offstage, meowing.)

LITTLE RED ANT: Stick must be the strongest. I will ask. Stick, are you the strongest of all?

STICK: No, I am not the strongest.

LITTLE RED ANT: Who is stronger than you?

STICK: Fire is stronger. When I am put into Fire, Fire burns me up! Here it comes!

(As Fire walks onstage, Stick hurries offstage.)

LITTLE RED ANT: Fire must be the strongest. I will ask. Fire, are you the strongest of all?

FIRE: No, I am not the strongest.

LITTLE RED ANT: Who is stronger than you?

FIRE: Water is stronger. When Water is poured on me, it kills me. Here it comes!

(As Water walks onstage, Fire hurries offstage.)

LITTLE RED ANT: Water must be the strongest. I will ask. Water, are you the strongest of all?

WATER: No, I am not the strongest.

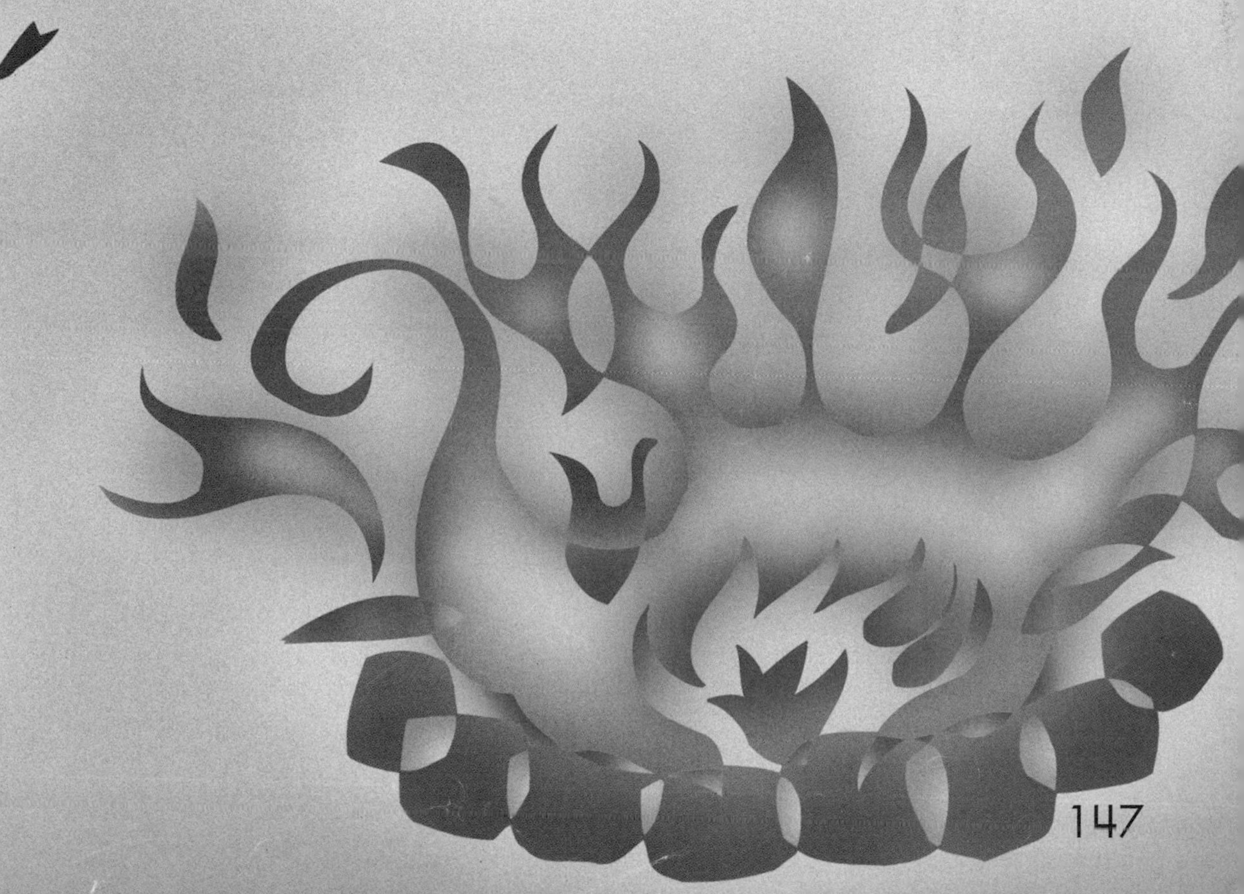

LITTLE RED ANT: Who is stronger than you?

WATER: Deer is stronger. When Deer comes, Deer drinks me. Here it comes!

(As Deer walks onstage, Water hurries offstage.)

LITTLE RED ANT: Deer must be the strongest. I will ask. Deer, are you the strongest of all?

DEER: No, I am not the strongest.

LITTLE RED ANT: Who is stronger than you?

DEER: Arrow is stronger. When Arrow strikes me, it can kill me. Here it comes!

(As Arrow walks onstage, Deer runs offstage with leaping bounds.)

LITTLE RED ANT: Arrow must be the strongest. I will ask. Arrow, are you the strongest of all?

ARROW: No, I am not the strongest.

LITTLE RED ANT: Who is stronger than you?

ARROW: Big Rock is stronger. When I am shot from the bow and I hit Big Rock, Big Rock breaks me.

LITTLE RED ANT: Do you mean the same Big Rock where the Red Ants live?

ARROW: Yes, that is Big Rock. Here it comes!

(As Big Rock walks onstage, Arrow runs offstage.)

LITTLE RED ANT: Big Rock must be the strongest. I will ask. Big Rock, are you the strongest of all?

BIG ROCK: No, I am not the strongest.

LITTLE RED ANT: Who is stronger than you?

BIG ROCK: You are stronger. Every day you and the other Red Ants come and carry little pieces of me away. Someday I will be gone.

Scene III: The Ant's Hole

NARRATOR: So Little Red Ant went back home and spoke to the ant people.

(The ants crouch together on the darkened stage.)

SECOND ANT: Little Red Ant has returned.

THIRD ANT: He has come back alive!

FOURTH ANT: Tell us about what you have learned. Who is the strongest of all?

LITTLE RED ANT: I have learned that everything is stronger than something else. And even though we ants are small, in some ways we are the strongest of all.

Talk About It You could perform this play as a dance or a puppet show. Tell how.

1. Use the pictures below to retell the story. Retell
2. Choose one of the characters Little Red Ant meets. How is this character strong? Why is it not the strongest of all? Classify and Categorize
3. Look at page 142. What is a word that means nearly the same as *chews*? Synonyms

TEST PRACTICE **Look Back and Write** What does Little Red Ant learn about being strong? Use details from the selection in your answer.

Retell

LS1.8 Retell stories, including characters, setting, and plot. **G3R1.6** Use sentence and word context to find the meanings of unknown words.

Meet the Author

Joseph Bruchac

As a child, Joseph Bruchac loved to explore nature—the animals, birds, insects, and plants around him. His grandfather, an Abenaki Indian, taught him many things about nature.

Today, Mr. Bruchac tells traditional Native American stories. "In the Abenaki Indian tradition," he says, "there is a story connected to just about every bird, animal, and plant." One message in many of these tales is that all parts of nature are important. Even tiny ants can make a difference!

Read more books by Joseph Bruchac.

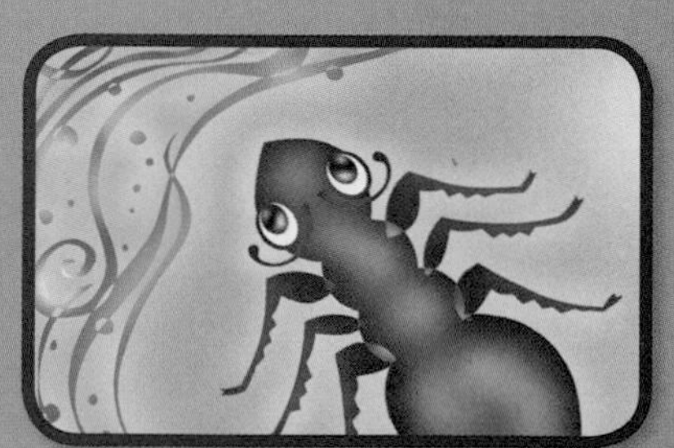

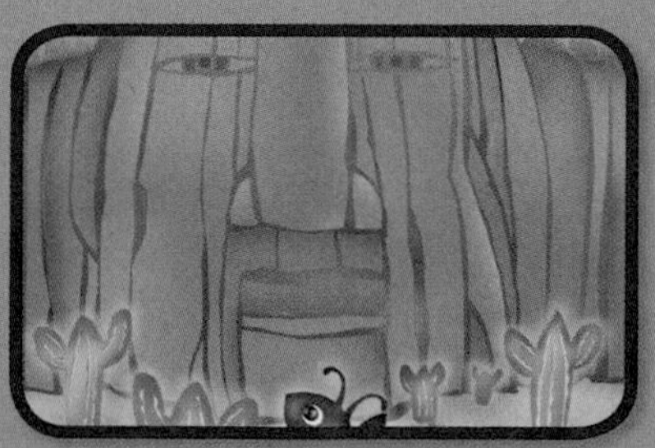

ANTEATERS

by John Jacobs

Have you ever heard of an anteater? Have you ever seen one? Let's learn more about them.

Where do they live?

Anteaters live mostly in South and Central America where there are lots of grasses, swamps, and rain forests. These are the kinds of places where many ants live. Anteaters explore these grasses, swamps, and rain forests all day looking for ants to eat.

What do they look like?

The giant anteater, which is the most common, looks like nothing you've ever seen before. It has a bushy tail and a fat body. It has a tiny mouth, small eyes, and small ears. Its most important body parts are its sharp claws and its long, long tongue. (Its tongue is almost two feet long. That's as long as two rulers put together!)

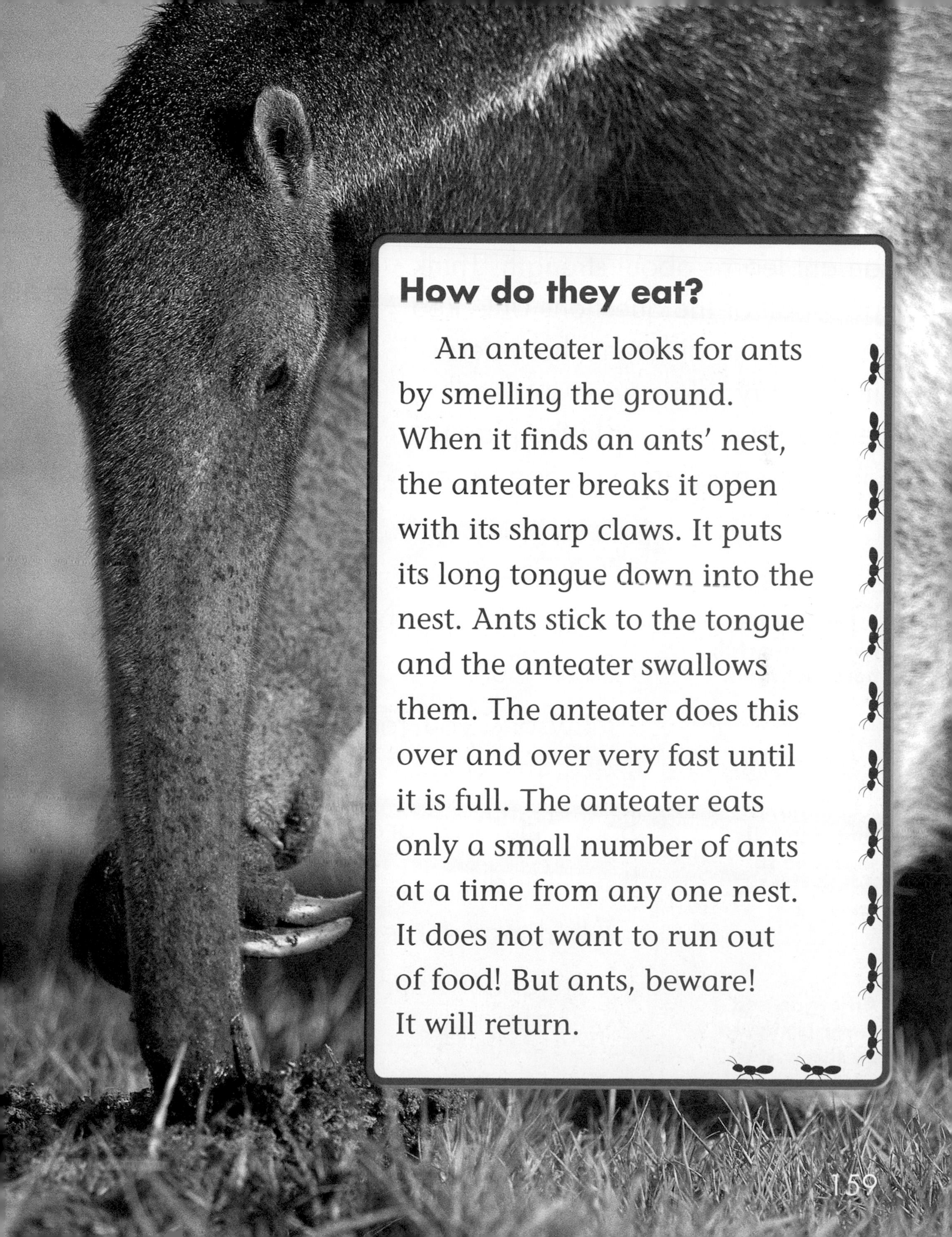

How do they eat?

An anteater looks for ants by smelling the ground. When it finds an ants' nest, the anteater breaks it open with its sharp claws. It puts its long tongue down into the nest. Ants stick to the tongue and the anteater swallows them. The anteater does this over and over very fast until it is full. The anteater eats only a small number of ants at a time from any one nest. It does not want to run out of food! But ants, beware! It will return.

Writing Friendly Letter

Prompt In *The Strongest One,* an ant learns about strength. Think about all of the questions Little Red Ant asks the different characters in the play. Now write a friendly letter to a character in the play to find out something you don't know.

Writing Trait

Organize your ideas in the form of a letter.

Student Model

A friendly letter has a cheerful, personal tone.

A command sentence tells someone to do something.

An organized letter is signed by the writer.

November 2, 2010

Dear Sun,

How are you today? I just learned that you are stronger than Snow. But you are not stronger than Wind!

What are some other things you are stronger than? Please tell me.

Your friend,

Sara

W2.2 Write a friendly letter complete with the date, salutation, body, closing, and signature.
LC1.4 Use commas in the greeting and closure of a letter and with dates and items in a series.

Writer's Checklist

- ✓ Does my letter have a friendly tone?
- ✓ Is my writing organized in the form of a letter?
- ✓ Do the commands in my sentences end with periods and the exclamations end with exclamation marks?

Grammar Commands and Exclamations

A **command** is a sentence that tells someone to do something. It usually ends with a **period(.)**.

Be careful out there**.**

An **exclamation** is a sentence that shows surprise or strong feeling, It ends with an **exclamation mark (!)**.

Practice Write a command and an exclamation from the letter. Circle the period and the exclamation mark.

Unit 2

Get Online!
PearsonSuccessNet.com

See It!

- Concept Talk Video
- Background Building Audio Slide Show
- *Picture It!* Animation
- e-Books

Hear It!

- Amazing Words *Sing with Me*
- Selection Snapshot and Response
- Paired Selection e-Text
- Grammar Jammer
- e-Books

Do It!

- Online Journal
- Story Sort
- New Literacies Activity
- Success Tracker

Working Together

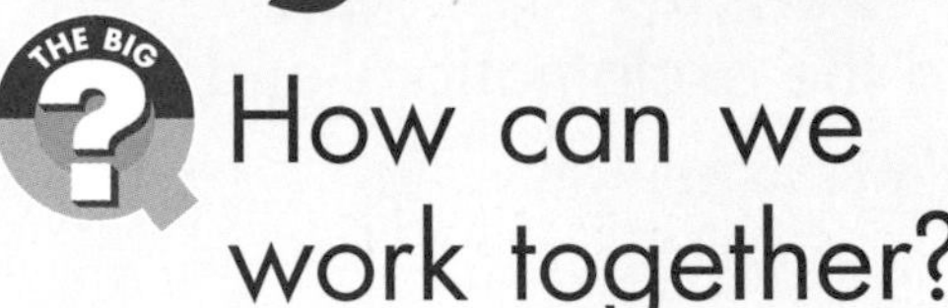

How can we work together?

Tara and Tiree, Fearless Friends
NARRATIVE NONFICTION

What makes Tara and Tiree fearless friends?

Paired Selection
Rescue Dogs PHOTO ESSAY

Abraham Lincoln BIOGRAPHY

What do you know about Abraham Lincoln?

Paired Selection
Lincoln POETRY

Scarcity EXPOSITORY NONFICTION

What happens when there are not enough oranges?

Paired Selection
Goods and Services WEB SITE

The Bremen Town Musicians
FAIRY TALE

Who are the Bremen Town Musicians?

Paired Selection
Animals Helping Animals WEB SITE

One Good Turn Deserves Another FABLE

How do a mouse and a coyote work together?

Paired Selection
The Lion and the Mouse FABLE

Let's Talk About Working Together

LS1.0 Students listen critically and respond appropriately to oral communication. They speak in a manner that guides the listener to understand important ideas by using proper phrasing, pitch, and modulation.

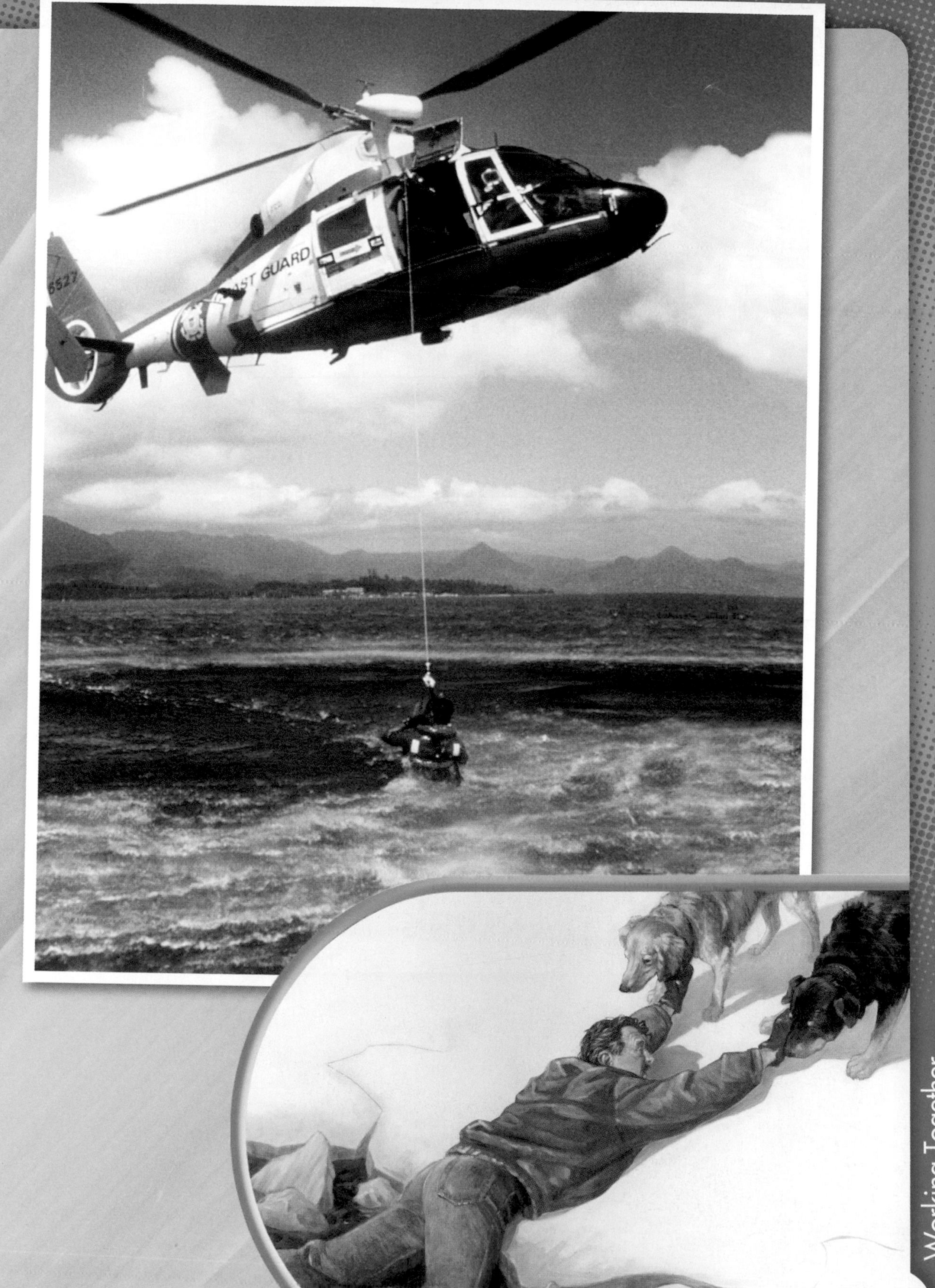
COAST GUARD
6527

Words to Read

family
pull
listen
once
heard
break

 G1R1.11 Read common, irregular sight words (e.g., *the, have, said, come, give, of*).

Read the Words

Tag is our family pet. He is a good dog. He will pull on my pant leg until I take him for a walk. He will listen and do what I say. Once he heard me call and came running so fast that I thought he would break a leg.

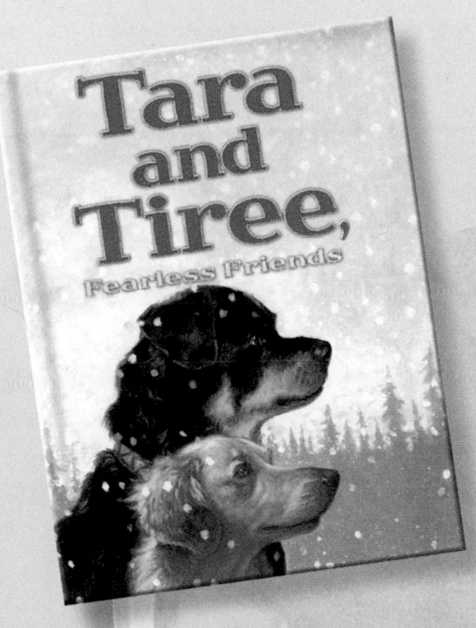

Genre: Narrative Nonfiction
Narrative nonfiction is true events told like a story. Now read about how two dogs saved their owner.

Tara and Tiree, Fearless Friends

by Andrew Clements
illustrated by Scott Gustafson

What makes Tara and Tiree fearless friends?

When Jim was a boy in Canada, his family had dogs. Jim loved those dogs. They were like part of his family.

When Jim grew up, he still loved dogs. He learned how to train them. He helped dogs learn to be good.

He always said, "There is no such thing as a bad dog." Training dogs became Jim's job.

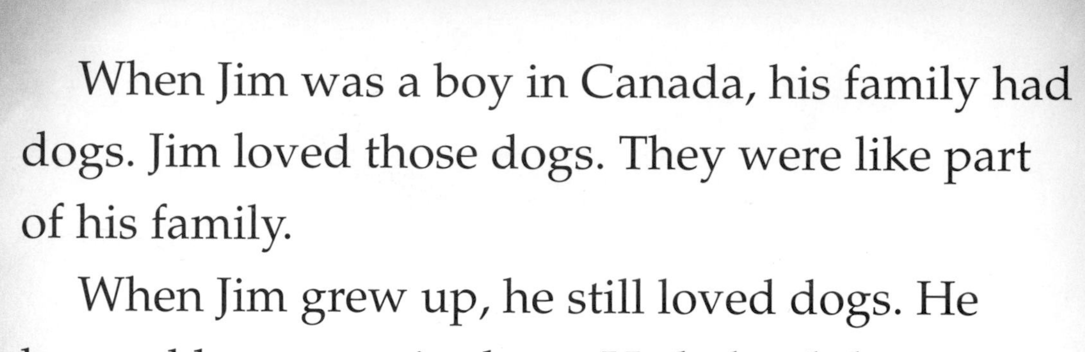

Jim had two dogs named Tara and Tiree.

Tara was mostly black. Tiree was mostly gold. Jim loved them both, and they loved him too. Jim and his dogs liked the winter time.

They had good coats to keep warm. They played in the snow. They went for long walks.

They liked going out, but they liked going back in too. It was good to sit by the fire and listen to the wind.

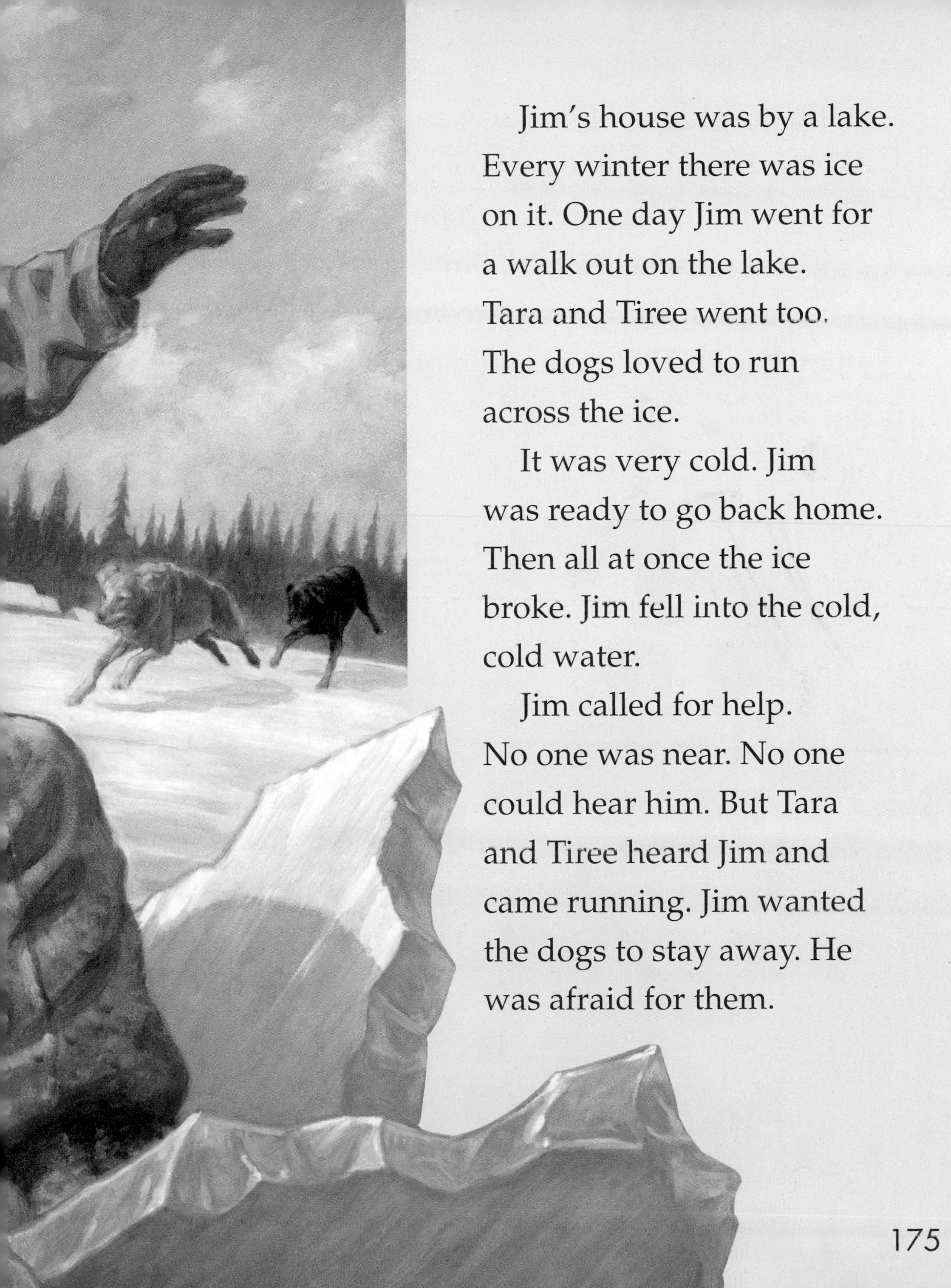

Jim's house was by a lake. Every winter there was ice on it. One day Jim went for a walk out on the lake. Tara and Tiree went too. The dogs loved to run across the ice.

It was very cold. Jim was ready to go back home. Then all at once the ice broke. Jim fell into the cold, cold water.

Jim called for help. No one was near. No one could hear him. But Tara and Tiree heard Jim and came running. Jim wanted the dogs to stay away. He was afraid for them.

But Tiree loved Jim. She wanted to help. When she came near the hole, the ice broke again. Tiree fell into the water with Jim.

The water was so cold. Jim knew he did not have much time. Jim tried to help Tiree get out. But the ice broke more and more.

Jim hoped Tara would run away. He did not want her to fall in the water too. But Tara did not run away. She wanted to help.

First Tara got down low. Then she came closer, little by little. The ice did not break.

Jim put out his hand. Tara got very close. Then Jim got hold of Tara's collar. Jim held on. Tara pulled back, but Jim was too big. He was still in the cold water.

Then Tiree did something very smart. She walked on Jim's back—up and out of the water!

Tiree was cold, but she was safe! Did she run off the ice? No. She loved Jim too much to run away.

Tiree got down on her belly like Tara. She got close to Jim. Jim held out his other hand. And he grabbed on to Tiree's collar!

The two dogs pulled back hard. They slipped, but they didn't stop. Slowly they pulled Jim up onto the ice. He was safe.

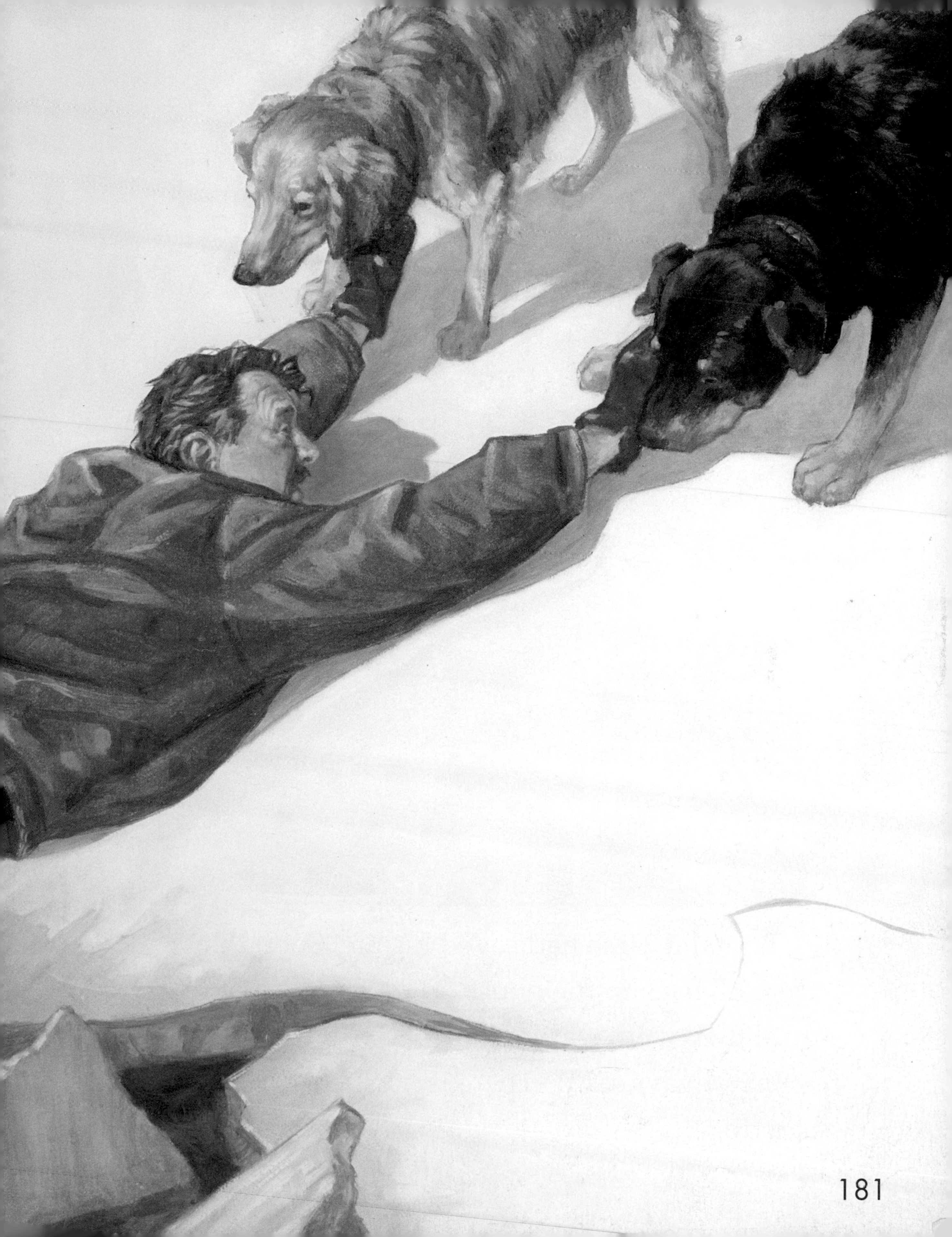

Tara and Tiree had saved his life! Soon they were all back in the house. They sat by the fire until they were warm again.

Jim always said, "There is no such thing as a bad dog."

Now Jim says something else too: "There *is* such a thing as a brave and wonderful dog!"

Jim is sure of this, because he has two of them—Tara and Tiree.

Talk About It Choose the most exciting part of this story. What makes it exciting? Read it.

1. Use the pictures below to retell the story. Retell
2. Tara seemed to know what to do when Jim fell into the water. What did she do first? What happened next? Sequence
3. Look at page 180. Read the words. How did you know what *slipped* means? Context Clues

TEST PRACTICE **Look Back and Write** What makes Tara and Tiree fearless friends? Use details from the selection in your answer.

Retell

LS1.8 Retell stories, including characters, setting, and plot. **G3R1.6** Use sentence and word context to find the meanings of unknown words.

Meet the Author

Andrew Clements

Andrew Clements says, "Every good writer I know started off as a good reader." When he was growing up, he loved to read. He remembers a school librarian who made him feel he was the "owner" of every book he read. He says, "That's one of the greatest things about reading a book—read it, and you own it forever."

Mr. Clements once taught school. Because he believes books make a difference, he read to his students in the classroom and to his four sons at home.

Read two more books by Andrew Clements.

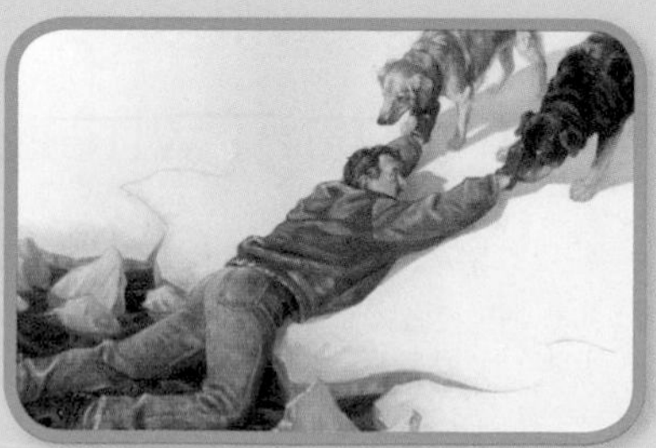

Rescue Dogs

by Rena Moran

Do you know that dogs can be trained to save lives? They are called rescue dogs. When people are in danger, rescue dogs are ready to help them.

Who do they help?

Rescue dogs find people who are lost or trapped. The dogs must be strong and smart. They must listen to the people who train and handle them. This dog's trainer is telling him where to go look for a person who is trapped in snow.

What dogs make good rescue dogs?

Some dogs, like bloodhounds and German shepherds, are good at following the scent trails of lost people. German shepherds are also good at finding people who are trapped under snow.

Newfoundlands are good swimmers. They do a great job with water rescues.

How do they do their jobs?

Like all dogs, rescue dogs have a very good sense of smell. They use their sense of smell to find a lost person.

A rescue dog can follows the scent trail a person has left.

Sometimes more than one person is lost. Rescue dogs can look for more than one person at a time.

Rescue dogs could not do their jobs without the people who train and handle them. Most of these people love working with dogs. They also like rescuing people in danger—just like their dogs do!

Writing Narrative Nonfiction

Prompt *Tara and Tiree* is about a dangerous rescue. Think about ways people work together in dangerous situations. Now write a narrative nonfiction paragraph about rescue workers.

Writing Trait

Voice shows how the writer feels about the topic.

Student Model

Every sentence has at least one noun.

Narrative nonfiction may include real quotes from people.

Voice shows how the writer felt.

Saving Spot

There was a fire at Mrs. Maxwell's house. Her dog Spot was trapped inside. The firefighters came. They tried to put out the fire. They heard Spot barking. "Save him, save him!" Mrs. Maxwell cried. It was so scary. Then two firefighters went inside. They saved Spot!

W2.1 Write brief narratives based on their personal experience. **LC1.3** Identify and correctly use various parts of speech, including nouns and verbs, in writing and speaking.

Writer's Checklist

- ✓ Is what I wrote realistic?
- ✓ Does my writing show my voice?
- ✓ Are my sentences complete, and do they use nouns?

Grammar Nouns

A **noun** names a person, place, animal, or thing.

The **boy** and his **dog** played with a **ball** in the **yard.**

Boy names a person.
Dog names an animal.
Ball names a thing.
Yard names a place.

Practice Look at the sentences in the model. Write the nouns in the sentences.

Let's Talk About Working Together

LS1.0 Students listen critically and respond appropriately to oral communication. They speak in a manner that guides the listener to understand important ideas by using proper phrasing, pitch, and modulation.

Words to Read

second
you're
either
laugh
worst
great
certainly

G1R1.11 Read common, irregular sight words (e.g., *the, have, said, come, give, of*).

Read the Words

Our second visit to Lincoln's Law Office worked out better than the first. The man at the door said, "You're going to get in this time. When you get to the museum at 8:00 A.M. you either have to wait or go someplace else for a while."

"It worked out okay." Dad said. "We had a good laugh about being early. We told the worst jokes and ate a great breakfast. But we are certainly glad to get in to see the office this time."

Genre: Biography
A biography tells about a real person's life. It is written by another person. Next read about some events from the life of a great President, Abraham Lincoln.

Abraham Lincoln

Written by Delores Malone
Illustrated by Stephen Costanza

What do you know about Abraham Lincoln?

It was clean up time in Ms. Grant's second grade class. Noah and Maya were putting away the big map of the United States. Suddenly, there was the worst ripping sound.

Everyone looked at Noah and Maya. The map was torn into two pieces.

"Look what you did!" said Noah.

"Me?" said Maya. "You're wrong! It's not my fault!"

Ms. Grant stepped in. "Please stop," she said. "I don't think either of you is at fault. We can fix that." They held up the two pieces of the map.

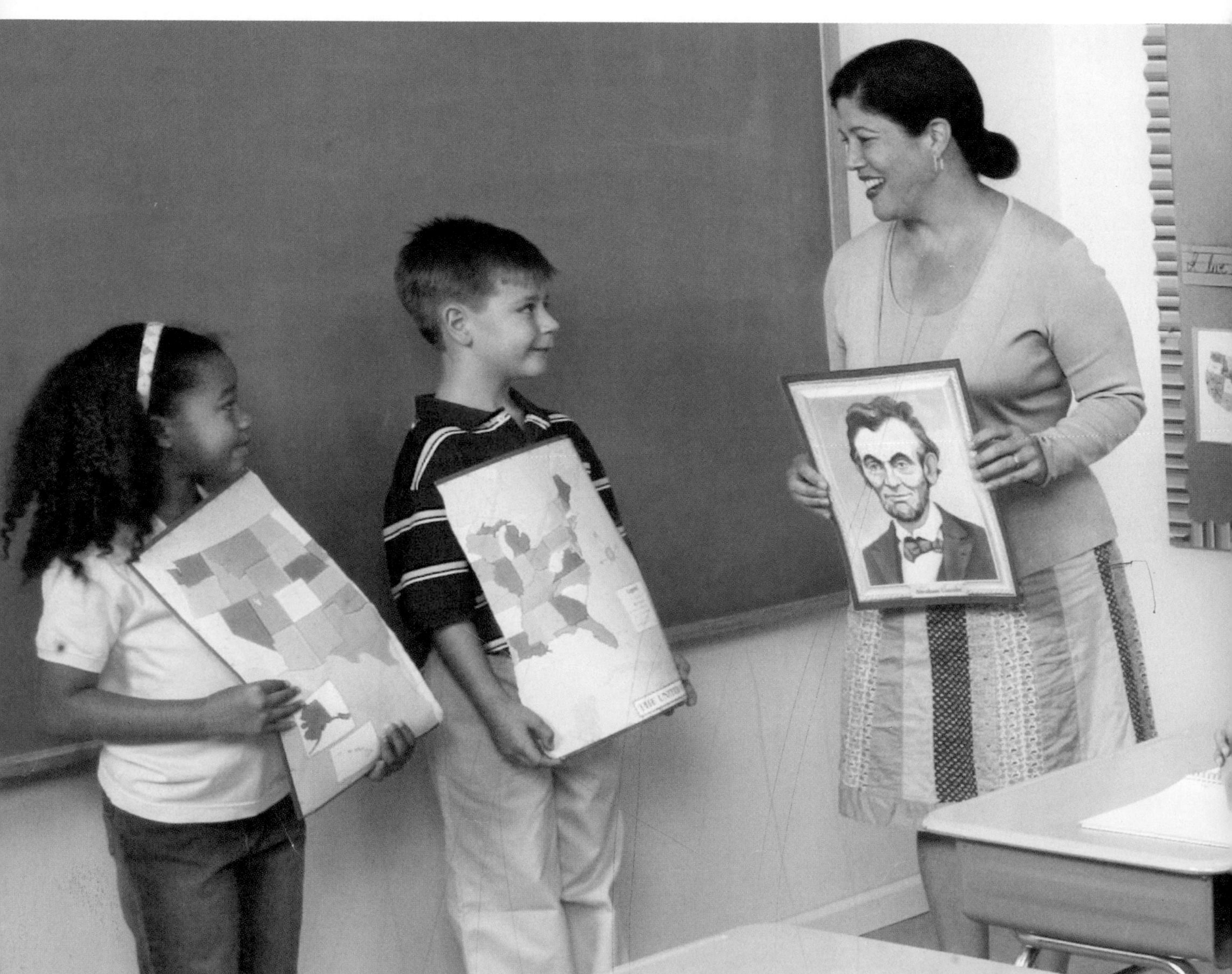

"Look! Our country has been torn in two. We need Abraham Lincoln!"

"Abraham Lincoln?" asked Noah. "You mean the President Lincoln from long ago?"

"Yes," said Ms. Grant. "I'll tell you about Abraham Lincoln and how he worked with other people to put our country back together."

Abraham Lincoln was born on February 12, 1809 in Kentucky. His family lived in a log cabin that had only one room. When Abraham Lincoln was a boy, everyone called him "Abe."

Abe and his family moved to Indiana in 1816. He was seven years old. Abe worked very hard on the farm.

One of his jobs was cutting wood. Wood was used for cooking and for heat. Wood was also used to make fences. When Abe grabbed the handle of his ax, a big log soon became firewood or fence rails.

Abe also plowed fields and planted corn. Young Abe carried a book with him wherever he went. Whenever he had time to rest, Abe took the book from his pocket and read.

As a young man, Abe worked in a store in New Salem, Illinois. One day a woman bought some things in the store. After she left, Abe noticed that he hadn't given enough money back to the woman. Abe walked many miles to give her the money. When his friends heard this story, they called him "Honest Abe."

Abe loved to read, tell stories, and make people laugh. Abe studied hard and passed a test to become a lawyer. In 1837, he opened a law office in Springfield, Illinois. Now people called him "Mr. Lincoln."

Abraham Lincoln was elected President of the United States on November 6, 1860. Now he was called "President Lincoln."

President Lincoln had a very big problem. People in the North wanted to end slavery. The people in the South wanted to form their own country and keep slavery. President Lincoln wanted to keep the country together.

1800 1810 1820 1830

1809 Abraham Lincoln is born in Kentucky.

1837 Lincoln opens his law office.

1816 Young Abe and his family move to Indiana.

The Civil War began on April 12, 1861. The armies of the North and the South fought each other. Many people died. President Lincoln had to find a way to stop the fighting.

The Civil War finally ended, on April 9, 1865. Abraham Lincoln worked very hard with many others to put our country back together. To this day, many people call Abraham Lincoln "American's Great President."

1861 The Civil War begins.

1860 Lincoln is elected president of the United States.

1865 The Civil War ends.

When Ms. Grant finished her story, Maya smiled at Noah and said, "Do you think we could put our country back together again?"

Noah nodded. "We certainly can."

When they finished, Maya and Noah held up the map for the class to see.

"Thank you," said Ms. Grant. "You did a terrific job. Now you have something in common with Abraham Lincoln. You worked together and you put our country back together."

Talk About It You have read about Abraham Lincoln. How is your life different from Lincoln's life as a child? Tell about it.

1. Use the pictures below to summarize what you learned. **Summarize**
2. Why do you think the author wrote this selection—to inform, entertain, or persuade? Explain. **Author's Purpose**
3. Did anything in this story confuse you? What did you do about it? **Monitor and Clarify**

TEST PRACTICE

Look Back and Write Look back at page 209. Why do you think people call Abraham Lincoln "America's Great President"?

Summarize

R2.3 Use knowledge of the author's purpose(s) to comprehend informational text.
R2.5 Restate facts and details in the text to clarify and organize ideas.

Meet the Author and the Illustrator

Delores Malone

Delores Malone has worked with small children most of her life. She now teaches others the best ways to work with young people. Ms. Malone lives in Evanston, Illinois with her husband, Roy.

Stephen Costanza

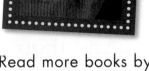

Stephen Costanza studied music before he studied art. He still loves music, but his chosen career is illustrator. You can see his illustrations in books, magazines, and advertising, as well as textbooks.

Mr. Costanza lives on the coast of Maine where he enjoys the out of doors.

Read more books by Stephen Costanza

LINCOLN

by Nancy Byrd Turner

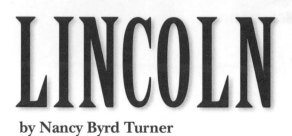

There was a boy of other days,
A quiet, awkward, earnest lad,
Who trudged long weary miles to get
A book on which his heart was set–
And then no candle had!

He was too poor to buy a lamp
But very wise in woodmen's ways.
He gathered seasoned bough and stem,
And crisping leaf, and kindled them
Into a ruddy blaze.

Then as he lay full length and read,
The firelight flickered on his face,
And etched his shadow on the gloom.
And made a picture in the room,
In that most humble place.

The hard years came, the hard years went,
But, gentle, brave, and strong of will,
He met them all. And when to-day
We see his pictured face, we say,
"There's light upon it still."

Writing Biography

Prompt In *Abraham Lincoln,* we read about someone who worked with others and changed history. Think about someone else in history who worked with others for change. Now write a biography of that person.

Writing Trait

Focus on one **idea** throughout a paragraph.

Student Model

Martin Luther King

Proper nouns should be capitalized.

Martin Luther King, Jr. spoke out for peace. He worked with others for change. King gave a famous speech. He said that he had a dream. His dream was that all people would be treated equally.

A biography tells about a real person.

Writing focuses on one idea.

G1W1.1 Group related ideas and maintain a consistent focus.
G1LC1.6 Capitalize all proper nouns, words at the beginning of sentences and greetings, months and days of the week, and titles and initials of people.

Writer's Checklist

- ☑ Did I write about a real person?
- ☑ Did I focus on one important idea?
- ☑ Did I capitalize all proper nouns?

Grammar Proper Nouns

Proper nouns are special names for people, places, animals, and things. They begin with capital letters.

Abraham Lincoln was born in February in Kentucky.

Days of the week, months of the year, and holidays also begin with capital letters.

Practice Look at the the model. Write the proper nouns from the sentences.

Let's Talk About Working Together

LS1.0 Students listen critically and respond appropriately to oral communication. They speak in a manner that guides the listener to understand important ideas by using proper phrasing, pitch, and modulation.

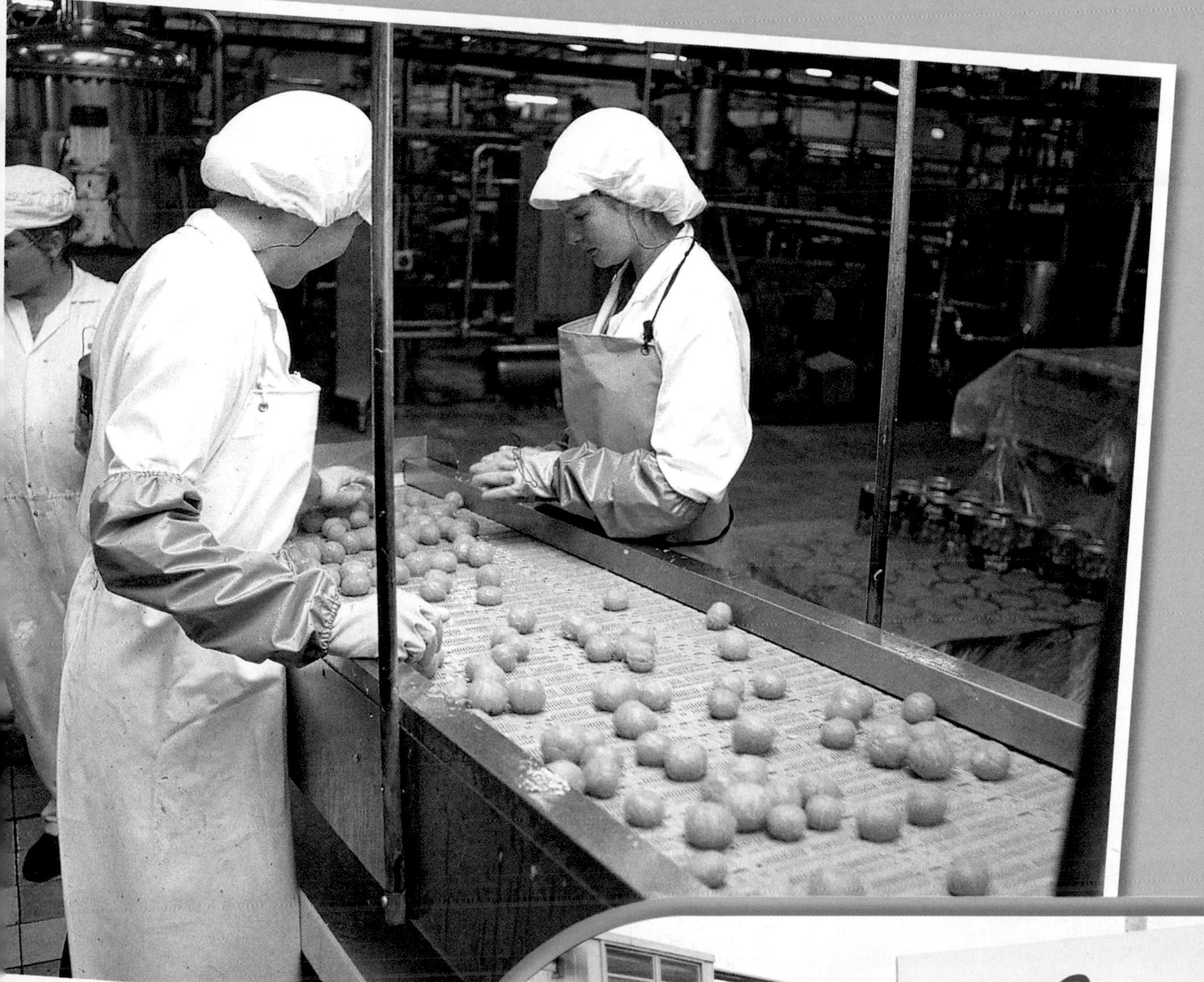

GAS
SHORTAGE!
Sales Limited to
10 GALS. OF GAS.
PER CUSTOMER

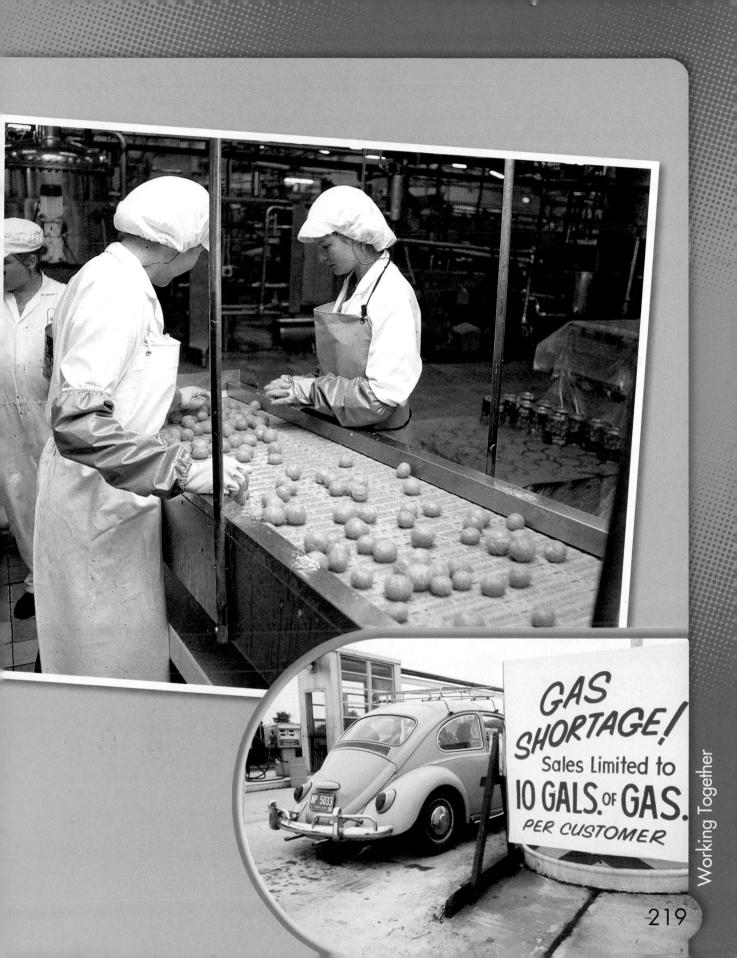

Words to Read

enough
word
ago
whole
above
toward

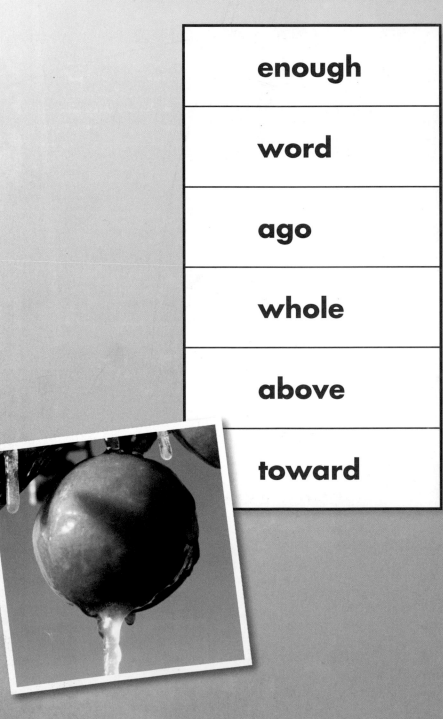

 G1R1.11 Read common, irregular sight words (e.g., *the, have, said, come, give, of*).

Read the Words

Do I have enough oranges for everyone? The word *oranges* kept going through my head. I had to get home and count them. Long ago our teacher told us we could bring fruit treats to school if we had enough for the whole class.

When I got home, the bag of oranges was on a shelf way above my head. I walked toward the living room to find Dad. He would help me.

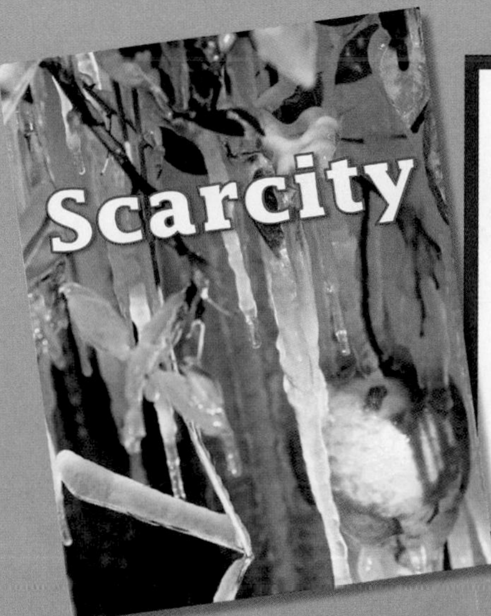

Genre: Expository Nonfiction

Expository nonfiction tells facts about a topic. Look for facts that help you understand what *scarcity* means.

Scarcity

By Janeen R. Adil

What happens when there are not enough oranges?

What Is Scarcity?

These three girls each want an orange. But only one orange is left. Not all the girls can get what they want.

Things people want and use are resources. Just like these girls, people want more resources than they can have. Sometimes there aren't enough resources for everyone. There is a word for this. It is *scarcity.*

Fact! All countries, rich and poor, have scarcity. No country has enough resources for everything it wants.

How Scarcity Happens

All resources can be scarce. But some resources become more scarce at times. For example, a few years ago, cold weather harmed orange trees.

Then farmers had fewer oranges to pick and sell. Oranges became scarce. There weren't enough oranges for everyone.

When There Isn't Enough

What happens when oranges are scarce? Then a food company must choose how to use them. The company could make orange juice. Or it could just sell whole, fresh oranges. The company might not be able to do both.

Fact! In 2004, four hurricanes in Florida harmed many fruit trees. Farmers had less fruit to pick and sell during 2005.

Making Trade-Offs

A food company might decide to sell just fresh, whole oranges. That means it's also deciding not to sell juice. The company is making a trade-off. To sell only fresh, whole oranges, it must give something up. The company gives up selling orange juice.

Prices

If oranges are scarce, not everyone can have them. But many people still want to buy oranges.

Stores raise the prices of scarce items. Oranges cost more money when they are scarce. If people want oranges, they must pay a higher price.

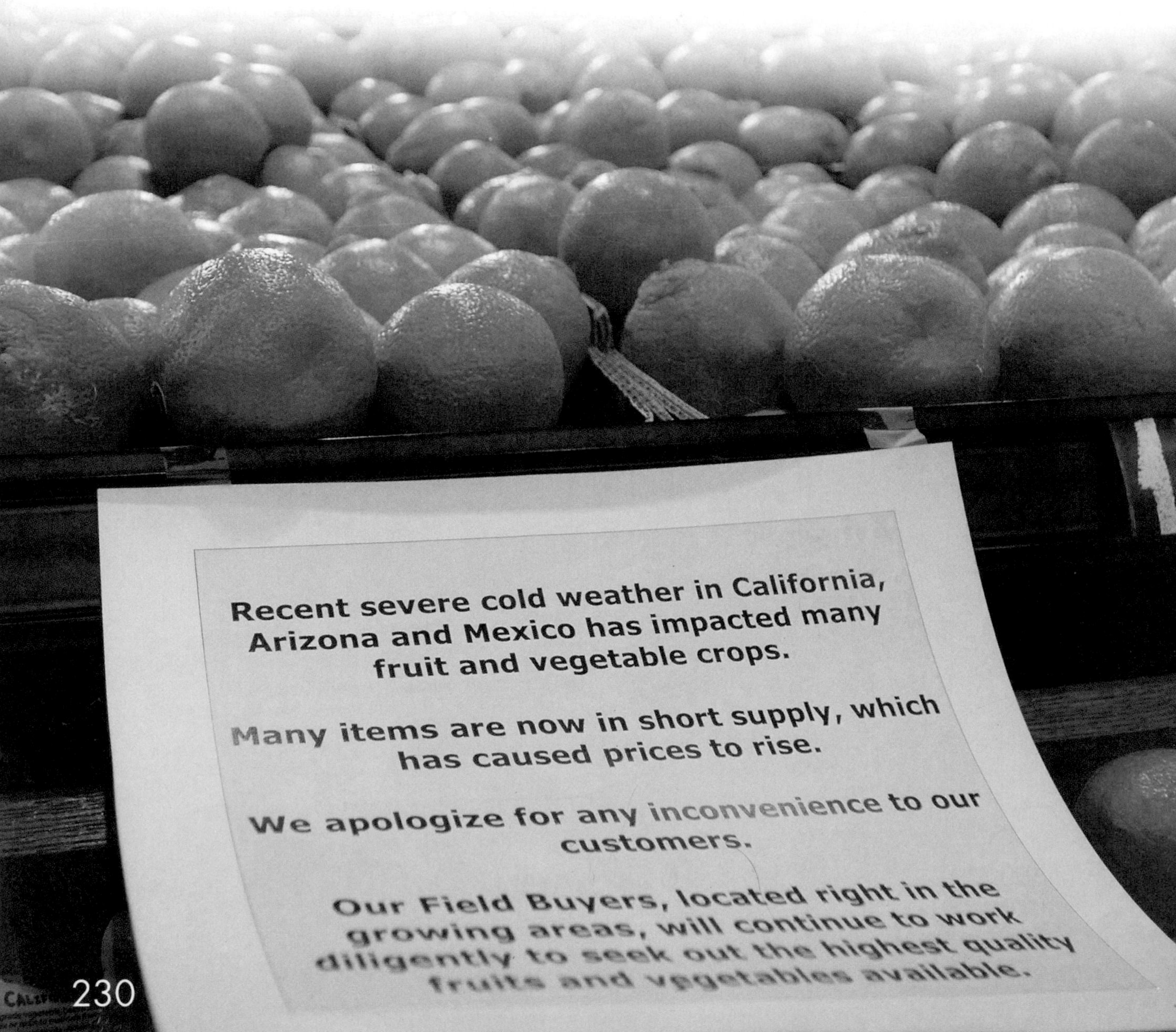

Recent severe cold weather in California, Arizona and Mexico has impacted many fruit and vegetable crops.
Many items are now in short supply, which has caused prices to rise.
We apologize for any inconvenience to our customers.
Our Field Buyers, located right in the growing areas, will continue to work diligently to seek out the highest quality fruits and vegetables available.

Fact! Orange prices were low before the 2004 Florida hurricanes damaged orange trees. After the hurricanes, the prices went up because oranges were scarce.

Making Choices

Scarcity means people have to make choices at the store. If oranges are scarce, what are the choices? People can pay a higher price for oranges. They can also try to find a better price at a different store. Or they can buy another fruit instead.

A Scarce Toy

Just like oranges, toys can be scarce. Ben wants to buy his sister a popular toy for her birthday. But the store near their house has sold out. The toy has become scarce.

Ben Must Choose

Ben looks at other stores around town. At last he finds the toy. But this store is charging a price above what Ben wants to pay.

Now Ben has to make a choice. Should he buy the toy at this high price? Should he keep looking for a better price? Or should he buy his sister something else? What would you do?

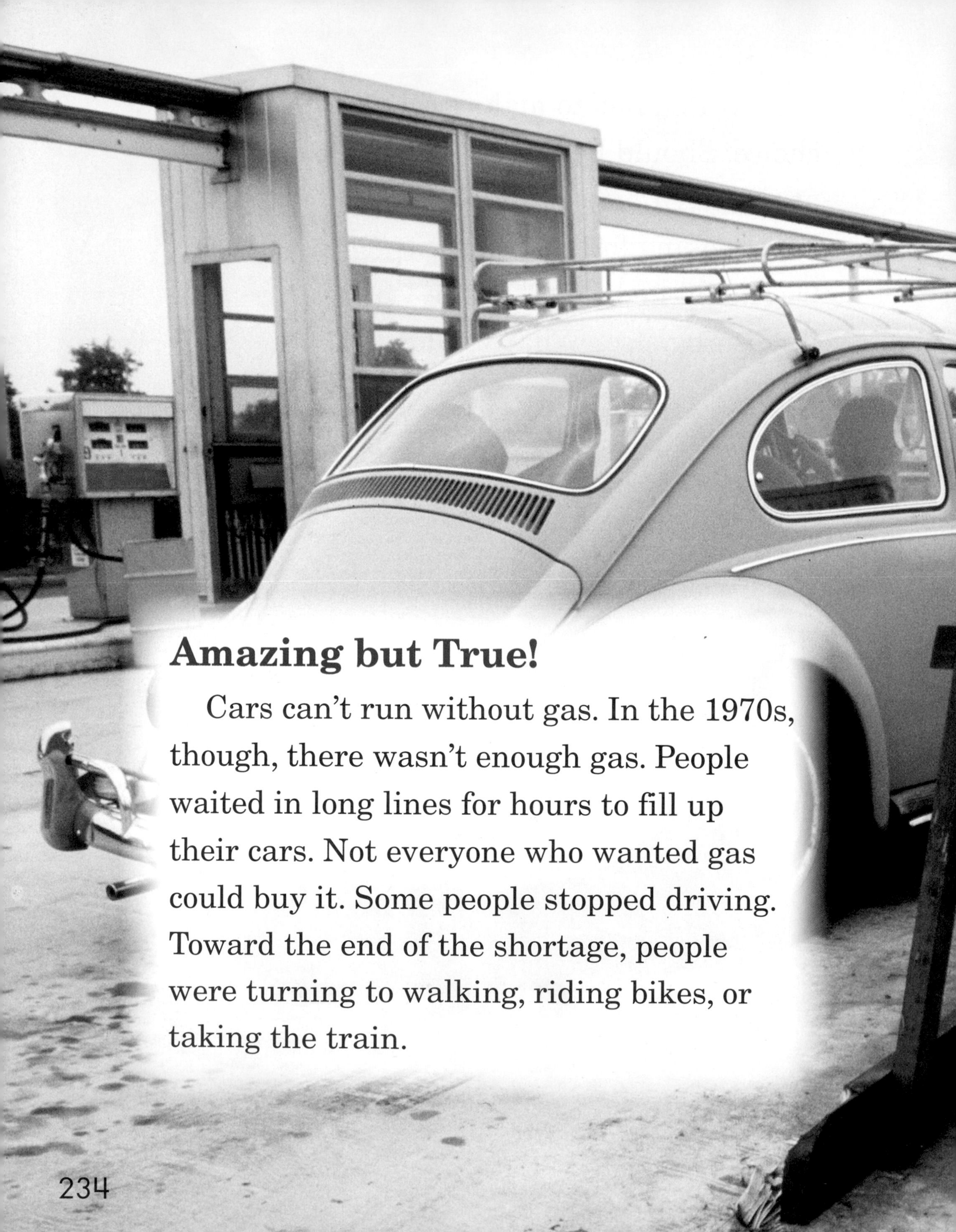

Amazing but True!

Cars can't run without gas. In the 1970s, though, there wasn't enough gas. People waited in long lines for hours to fill up their cars. Not everyone who wanted gas could buy it. Some people stopped driving. Toward the end of the shortage, people were turning to walking, riding bikes, or taking the train.

GAS
SHORTAGE!
Sales Limited to
10 GALS. OF GAS.
PER CUSTOMER

Talk About It What would you do if something you wanted to buy was not at the store? Explain.

1. Use the pictures below to summarize what you learned. **Summarize**
2. Why do you think the author wrote this selection—to inform, entertain, or persuade? Explain. **Author's Purpose**
3. Did anything in the story confuse you? What questions did you ask yourself as you read? **Ask Questions**

TEST PRACTICE

Look Back and Write Look back at pages 222–223. What are some things that happen when oranges become scarce? Use details from the selection.

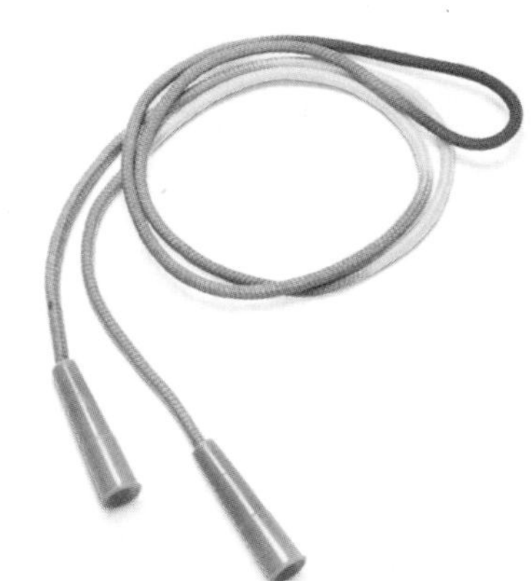

Summarize

Recent severe cold weather in California, Arizona and Mexico has impacted many fruit and vegetable crops.
Many items are now in short supply, which has caused prices to rise.
We apologize for any inconvenience to our customers.
Our Field Buyers, located right in the growing areas, will continue to work

R2.3 Use knowledge of the author's purpose(s) to comprehend informational text. **R2.4** Ask clarifying questions about essential textual elements of exposition (e.g., *why, what if, how*). **R2.5** Restate facts and details in the text to clarify and organize ideas.

Meet the Author

Janeen R. Adil

Janeen R. Adil grew up in a Connecticut farmhouse that is almost 300 years old. In her house, books were everywhere. Her writing grew naturally out of her love of reading.

Ms. Adil especially likes to write nonfiction for young people. She says, "What could be better than showing and sharing the wonders of our world?"

More books to read by Janeen R. Adil

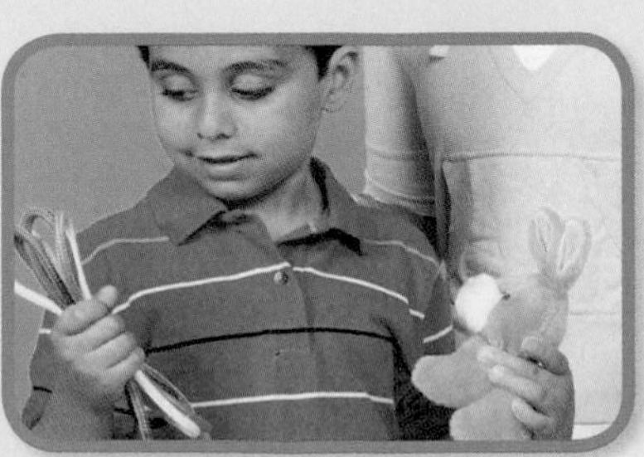

Goods and Services

After reading *Scarcity,* Jordan wants to learn more about economics. Economics is the science that deals with money, goods, and services. Jordan searches the Web. His parents help him. They find a Web site with many links.

Jordan clicks on one link, Economics. A new Web page opens. He finds these choices:

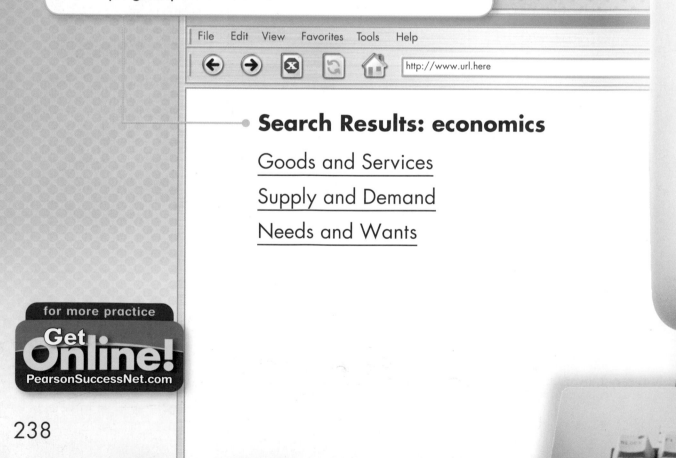

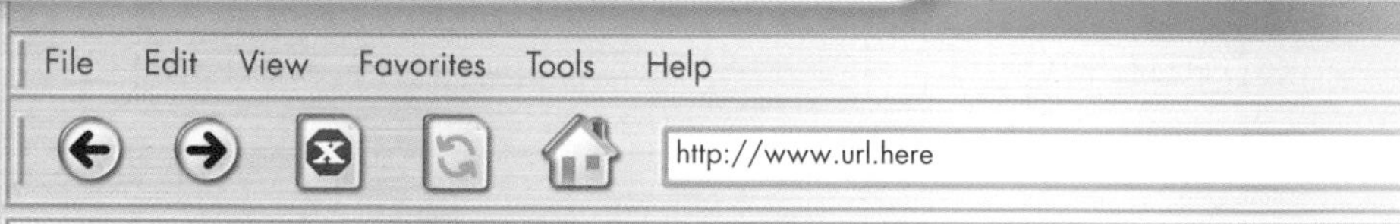

Search Results: economics

Goods and Services

Supply and Demand

Needs and Wants

Jordan chooses the link Goods and Services. This link opens to a new Web page.

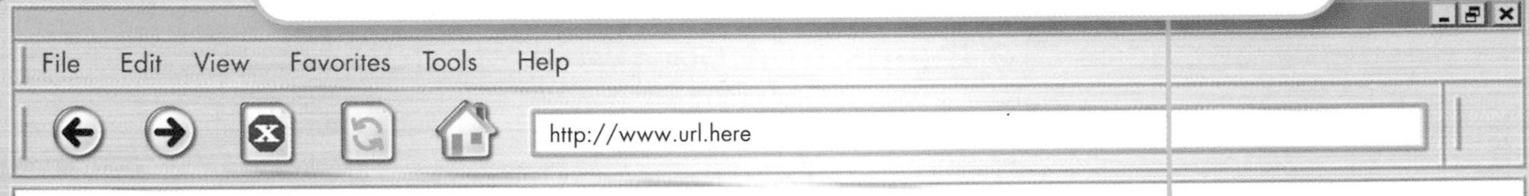

Goods and Services

Goods and services are important parts of economics.

Goods are things that people use. A good may be something people need to live, like food. A good may also be something people want, just for fun, like a bicycle. Goods can be bought or sold.

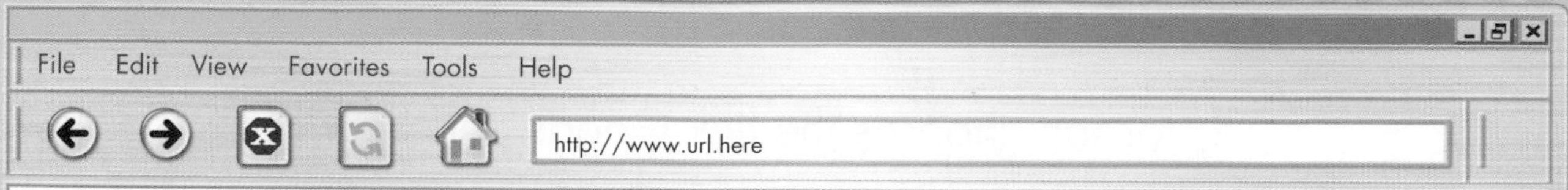

Services are things that people do for others. People who provide a service usually do it as part of their jobs. Doctors provide a service by helping people get well. Bus drivers provide a service by taking people to work or to school.

Jordan uses the scroll bar on the right-hand side of the Web page to find out more about goods and services.

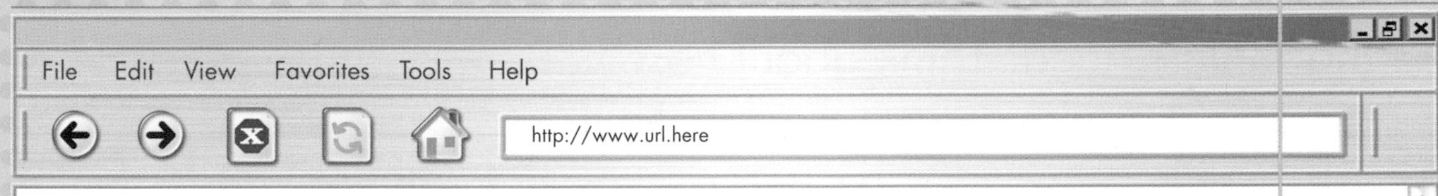

Sometimes one place sells both goods and services. This is a shop where people can buy shampoo and other things for their hair. These are goods. People can also get their hair cut here. The haircuts are a service.

Writing Expository Nonfiction

Prompt In *Scarcity,* many people work together to provide things that others need. Think about how working together meets the needs of others. Now write an informational paragraph explaining how working together could help someone.

Writing Trait

Choose words that give exact information.

Student Model

Working Together

Our little league team needed new uniforms. The whole neighborhood helped to raise money. Last Saturday, we had a big rummage sale. It was in the school gym. We sold old coats, books, and games. We raised enough money for new uniforms.

Expository nonfiction tells about real people, places, or events.

Choosing exact words makes meaning clearer.

Plural nouns end with -s.

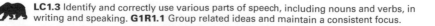

LC1.3 Identify and correctly use various parts of speech, including nouns and verbs, in writing and speaking. **G1R1.1** Group related ideas and maintain a consistent focus.

Writer's Checklist

- ☑ Did I tell about real people, places, and events?
- ☑ Did I choose words that make my meaning clear?
- ☑ Did I use singular and plural nouns correctly?

Grammar **Singular and Plural Nouns**

A **singular noun** names one person, place, animal, or thing.

We sold a **book.**

A noun that names more than one is called a **plural noun.**

We sold many **books.**

Add -s to most nouns to show more than one.

Practice Write the singular nouns from the model in one list. Write the plural nouns in another list.

Let's Talk About Working Together

LS1.0 Students listen critically and respond appropriately to oral communication. They speak in a manner that guides the listener to understand important ideas by using proper phrasing, pitch, and modulation.

Words to Read

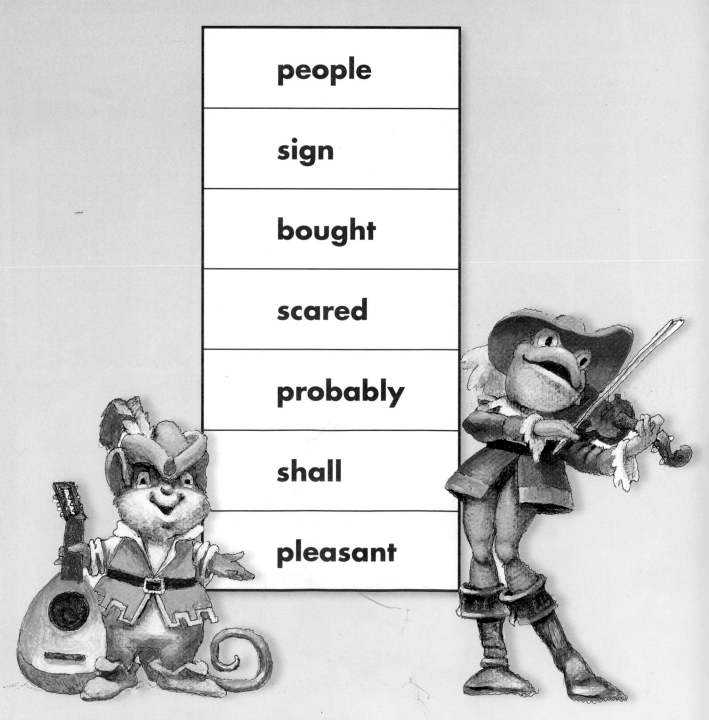

people
sign
bought
scared
probably
shall
pleasant

Read the Words

People waited for hours to get tickets for the big concert. One man made a sign asking for extra tickets! Some wise fans bought their tickets months ago. They were scared by all the talk that the concert would probably be sold out.

"I shall do my best," one singer said. "I think this will be a very pleasant concert."

Genre: Fairy Tale
A fairy tale usually takes place long ago and far away and has fantastic characters. Next you will read about four animals that become friends and travel to a faraway town.

The Bremen Town Musicians

retold as a play by Carol Pugliano-Martin
illustrated by Jon Goodell

Who are the Bremen Town Musicians?

NARRATOR 1: Once there was a donkey. He worked hard for his owner for many years. Day after day he carried heavy bags of grain to the mill.

NARRATOR 2: But the donkey grew old. He could no longer work hard. One day he heard his owner talking about him. He said he was going to get rid of the donkey. The donkey was worried.

DONKEY: Oh, no! What will happen to me? I must run away. I'll go to Bremen. There I can be a fine musician. (The donkey sings this song:)

Off I go to Bremen Town.
It's the place to be!
I will play my music there.
People will love me!
With a hee-haw here,
And a hee-haw there.
Here a hee, there a haw,
Everywhere a hee-haw.
Off I go to Bremen Town.
It's the place to be!

NARRATOR 1: So the donkey left that night. He had not gone far when he saw a dog lying on the ground.

NARRATOR 2: The dog looked weak. He also looked sad. The donkey knelt down to speak to the dog.

DONKEY: What is the matter, my friend?

DOG: Ah, me. Now that I am old and weak, I can no longer hunt. My owner wants to get rid of me. I got scared, so I ran away. Now I don't know what I will do.

DONKEY: You can come with me to Bremen. I am going to be a musician. Will you join me?

DOG: I'd love to! I can bark very pleasant tunes.

DOG AND DONKEY: Off we go to Bremen Town. It's the place to be! We will play our music there. We'll be filled with glee!

DONKEY: With a hee-haw here, and a hee-haw there. Here a hee, there a haw, everywhere a hee-haw.

DOG: With a bow-wow here and a bow-wow there. Here a bow, there a wow, everywhere a bow-wow.

DOG AND DONKEY:
Off we go to Bremen Town.
It's the place to be!

NARRATOR 1: So, the donkey and the dog set off for Bremen. Soon, they saw a cat sitting by the road.

NARRATOR 2: The cat had the saddest face the donkey and the dog had ever seen. They stopped to find out what was wrong.

DOG: Hello there. Why so glum?

CAT: Ho, hum. Now that I am old and my teeth are not sharp, I cannot catch mice. My owner wants to get rid of me. I don't know what I will do.

DONKEY: You'll come to Bremen with us, that's what! We are going to become musicians. Won't you join us?

CAT: Sure I will! I love to meow.

DONKEY, DOG, AND CAT:
Off we go to Bremen Town.
It's the place to be!
We will play our music there.
We're a gifted three!

DONKEY: With a hee-haw here,
and a hee-haw there.
Here a hee, there a haw,
everywhere a hee-haw.

DOG: With a bow-wow here,
and a bow-wow there.
Here a bow, there a wow,
everywhere a bow-wow.

CAT: With a meow-meow here,
and a meow-meow there.
Here a meow, there a meow,
everywhere a meow-meow.

ALL: Off we go to Bremen Town.
It's the place to be!

NARRATOR 1: The three musicians walked along some more. They came to a farmyard. There they heard a rooster crowing sadly.

ROOSTER: Cock-a-doodle-doo! Cock-a-doodle-doo!

DONKEY: My, you sound so sad. What is wrong?

ROOSTER: I used to crow to wake up the farmer each morning. But he just bought an alarm clock. Now he doesn't need my crowing so he wants to get rid of me. Now I'm a cock-a-doodle-*don't!* Oh, what will I do?

DOG: Come with us to Bremen. We're going to be musicians.

CAT: With your fine crowing, we'll make a wonderful group!

ROOSTER: I *cock-a-doodle-do* think that's a wonderful idea! Let's go!

DONKEY, DOG, CAT, AND ROOSTER:
Off we go to Bremen Town. It's the place to be!
We will play our music there. We're a sight to see!

DONKEY: With a hee-haw here, and a hee-haw there.
Here a hee, there a haw, everywhere a hee-haw.

DOG: With a bow-wow here, and a bow-wow there.
Here a bow, there a wow, everywhere a bow-wow.

CAT: With a meow-meow here, and a meow-meow there. Here a meow, there a meow, everywhere a meow-meow.

ROOSTER: With a cock-a-doodle here, and a cock-a-doodle there. Here a doodle, there a doodle, everywhere a cock-a-doodle.

ALL: Off we go to Bremen Town. It's the place to be!

NARRATOR 2: The four musicians walked until it got dark. Finally, they saw a sign that said Bremen Town. They danced with excitement, but they were also very tired. They wanted to rest.

NARRATOR 1: They saw light coming from a little house up the road. They walked up to the window, but none of the animals was tall enough to see inside. So, the dog stood on the donkey's back, the cat stood on the dog's back, and the rooster stood on the cat's back and peeked inside.

DOG: What do you see, rooster?

ROOSTER: I think there are three robbers in there! They are sitting at a table full of delicious-looking food!

CAT: Food? I'm starving! What shall we do? We must get them out of that house!

ROOSTER: I have a plan. Listen closely.

NARRATOR 2: The rooster whispered his plan to the others.

NARRATOR 1: All of a sudden, the four began singing. They made quite a noise. When the robbers heard the animals, they ran out of the house screaming!

NARRATOR 2: The four musicians went inside the house. There they ate and ate until they were full. Then, it was time for bed.

NARRATOR 1: The donkey slept in the soft grass in the yard. The dog slept behind the front door. The cat slept near the warmth of the fireplace. And the rooster slept high on a bookshelf.

NARRATOR 2: After a while, the robbers returned to finish eating their feast.

ROBBER 1: That noise was probably just the wind. Besides, I can't wait to eat the rest of that roast beef!

ROBBER 2: I can taste those mashed potatoes now!

ROBBER 3: I'll go first just to make sure it's safe.

NARRATOR 1: So the robber went inside. He was cold, so he went to the fireplace to warm himself. There he surprised the cat, who scratched his face.

NARRATOR 2: The robber ran to the front door. The dog was startled and bit his leg. The robber ran outside. He tripped over the donkey, who kicked him.

NARRATOR 1: All this noise woke the rooster up. He started screeching, "Cock-a-doodle-doo!" The robber ran back to his friends.

ROBBER 3: There are four horrible monsters in there! One scratched me with its long nails. Another bit me. Another kicked me. And the fourth one screamed, "Coming to get yooouuuuu!"

ROBBER 1: Four monsters! Let's get out of here!

NARRATOR 2: And the robbers ran off, never to be heard from again.

NARRATOR 1: But the four musicians stayed there. They sang every night in Bremen, where they became the famous Bremen Town Musicians!

Talk About It You have seen the Bremen Town Musicians perform. Tell about the show they put on.

1. Use the pictures below to retell the story. **Retell**
2. The animals wanted to chase the robbers out of the house. What did they do first? What happened next? **Sequence**
3. Look at page 260. Read the words. How did you know what *excitement* means? **Context Clues**

TEST PRACTICE

Look Back and Write Who are the Bremen Town Musicians? Use details from the story in your answer.

Retell

LS1.8 Retell stories, including characters, setting, and plot. **G3R1.6** Use sentence and word context to find the meanings of unknown words.

Meet the Author

Carol Pugliano-Martin

Carol Pugliano-Martin has written many plays for schoolchildren to perform. Some of her plays are about real Americans. Others tell about the heroes of American folk tales. Ms. Pugliano-Martin lives in White Plains, New York.

Here are two books by Carol Pugliano-Martin with plays you may want to perform.

Animals Helping Animals

Did you know that some animals help one another? Sometimes they do this in surprising ways. Click on the pictures below to see how these animals help each other.

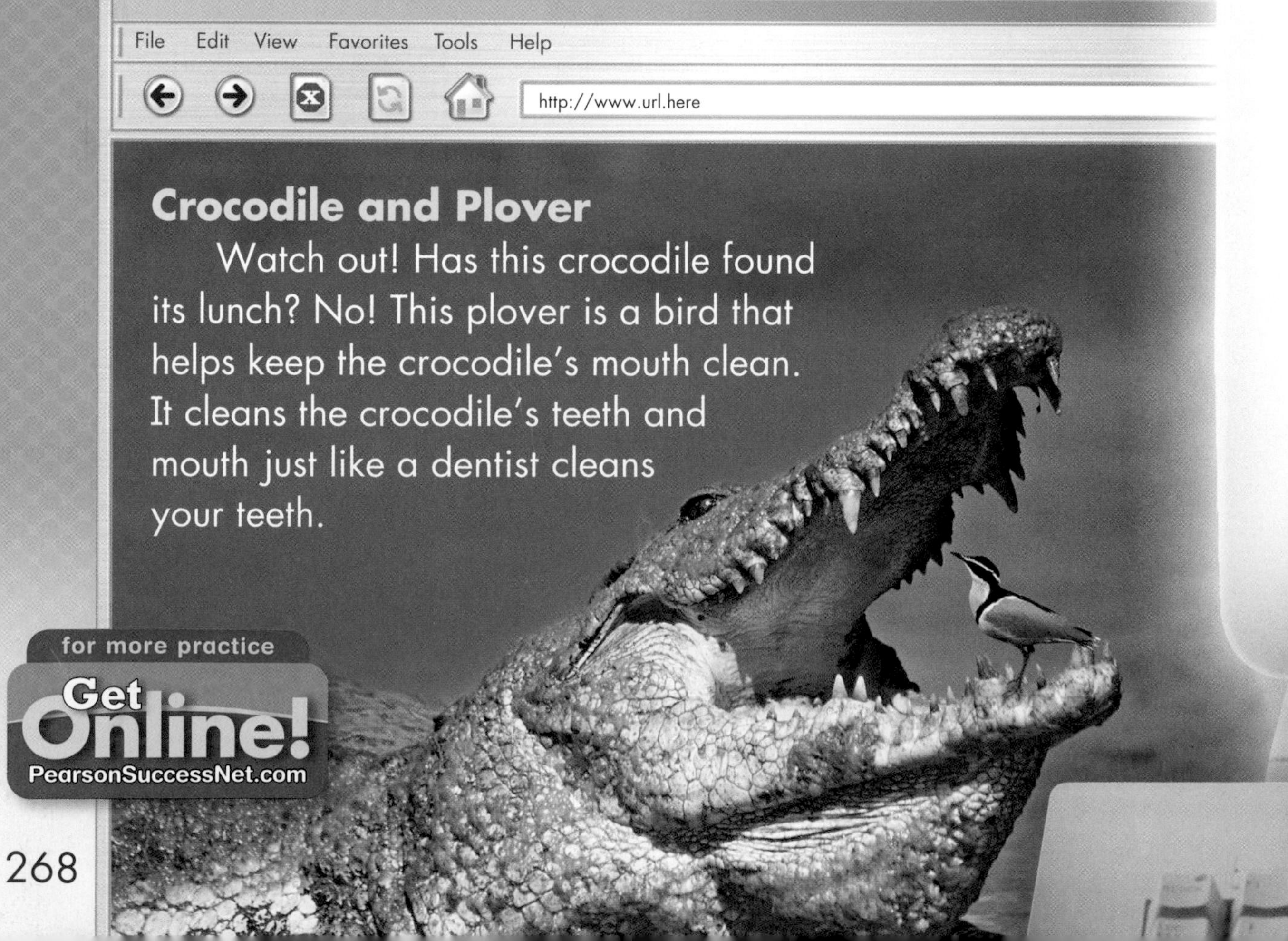

Crocodile and Plover

Watch out! Has this crocodile found its lunch? No! This plover is a bird that helps keep the crocodile's mouth clean. It cleans the crocodile's teeth and mouth just like a dentist cleans your teeth.

for more practice
Get Online!
PearsonSuccessNet.com

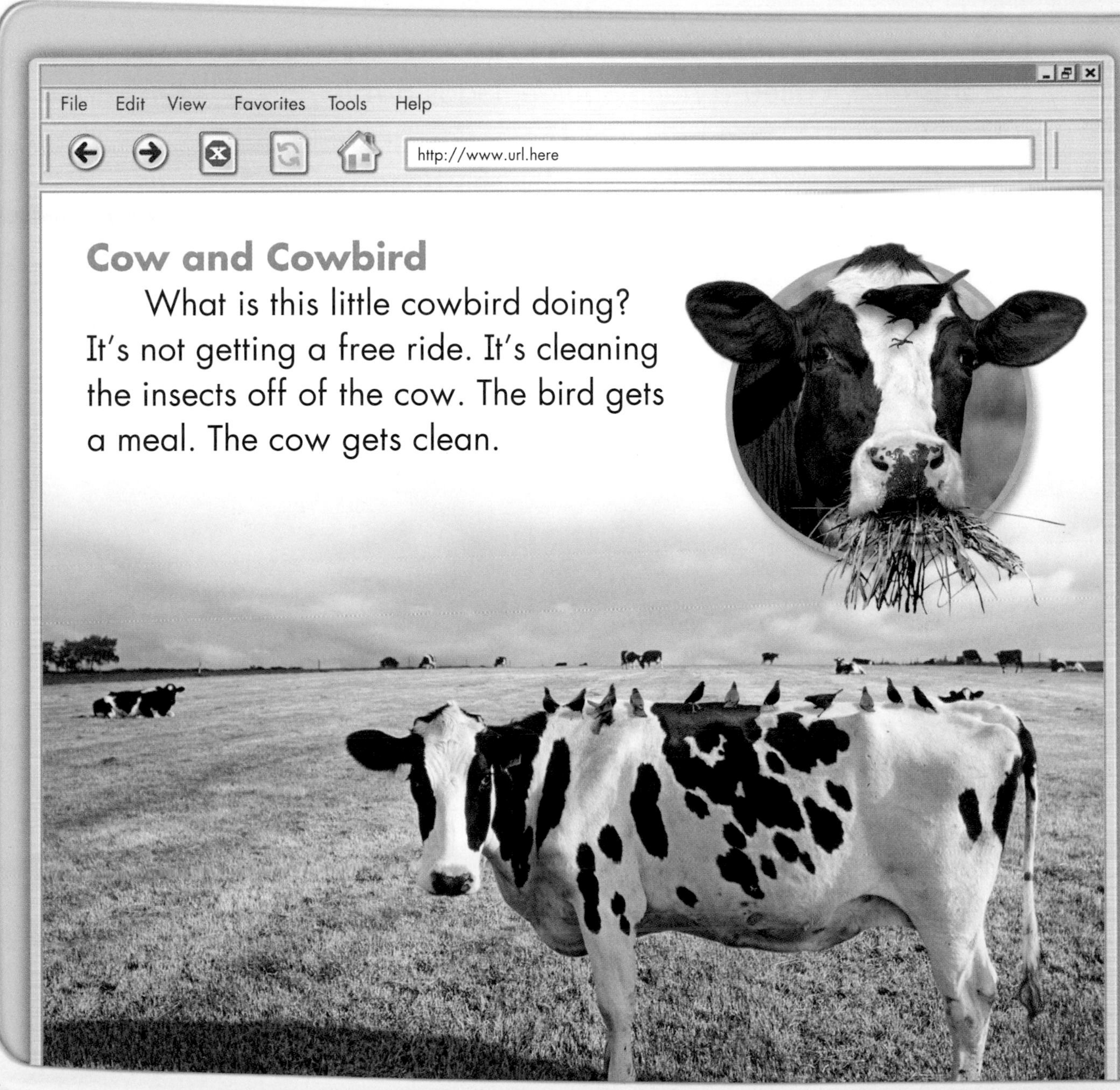

Cow and Cowbird

What is this little cowbird doing? It's not getting a free ride. It's cleaning the insects off of the cow. The bird gets a meal. The cow gets clean.

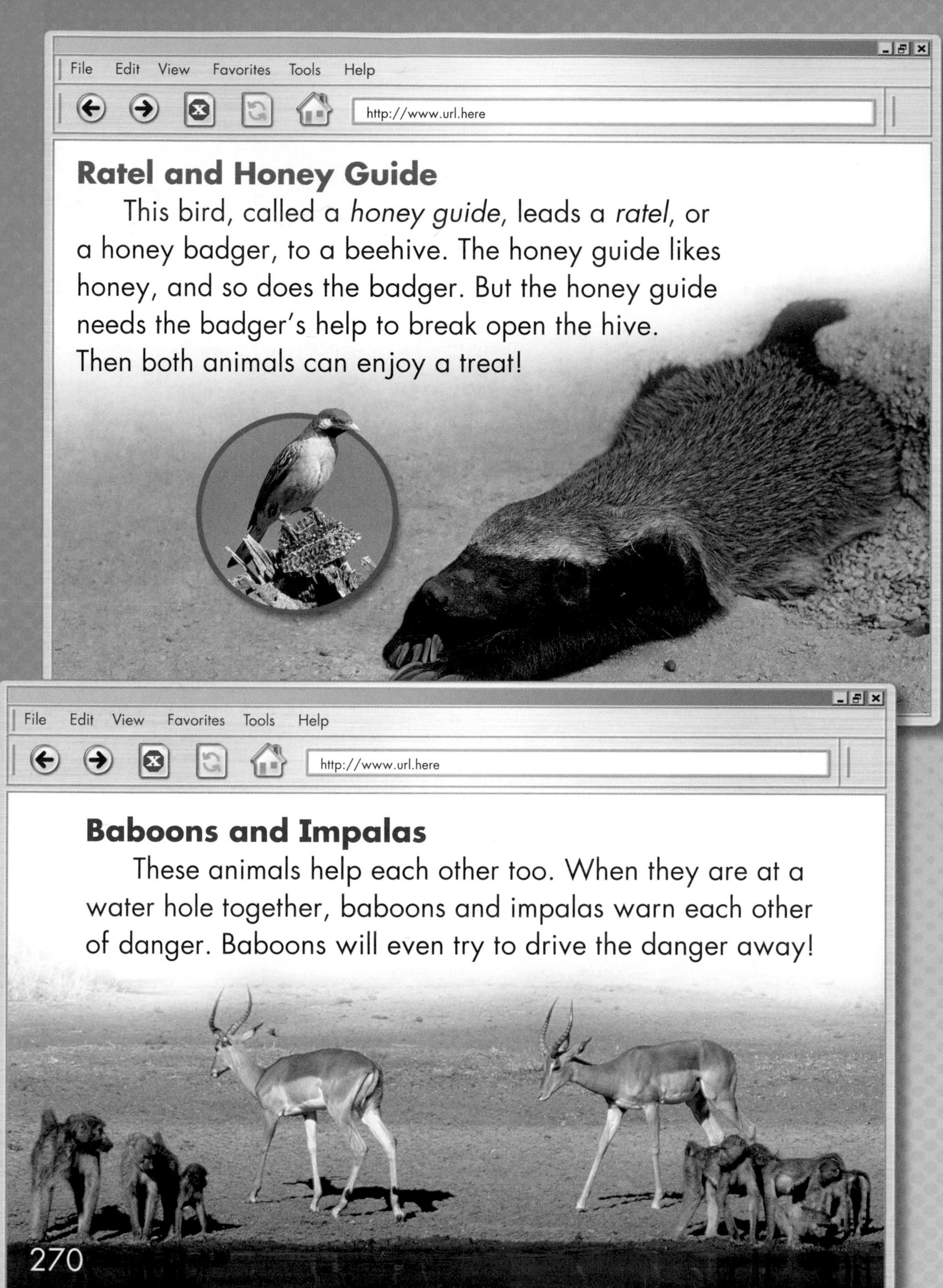

Ratel and Honey Guide

This bird, called a *honey guide*, leads a *ratel*, or a honey badger, to a beehive. The honey guide likes honey, and so does the badger. But the honey guide needs the badger's help to break open the hive. Then both animals can enjoy a treat!

Baboons and Impalas

These animals help each other too. When they are at a water hole together, baboons and impalas warn each other of danger. Baboons will even try to drive the danger away!

File Edit View Favorites Tools Help

http://www.url.here

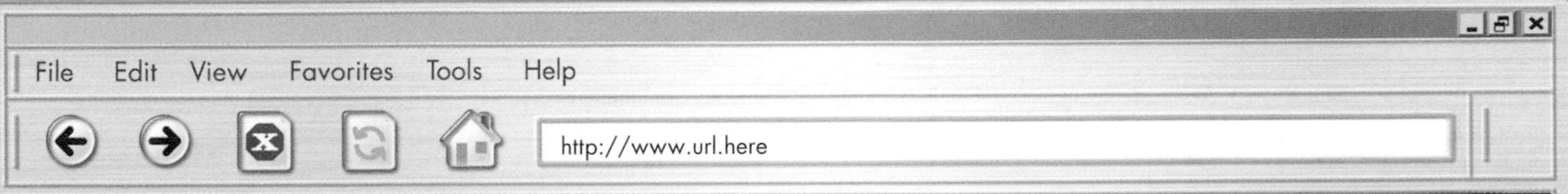

Clown Fish and Sea Anemone

The sea animal that looks like a plant is called a *sea anemone*. The anemone will sting almost any fish that comes near it but not the clown fish. For some reason, the anemone does not hurt the clown fish. The clown fish can swim among the waving arms of the anemone and be safe from other fish that might try to hurt it.

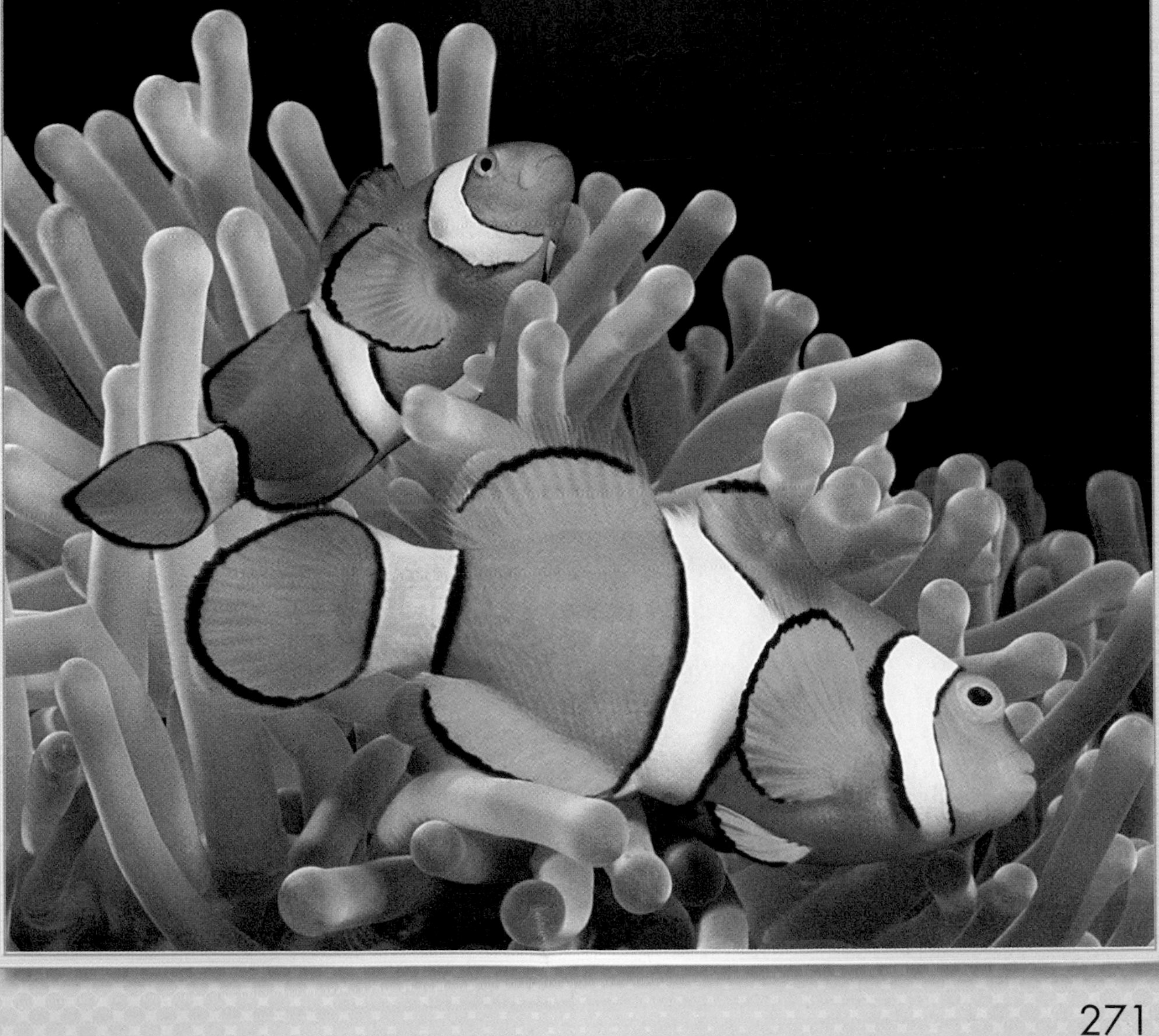

Writing Fairy Tale

Prompt *The Bremen Town Musicians,* is a fairy tale about animals that sing together to solve a problem. Think about another fairy tale in which the characters work together. Now write your own fairy tale about characters who work together.

Writing Trait

All sentences should **focus** on one **idea.**

Student Model

A New Mouse House

Fairy tales tell about magical characters.

Once there was a family of mice. They lived near the woods. Father mouse said, "We need a new home." Mother mouse agreed.

Some plural nouns change spelling.

The mice started a new home. Children helped dig the hole. Then they used leaves and twigs to line the nest. The mouse family lived in the new home happily ever after.

Writer focuses on one idea throughout the story.

W2.1 Write brief narratives based on their experiences. **G1W1.1** Group related ideas and maintain a consistent focus. **G1LC.1.7** Spell frequently used, irregular words correctly (e.g., *was, were, says, said, who, what, why*).

Writer's Checklist

- ✓ Is my story a fairy tale?
- ✓ Does my writing focus on one main idea?
- ✓ Are the plural nouns spelled correctly?

Grammar Plural Nouns That Change Spelling

A **plural noun** names more than one person, place, animal, or thing. Some nouns change spelling to name more than one.

one **mouse**	two **mice**
one **man**	two **men**
one **child**	two **children**

Practice Look at the model. Write the plural nouns that change spelling. Write the singular form of each noun.

Let's Talk About
Working Together

LS1.0 Students listen critically and respond appropriately to oral communication. They speak in a manner that guides the listener to understand important ideas by using proper phrasing, pitch, and modulation.

Words to Read

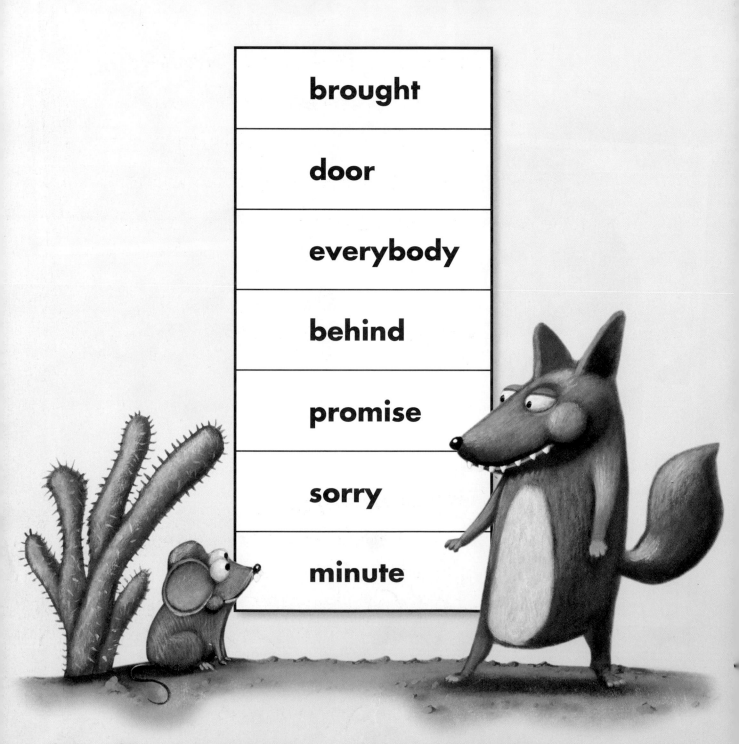

brought
door
everybody
behind
promise
sorry
minute

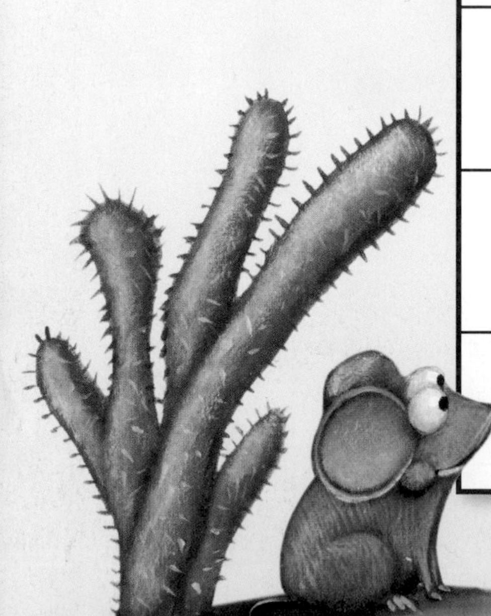

Read the Words

Coyote brought the box to Mouse's door. Everybody wondered what was inside the box. From behind a bush a voice shouted. "I made Mouse promise not to open it until I got here. I'm sorry. You'll have to wait a minute."

One Good Turn Deserves Another Mexico

Genre: Fable
A fable is a story that teaches a lesson. Now read to find out what lesson Mouse learns.

One Good Turn Deserves Another Mexico

Told by Judy Sierra
Illustrated by Will Terry

How do a mouse and
a coyote work together?

Hop, stop, sniff. Hop, stop, sniff. A mouse was going across the desert. Suddenly, she heard a voice, "Help! Help me!" The sound came from under a rock. "Pleasssse get me out of here," said the voice with an unmistakable hiss.

The mouse placed her front paws against the rock. She was small, but she brought her best to the job. The rock rolled aside like a door opening. Out slid a snake.

“Thank you sssso much,” said the snake as he coiled around the mouse. “I was stuck under that rock for a long time. I am very hungry.”

"But you wouldn't eat me," squeaked the mouse.

"Why not?" the snake asked.

"Because I moved the rock," said the mouse. "I saved your life."

"So?" hissed the snake.

"So, one good turn deserves another," the mouse said hopefully.

The snake moved his head from side to side. "You are young," he said. "You don't know much about the world. Good is often repaid with evil."

"That's not fair!" cried the mouse.

"Everybody knows I am right," said the snake. "If you find even one creature who agrees with you, I promise to set you free."

A crow flew up behind them. “Uncle,” said the snake to the crow, “Help us settle an argument. I was trapped under a rock, and this silly mouse set me free. Now she thinks I shouldn’t eat her.”

“He should be grateful,” the mouse insisted.

“Well, now,” said the crow. “I’ve flown high an I’ve flown low. I’ve been just about everywhere. This morning, I ate some grasshoppers that were destroying a farmer’s crops. Was he grateful? No, he used me for target practice! Good is often repaid with evil.” And off he flew.

An armadillo ambled by. "What's all the noise?" she asked.

"Merely a minute of conversation before dinner," replied the snake. "My young friend moved a rock and set me free. Now she thinks I shouldn't eat her."

"One good turn deserves another," said the mouse.

"Wait a minute," said the armadillo. "Did you know he was a snake before you moved that rock?

"I guess I did, but..."

"Sorry, a snake is always a snake," the armadillo declared as she waddled away.

"That settles it," said the snake. "Everybody agrees with me."

“Can’t we ask just one more creature?” the mouse pleaded.

“I don’t think you’ll ever understand,” groaned the snake.

A coyote trotted up. “Understand what?” he asked.

“The snake was trapped under that rock,” the mouse explained.

“Which rock?” asked the coyote.

“Over there. That rock,” said the snake.

"Oh," said the coyote. "The mouse was under that rock."

"No, I was under that rock!" said the snake.

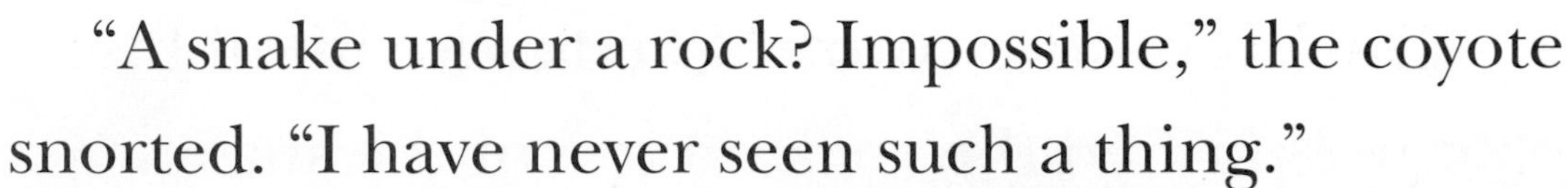

"A snake under a rock? Impossible," the coyote snorted. "I have never seen such a thing."

The snake slid into the hole where he had been trapped. "I was in this hole," he hissed, "and that rock was on top of me!"

"This rock?" the coyote asked as he lifted his paw and pushed the rock on top of the snake.

"Yess!" hissed the snake. "Now show him, little mouse! Show him how you set me free."

But the mouse was already far away. “Thank you, cousin,” she called as she ran. “I’ll return the favor someday.”

“Yes, indeed,” said the coyote. “One good turn deserves another.”

Talk About It Pretend you are the mouse in the story. Tell why you helped set the snake free.

1. Use the pictures below to retell the story. **Retell**
2. What message do you think the author is trying to give you in this story? **Author's Purpose**
3. Look at page 281. Read the words. How did you know what *coiled* means? **Context Clues**

TEST PRACTICE

Look Back and Write Look back at the story. What does the mouse mean by "one good turn deserves another"? Write why you think this.

Retell

R2.2 State purpose for reading. **R2.3** Use knowledge of author's purpose. **R2.5** Restate facts and details. **G1R2.4** Use context for meaning.

Meet the Author and the Illustrator

Judy Sierra

As a child, Judy Sierra loved telling stories and putting on shows. She still does. Her books draw on this experience. She says, "Writing is a job, and there are many difficult and frustrating times. The most enjoyable part of being a writer is spending time with children and adults who love to read."

Read more books written by Judy Sierra and illustrated by Will Terry.

Will Terry

Will Terry studied illustration in college, and his pictures have appeared in books, magazines, and advertising. Mr. Terry and his family love snow boarding, mountain biking, and camping.

The Lion and the Mouse

retold by Claire Daniel
Illustrated by Dan Andreasen

One day Mouse bumped into Lion by mistake and woke him up. Lion caught Mouse and dangled him by his tail.

"Do not eat me!" Mouse cried. "One day I will return the favor."

Lion laughed so hard that he dropped Mouse. Lion said, "How can a tiny mouse ever help a mighty lion like me?"

The next day Lion fell into a hunter's trap. He was covered with a net. Lion's roars shook the ground.

Other animals heard Lion, but no one wanted to come near an angry lion. Only Mouse ran toward Lion.

Mouse said, "I will help you."

Lion roared, "You are too small to help me!"

Mouse just said, "Lion, be quiet."

Mouse chewed the net. He chewed for a long time. Finally, Mouse made a hole. Lion was free!

Just then the hunters returned. Lion roared at the men, and they ran away.

One hunter looked back. He saw the proud Lion walking away. The hunter rubbed his eyes. Could it be? A mouse was riding on the lion's back!

Lion and Mouse became best friends. Lion liked to say, "Little friends can make the best friends."

Writing Folk Tale

Prompt A mouse needs help in *One Good Turn Deserves Another.* Think about problems that happen when we don't work together. Now write a folk tale about animals that won't work together.

Writing Trait

Sentences have words in the correct order.

Student Model

Acorns

Singular possessive nouns end in -'s.

Words in the sentences are in the correct order.

In folk tales, bad is often punished.

Mouse went to Squirrel's house for dinner. Squirrel put acorns in a pot. Mouse took the acorns out.

"I do not like acorns," Mouse said.

"I love acorns," said Squirrel.

"I will not eat acorns!" said Mouse.

"I will eat only acorns!" said Squirrel. The animals' fight did not stop. So they both went without dinner.

G2W2.1 Write brief narratives based on their personal experience. **G1LC1.2** Recognize and use the correct word order in written sentences. **G1LC1.3** Identify and correctly use various parts of speech, including nouns and verbs, in writing and speaking.

Writer's Checklist

- ✓ Is my story like a folk tale?
- ✓ Are the words in my sentences in the correct order?
- ✓ Are the possessive nouns spelled correctly?

Grammar Possessive Nouns

A noun that shows who or what owns something is a **possessive noun.** To show ownership, add an **apostrophe (')** and **-s** when the noun is singular.

the squirrel's acorn (one squirrel)

Add just an **apostrophe** when the noun is plural.

the squirrels' acorn (more than one squirrel)

Practice Write the possessive nouns in the model. Which is singular? How do you know?

Unit 3

Get Online!

PearsonSuccessNet.com

See It!

- Concept Talk Video
- Background Building Audio Slide Show
- *Picture It!* Animation
- e-Books

Hear It!

- Amazing Words *Sing with Me*
- Selection Snapshot and Response
- Paired Selection e-Text
- Grammar Jammer
- e-Books

Do It!

- Online Journal
- Story Sort
- New Literacies Activity
- Success Tracker

Creative Ideas

What does it mean to be creative?

Pearl and Wagner: Two Good Friends
ANIMAL FANTASY

What creative idea will help Pearl and Wagner remain good friends?

Paired Selection
Robots at Home EXPOSITORY NONFICTION

Dear Juno REALISTIC FICTION

Who has written a letter to Juno?

Paired Selection
Saying It Without Words: Signs and Symbols EXPOSITORY NONFICTION

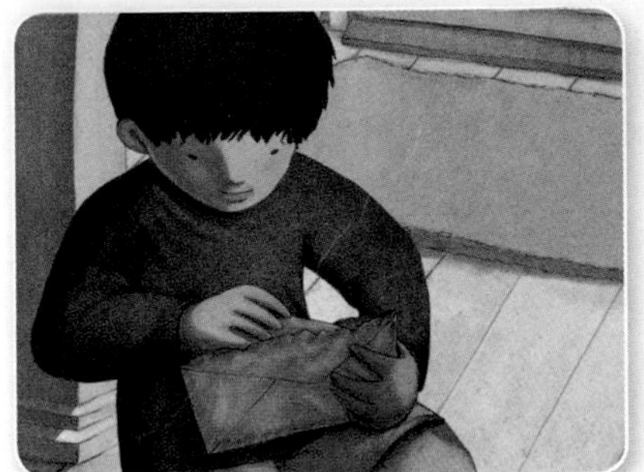

Anansi Goes Fishing FOLK TALE

What will Anansi catch when he goes fishing?

Paired Selection
Do spiders stick to their own webs? POETRY

Rosa and Blanca REALISTIC FICTION

Who are Rosa and Blanca, and what is their creative idea?

Paired Selection
The Crow and the Pitcher FABLE

A Weed Is a Flower BIOGRAPHY

Who was George Washington Carver?

Paired Selection
What's Made from Corn? SEARCH ENGINES

Let's Talk About Creative Ideas

LS1.0 Students listen critically and respond appropriately to oral communication. They speak in a manner that guides the listener to understand important ideas by using proper phrasing, pitch, and modulation.

Trash-eating
Robot
New &
improved

Words to Read

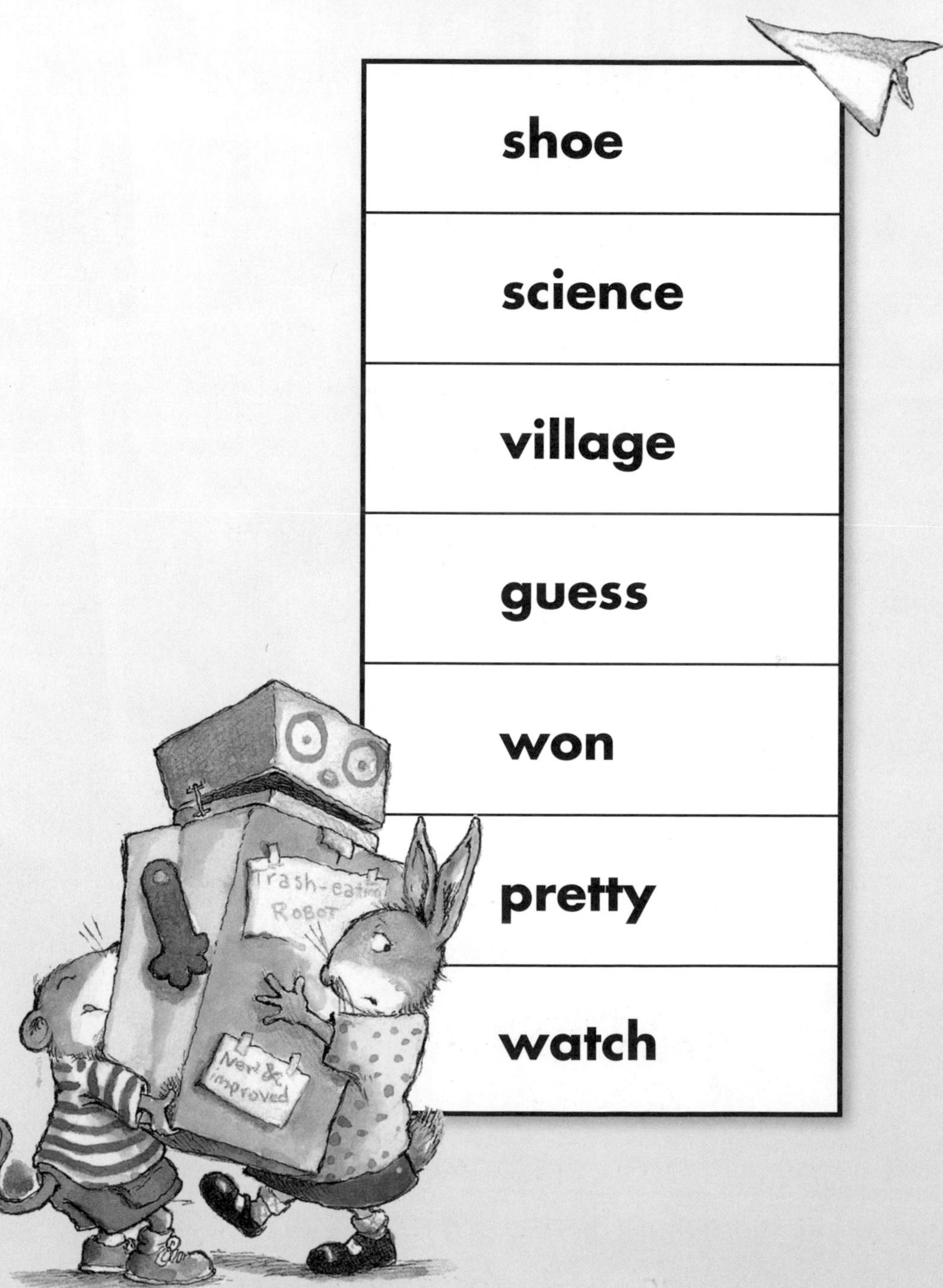

shoe
science
village
guess
won
pretty
watch

 G1R1.11 Read common, irregular sight words (e.g., *the, have, said, come, give, of*).

Read the Words

"Pearl?" Wagner asked. "Did you ever find your shoe?"

"Yes," Pearl said. "I lost it at the science fair when you opened the ant village."

"I guess setting the ants free was a bad idea. I just wanted to win a prize."

"Well, nobody won because ants were everywhere," said Pearl. "It wasn't a pretty sight."

"I guess it's better to watch ants from the outside in," Wagner said.

"I guess it is," Pearl replied.

Genre: Animal Fantasy
In an animal fantasy, the animal characters act like humans. Next you will read about Pearl and Wagner at the science fair.

Pearl and Wagner
Two Good Friends

by Kate McMullan · illustrated by R.W. Alley

Trash-eating Robot
New & improved
Look at the ANTS
The ants dig and dig and dig to make tunnels. It's a good life

What creative idea will help Pearl and Wagner remain good friends?
Plants love music
See the effect of music on planted in the pot marigolds.
DANGER KEEP AWAY

The Robot

Everyone in Ms. Star's class was talking about the Science Fair.

"I am going to make a robot," said Pearl.

"I am going to win a prize," said Wagner.

Pearl got to work. She taped up the flaps of a great big box. She cut a hole in the top. Then she cut a hole in the lid of a shoe box. She glued the shoe box lid to the top of the great big box. Wagner held the boxes together while the glue dried.

"Maybe I will make a walkie-talkie," he said.

Pearl punched a hole in one end of the shoe box. She stuck string through the hole. She tied the string in a knot.

"Maybe I will make a brain out of clay," said Wagner.

"Cool," said Pearl.

She drew eyes and a nose on the shoe box. Wagner looked at the shoe box.

"The eyes are too small," he said.

Pearl made the eyes bigger.

"Maybe I will make a rocket," said Wagner. "*Vrooom!* Blast off!"

Pearl put the shoe box onto the lid.

“There!” she said. “Finished!”

Pearl pulled the string.
The robot’s mouth opened.
She threw in a wad of paper.
Then she let go of the string.
The robot’s mouth shut.

“Wow!” said Wagner.
“A trash-eating robot!”

“Let’s see what everyone has made,” said Ms. Star.

“Uh-oh,” said Wagner. He had not made anything yet.

Lulu raised her hand. “I made a walkie-talkie,” she said.

“I was going to do that!” said Wagner.

“I made paper airplanes,” said Bud. “This chart shows how far they flew.”

Wagner slapped his head. “Why didn’t *I* think of that?”

Henry showed how to get electricity from a potato.

"Henry is a brain," said Pearl.

"Pearl?" Wagner said. "Remember how I held the boxes together while the glue dried?"

"I remember," said Pearl.

"Remember how I told you to give the robot bigger eyes?" asked Wagner.

Pearl nodded. "I remember."

“Your turn, Pearl,” said Ms. Star.

“I made a trash-eating robot,” said Pearl. She looked at Wagner. He was slumped down in his seat.

“Wagner and I made it together,” said Pearl.

Wagner sat right up again.

Pearl pulled the robot's string. She pulled too hard. The robot's head fell off.

"Uh-oh," said Wagner.

"I guess you two friends have more work to do," said Ms. Star.

"I guess so," said Pearl. "But I don't mind, because Wagner and I will do all of the work together."

"Uh-oh," said Wagner.

The Science Fair

On Science Fair Day, Pearl and Wagner were still working on their robot. Pearl stretched rubber bands. She held them tight. Wagner stapled them onto the shoe box and the lid.

"That should do it," he said.

Pearl and Wagner hurried to the gym with their robot. They passed a boy with an ant village. They passed a girl playing music for plants. They passed Henry. He had his electric potato hooked up to a tiny Ferris wheel.

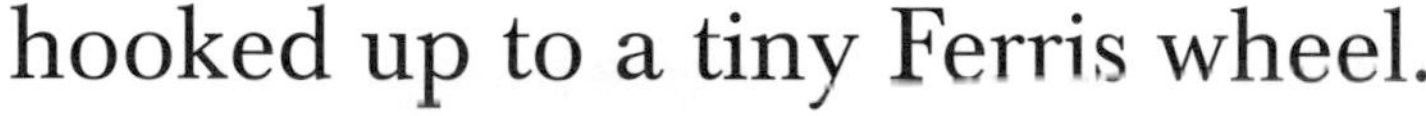

Pearl and Wagner set up their robot.

A judge came over.

"Watch this," said Pearl. Pearl pulled the robot's string. Nothing happened. She pulled harder. The robot's mouth popped open. The rubber bands flew everywhere.

"Yikes!" said the judge.

"Oh, no!" said Wagner. "There goes our prize!"

"We are not quite ready," Pearl told the judge.

"I will come back in five minutes," said the judge.

"I have more rubber bands in my desk," said Pearl. She raced off to get them.

Wagner tapped his foot. He bit his nails. Pearl was taking forever! The judge would be back any second. He had to *do* something.

Wagner looked around. No one was watching him. He pulled the tape off the big box. He opened the back of the robot and slipped inside.

The judge came back. She did not see Pearl and Wagner. She started to leave.

"Wait!" said the robot.

"Oh, my stars!" said the judge. "A talking robot!"

Just then Pearl came back.

"You have a nice smile," the robot was telling the judge. "And such pretty eyes."

"Do you think so?" said the judge.

Pearl could not believe her ears.

"Your robot is so smart!" said the judge. "How does it work?"

"Uh . . ." said Pearl. "It is hard to explain."

The judge opened the robot's mouth. She looked inside.

"Hi there!" said Wagner.

"Uh-oh," said Pearl.

The judge gave out the prizes. The girl who played music for plants won first prize. Henry and his electric potato won second prize. The trash-eating robot did not win any prize at all.

“I was only trying to help,” Wagner told Pearl.

“I know,” said Pearl. “You are a good friend, Wagner. And you were a pretty good robot too.”

Talk About It Do you think this story has a sad or happy ending? Why do you think so?

1. Use the pictures below to retell the story. Retell
2. How are Pearl and Wagner alike? How are they different? Compare and Contrast
3. What happens when the judge comes to see Pearl and Wagner's robot? Reread pages 322–325 to check. Monitor and Clarify

TEST PRACTICE

Look Back and Write Look back at pages 308–309. What creative idea will help Pearl and Wagner remain good friends? Write your answer using details from the selection.

Retell

 LS1.8 Retell stories, including characters, setting, and plot.

Meet the Author and the Illustrator

Kate McMullan

Kate McMullan loves to read. When asked what she wanted to be when she grew up, she always said, "A reader." When she decided to try writing, she moved to New York City.

Read more books by Kate McMullan.

R. W. Alley

R. W. Alley has illustrated many books for children. He says Kate McMullan had been thinking of a dog and a cat as Pearl and Wagner. But when she saw his mouse and his rabbit, she approved.

Robots at home

from *Robots* by Clive Gifford

Robots are coming home. The latest robots are doing useful chores around the house. Home robots need to know their way around a house and be able to communicate with their owners.

Ready for breakfast?

Robots cannot cook your meals yet, but they can carry them to you. Home robots often hold a map of the house in their memory. They also need sensors to know when household objects are in their way.

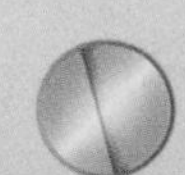

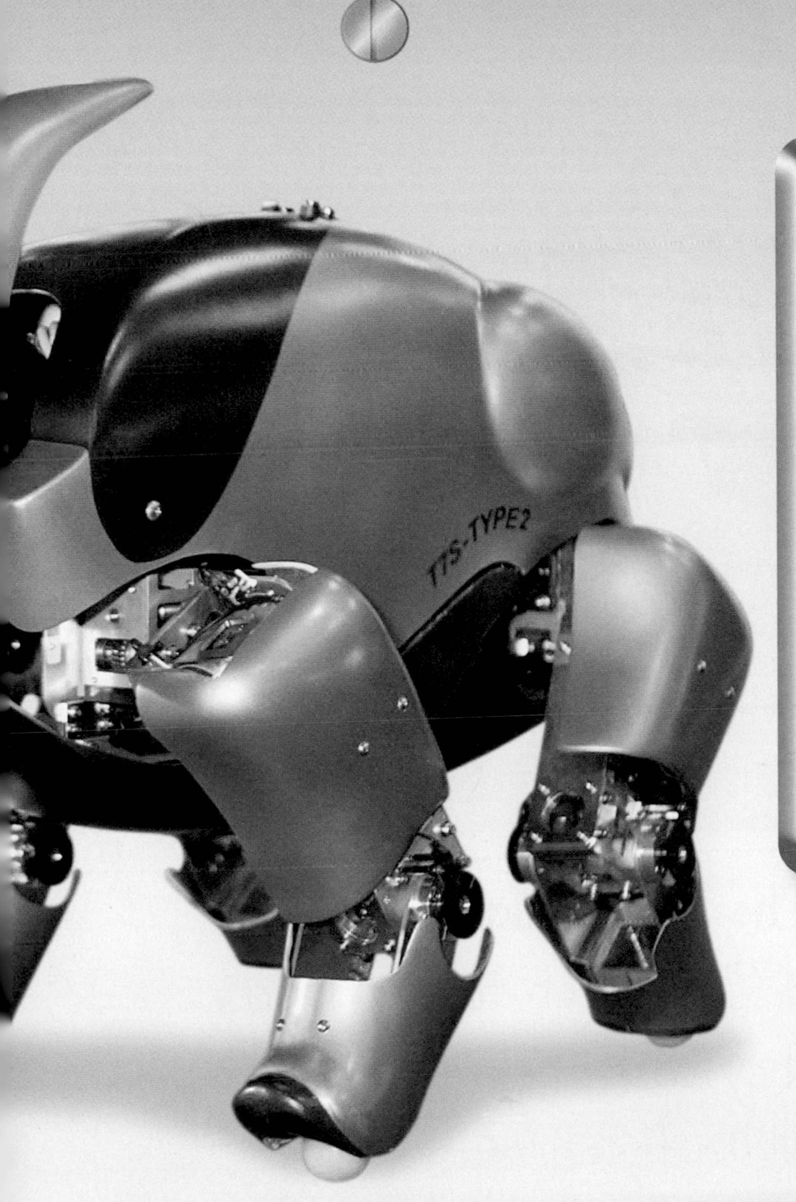

Beware of the dog.

This robot guard dog patrols the house, checking that everything is safe. If it notices anything wrong, it can take pictures and send them to the owner's cell phone.

Home playmates

PaPeRos wander around the house looking for people to talk to. They can recognize 650 different words and phrases and can speak up to 3,000 words. They can even dance!

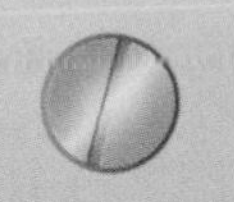

Writing Animal Fantasy

Prompt Two friends create a robot in *Pearl and Wagner.* Think about how others help with creative ideas. Now write a story about animals who create something together.

Writing Trait

Voice shows how the writer feels about the topic.

Student Model

Verbs show action.

Animal fantasy tells about animals doing impossible things.

The writer uses a playful voice.

The Flying Machine

Dog and Cat watch the birds in the sky. They wish they could fly too.

"Let's build a flying machine!" says Dog.

First they make a place to sit. Then they add wings. Next Dog and Cat wait for the wind. The wind carries them up into the air.

"We're flying!" says Cat.

W2.1 Write brief narratives based on their personal experience. **LC.1.3** Identify and correctly use various parts of speech, including nouns and verbs, in writing and speaking.

Writer's Checklist

- ✓ Did I tell a story about animals that do impossible things?
- ✓ Did I use a clear voice in my writing?
- ✓ Did I use verbs correctly?

Grammar Verbs

A word that shows action is a **verb.**

Pearl and Wagner **make** a robot.

The word **make** is a verb. It tells what Pearl and Wagner do.

Practice Look at the model. Name three verbs that show action.

Let's Talk About
Creative Ideas

LS1.0 Students listen critically and respond appropriately to oral communication. They speak in a manner that guides the listener to understand important ideas by using proper phrasing, pitch, and modulation.

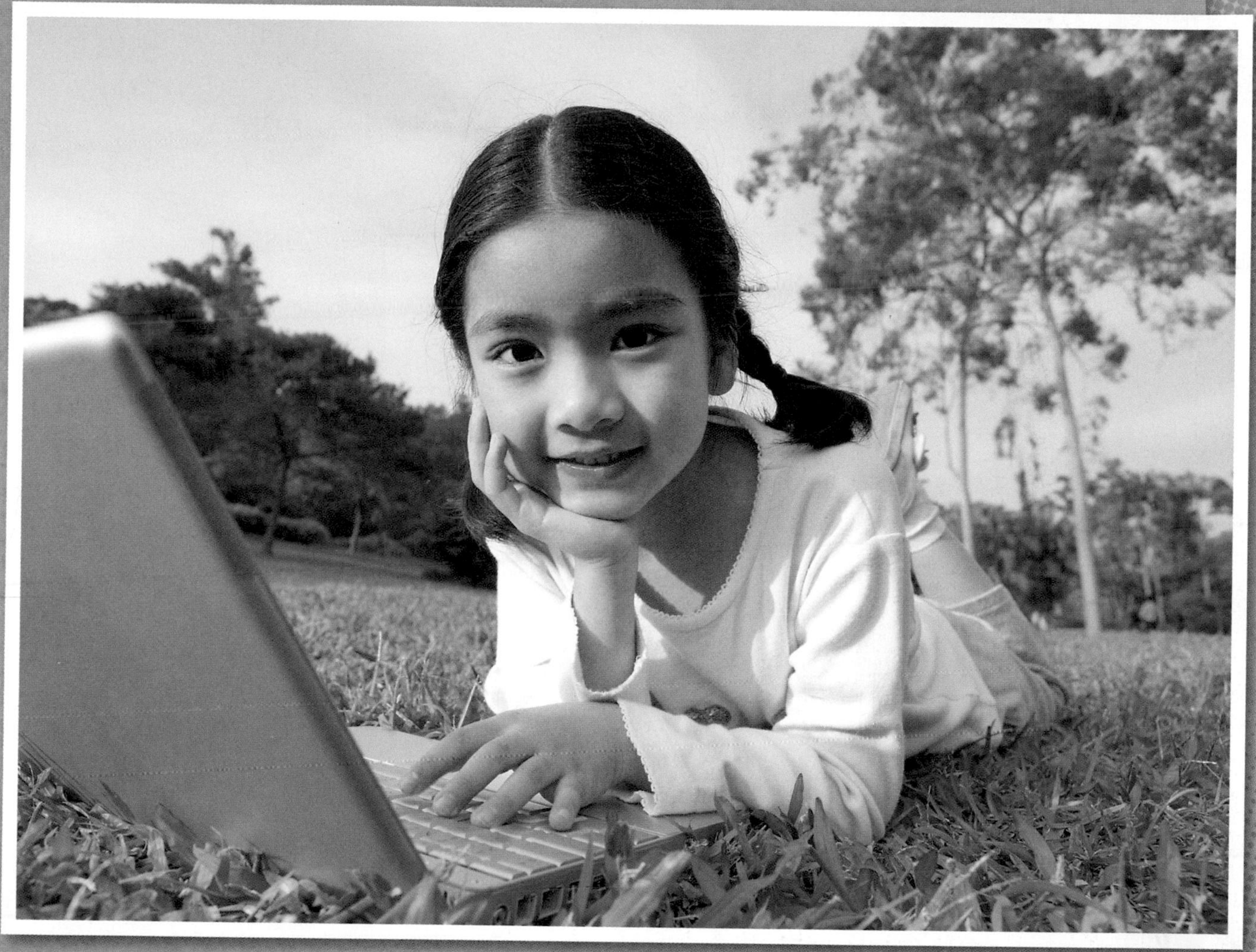

Words to Read

picture
school
answer
faraway
parents
wash
company

G1R1.11 Read common, irregular sight words (e.g., *the, have, said, come, give, of*).

Read the Words

Dear Grandma,

Thank you for your letter and the picture. I took them to school. I had to answer many questions from my friends. I told them that you lived in a faraway place called Korea. I told them that my parents will take me there soon.

I must go now and wash my hands. We are having company for dinner.

Love,

Juno

Genre: Realistic Fiction
Realistic fiction has characters, a setting, and a plot that could be real. This next story is about Juno, a boy who finds a creative way to write to his grandmother.

Dear Juno

by Soyung Pak

illustrated by Susan Kathleen Hartung

Who has written a letter to Juno?

Juno watched as the red and white blinking lights soared across the night sky like shooting stars, and waited as they disappeared into faraway places. Juno wondered where they came from. He wondered where they were going. And he wondered if any of the planes came from a little town near Seoul where his grandmother lived, and where she ate persimmons every evening before bed.

Juno looked at the letter that came that day. It was long and white and smudged. He saw the red and blue marks on the edges and knew the letter came from far away. His name and address were neatly printed on the front, so he knew the letter was for him. But best of all, the special stamp on the corner told Juno that the letter was from his grandmother.

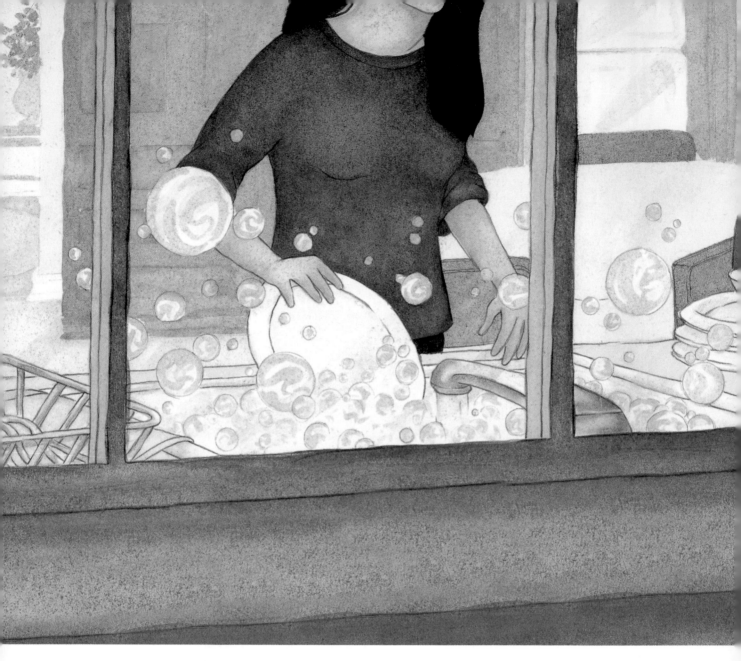

Through the window Juno could see his parents. He saw bubbles growing in the sink. He saw dirty dishes waiting to be washed. He knew he would have to wait for the cleaning to be done before his parents could read the letter to him.

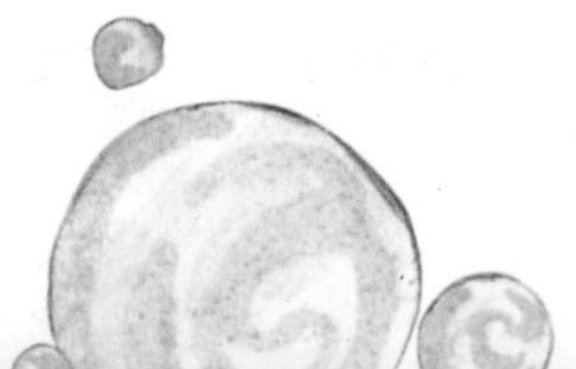

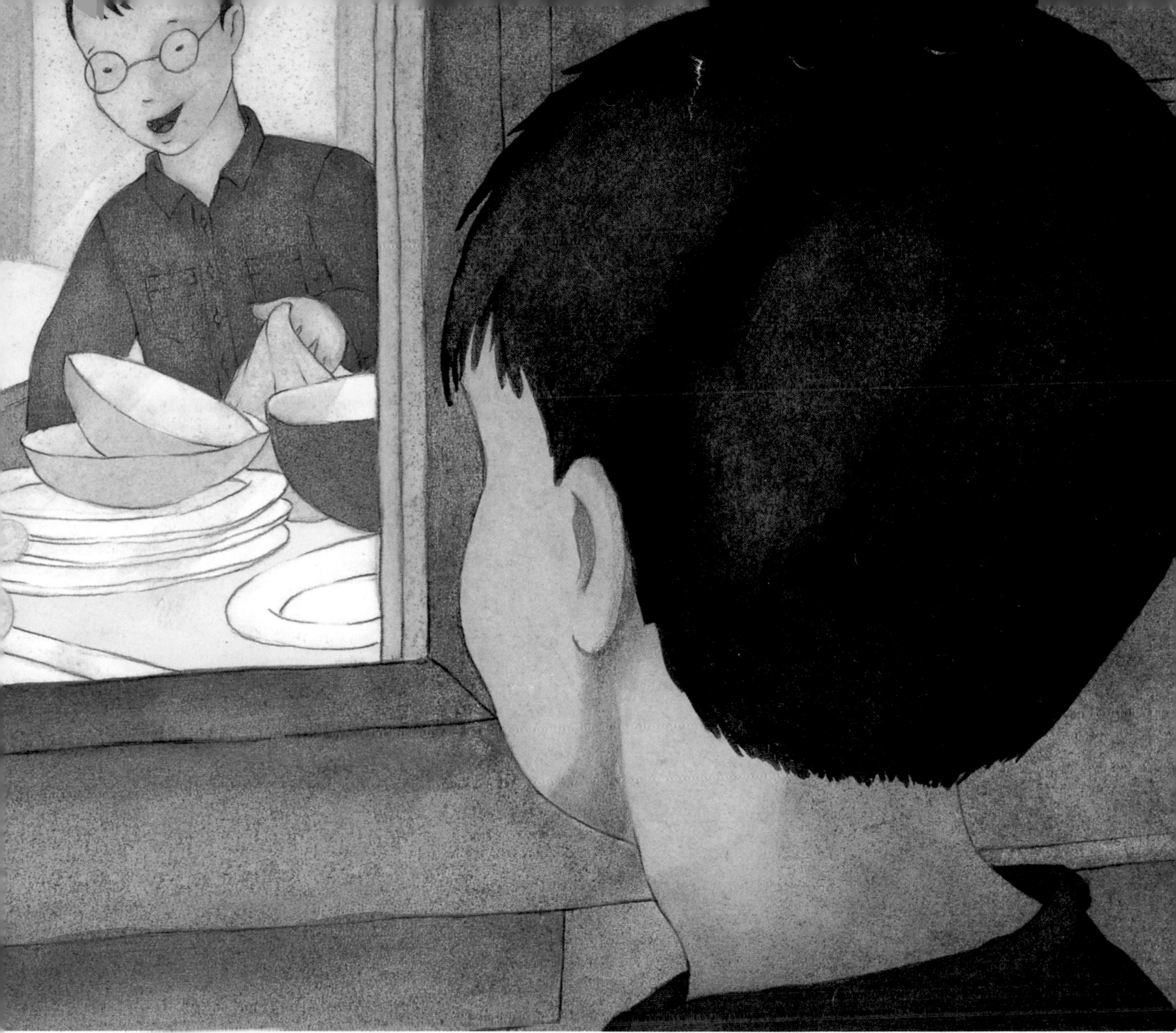

“Maybe I can read the inside too,” Juno said to his dog, Sam. Sam wagged his tail. Very carefully, Juno opened the envelope. Inside, he found a letter folded into a neat, small square.

He unfolded it. Tucked inside were a picture and a dried flower.

Juno looked at the letters and words he couldn't understand. He pulled out the photograph. It was a picture of his grandmother holding a cat. He pulled out the red and yellow flower. It felt light and gentle like a dried leaf. Juno smiled. "C'mon, Sam," Juno said. "Let's find Mom and Dad."

주노야,
잘 지내고 있느냐? 나에게는 친구가 되어
주는 고양이가 한마리 있단다.
네 이름을 따서 주노라고 부른단다.
이 고양이는 내가 잡초 뽑는것은
돕지 못하지만 그래도 덕분에
가 내가 키우는 꽃을
것을 막아 준단다.

"Grandma has a new cat," Juno said as he handed the letter to his mother. "And she's growing red and yellow flowers in her garden."

"How do you know she has a new cat?" Juno's father asked.

"She wouldn't send me a picture of a strange cat," said Juno.

"I guess not," said Juno's father.

"How do you know the flower is from her garden?" asked Juno's mother.

"She wouldn't send me a flower from someone else's garden," Juno answered.

"No, she wouldn't," said Juno's mother.

Then Juno's mother read him the letter.

Dear Juno,

How are you? I have a new cat to keep me company. I named him Juno after you. He can't help me weed, but the rabbits no longer come to eat my flowers.

Grandma

"Just like you read it yourself," Juno's father said.

"I did read it," Juno said.

"Yes, you did," said his mother.

At school, Juno showed his class his grandmother's picture and dried flower. His teacher even pinned the letter to the board. All day long, Juno kept peeking at the flower from his grandmother's garden. He didn't have a garden that grew flowers, but he had a swinging tree.

Juno looked at the letter pinned to the board. Did his grandmother like getting letters too? Yes, Juno thought. She likes getting letters just like I do. So Juno decided to write one.

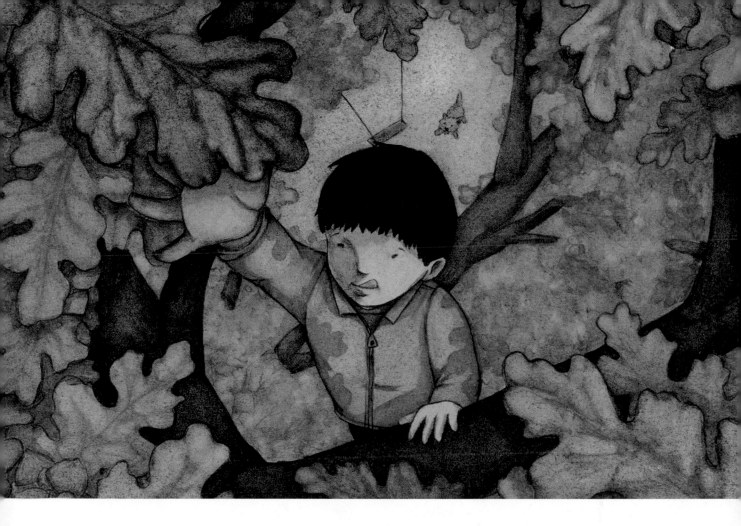

After school, Juno ran to his backyard. He picked a leaf from the swinging tree—the biggest leaf he could find.

Juno found his mother, who was sitting at her desk. He showed her the leaf. "I'm going to write a letter," he told her.

"I'm sure it will be a very nice letter," she answered, and gave him a big yellow envelope.

"Yes it will," Juno said, and then he began to draw.

First, he drew a picture of his mom and dad standing outside the house. Second, he drew a picture of Sam playing underneath his big swinging tree. Then very carefully, Juno drew a picture of himself standing under an airplane in a starry, nighttime sky. After he was finished, he placed everything in the envelope.

"Here's my letter," Juno announced proudly. "You can read it if you want."

Juno's father looked in the envelope.

He pulled out the leaf. "Only a big swinging tree could grow a leaf this big," he said.

Juno's mother pulled out one of the drawings. "What a fine picture," she said. "It takes a good artist to say so much with a drawing."

Juno's father patted Juno on the head. "It's just like a real letter," he said.

"It is a real letter," Juno said.

"It certainly is," said his mother. Then they mailed the envelope and waited.

One day a big envelope came. It was from Juno's grandmother. This time, Juno didn't wait at all. He opened the envelope right away.

Inside, Juno found a box of colored pencils. He knew she wanted another letter.

Next, he pulled out a picture of his grandmother. He noticed she was sitting with a cat and two kittens. He thought for a moment and laughed. Now his grandmother would have to find a new name for her cat—in Korea, Juno was a boy's name, not a girl's.

Then he pulled out a small toy plane.

Juno smiled. His grandmother was coming to visit.

“Maybe she’ll bring her cat when she comes to visit,” Juno said to Sam as he climbed into bed. “Maybe you two will be friends.”

Soon Juno was fast asleep. And when he dreamed that night, he dreamed about a faraway place, a village just outside Seoul, where his grandmother, whose gray hair sat on top of her head like a powdered doughnut, was sipping her morning tea.

The cool air feels crisp against her cheek. Crisp enough to crackle, he dreams, like the golden leaves which cover the persimmon garden.

Talk About It Plan a letter without words to someone. Put three things in the envelope, but only one can be a picture. What will you send?

1. Use the pictures below to retell the story. Retell
2. Can you tell how Juno feels about his grandmother? What makes you think that? Draw Conclusions
3. Look at page 342. Read the words. How did you know what *photograph* means? Context Clues

TEST PRACTICE

Look Back and Write Reread page 339. How did Juno know who sent the letter? Use information from the story to write your answer.

Retell

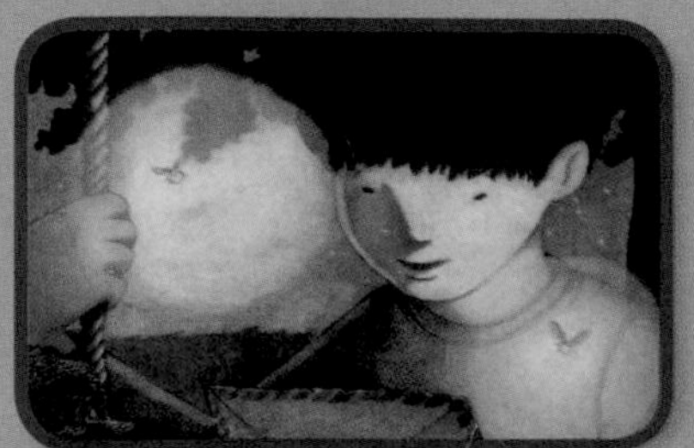

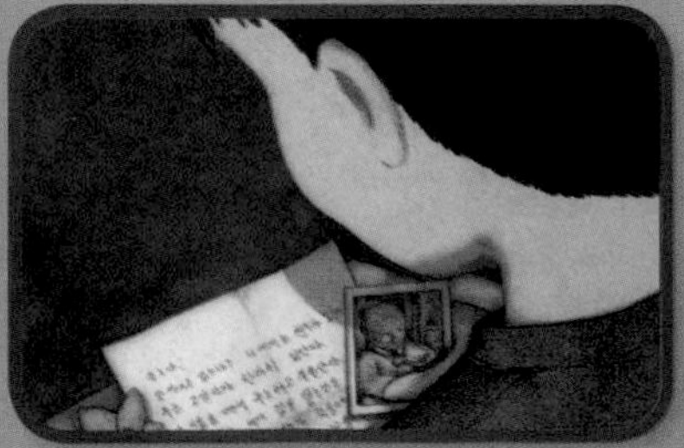

LS1.8 Retell stories, including characters, setting, and plot. **G3R1.6** Use sentence and word context to find the meanings of unknown words.

Meet the Author and the Illustrator

Soyung Pak

Soyung Pak was born in South Korea. When she was two years old, she moved to New Jersey. When a plane flew overhead, her family waved. They pretended Grandmother was on the plane, coming from Korea.

Read more books by Soyung Pak.

Susan Kathleen Hartung

Susan Hartung has always loved to draw. As a child, she sometimes got in trouble for her pictures. Finally she learned to do her drawings on paper!

SAYING IT WITHOUT WORDS
Signs and Symbols

by Arnulf K. Esterer and Louise A. Esterer

Have you seen signs like these:

- the arrow on a one-way street?
- the EXIT sign over doors in the school auditorium?
- the big letter *M* over a hamburger shop downtown?

ONE WAY

EXIT

These are a few examples of signs. You have seen many more all around you. A sign tells you exactly what to do or what is there.

Have you seen:

- a happy face on your milk mug?
- the flag of our country waving from a building?
- a drawing of the atom in advertising?

These are a few examples of symbols. They tell about something. Symbols are like pictures of ideas.

Look around. See how many signs and symbols you can find. We use them every day. See how much they help you to know what to do or where to go.

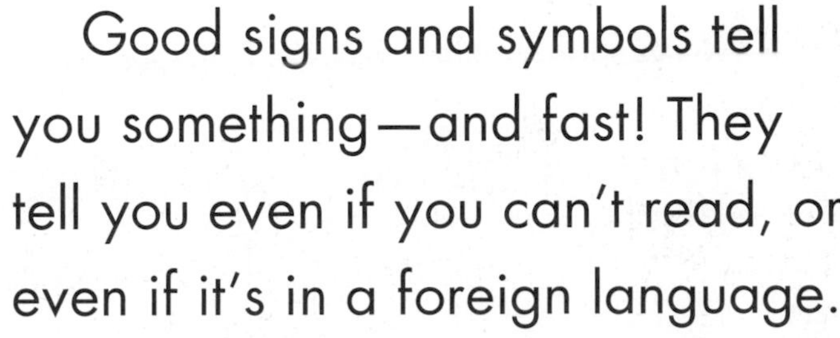

Good signs and symbols tell you something—and fast! They tell you even if you can't read, or even if it's in a foreign language.

One look is all you usually need. One look tells it.

Writing Friendly Letter

Prompt In *Dear Juno,* a boy and his grandmother exchange friendly letters. Think about the different ways people communicate. Now write a friendly letter about a new way to communicate.

Writing Trait

Each sentence should **focus** on one **idea.**

Student Model

January 10, 2010

Dear Sam,

Today I learned that dogs use actions to talk, not words. A happy dog wags its tail. A dog bows on its front legs when it wants to play. It also puts its ears back if it is scared. Dogs are so smart!

Your friend,

Danny

The writer focuses on one idea.

Singular nouns use verbs with *-s*.

A friendly letter tells the writer's ideas and feelings.

W2.2 Write a friendly letter complete with the date, salutation, body, closing, and signature. **LC.1.3** Identify and correctly use various parts of speech, including nouns and verbs, in writing and speaking.

Writer's Checklist

- ✓ Did I write a friendly letter?
- ✓ Does each sentence focus on one idea?
- ✓ Did I spell verbs correctly?

Grammar Verbs with Singular and Plural Nouns

Add **–s** to a verb to tell what one person, animal, or thing does. Do not add **–s** to a verb that tells what two or more people, animals, or things do.

Grandma **mails** a letter to Juno.
The pictures **tell** a story.

Practice Look at the model. Write the verbs from the sentences. Circle the verbs that tell what one dog does.

Let's Talk About Creative Ideas

  **LS1.0** Students listen critically and respond appropriately to oral communication. They speak in a manner that guides the listener to understand important ideas by using proper phrasing, pitch, and modulation.

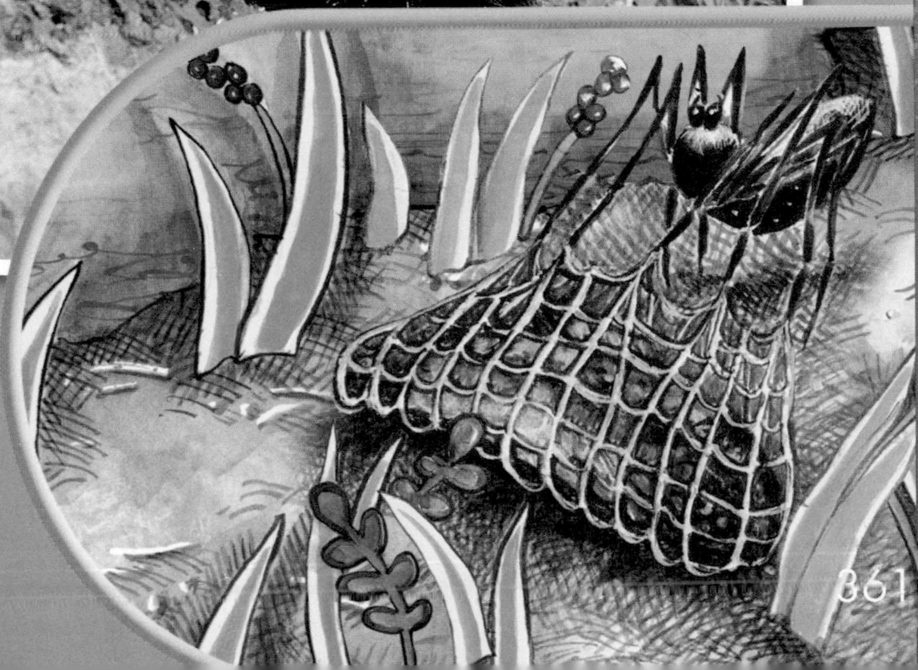

Words to Read

believe
caught
finally
been
whatever
today
tomorrow

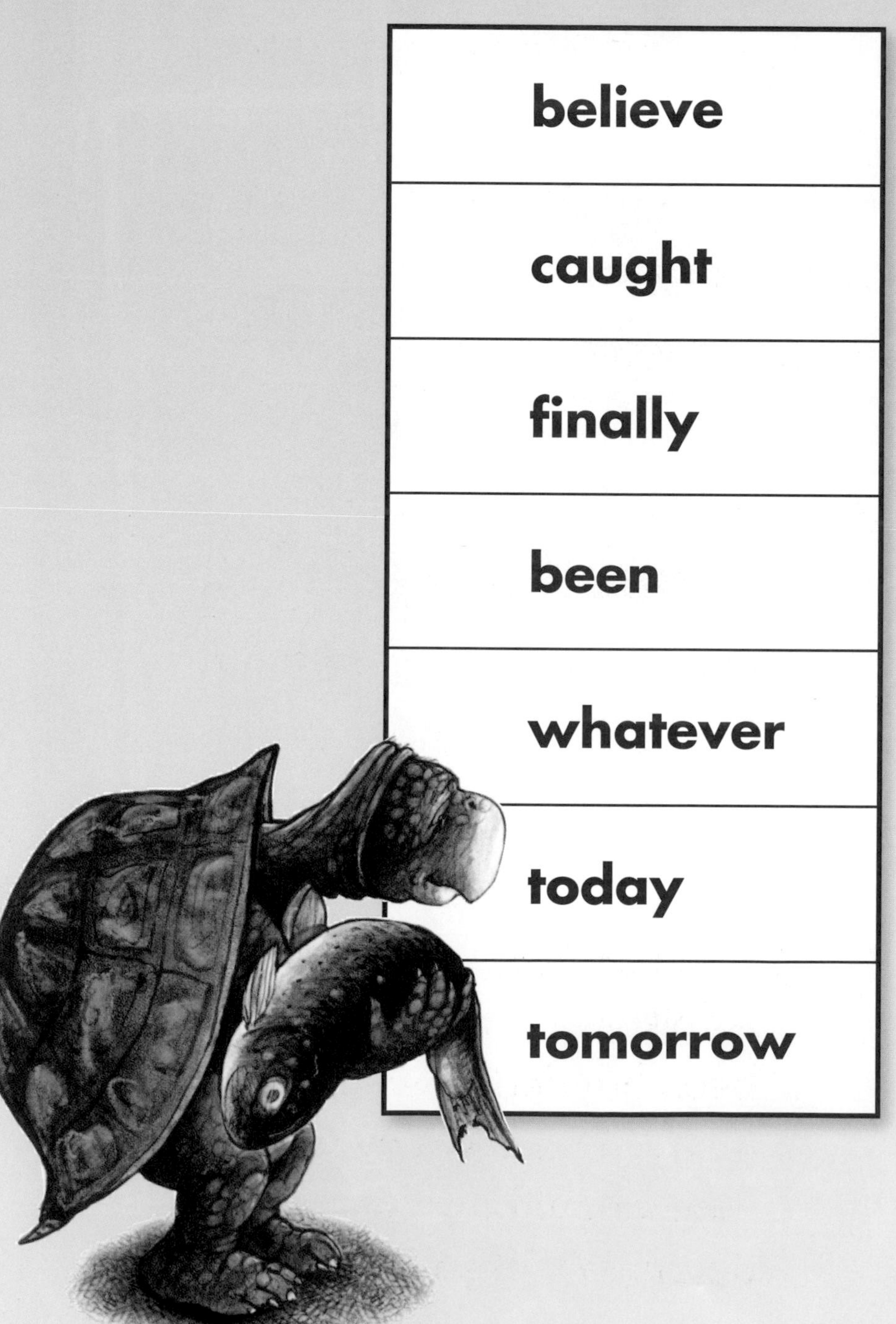

 G1R1.11 Read common, irregular sight words (e.g., *the, have, said, come, give, of*).

Read the Words

"I do believe you are stuck," said the spider to the fly who was caught in his web.

"Finally," said the clever fly to the spider. "I've been waiting for you."

"Whatever do you mean?" the spider asked, surprised.

"You invited me over today," the fly said. "Why would you set a trap for your friend?"

The confused spider helped free the fly. As the fly flew off, he called, "Better clever today than lunch tomorrow!"

Genre: Folk Tale
A folk tale is a story that has been handed down over many years. Now you will read about how Anansi the Spider is tricked by Turtle.

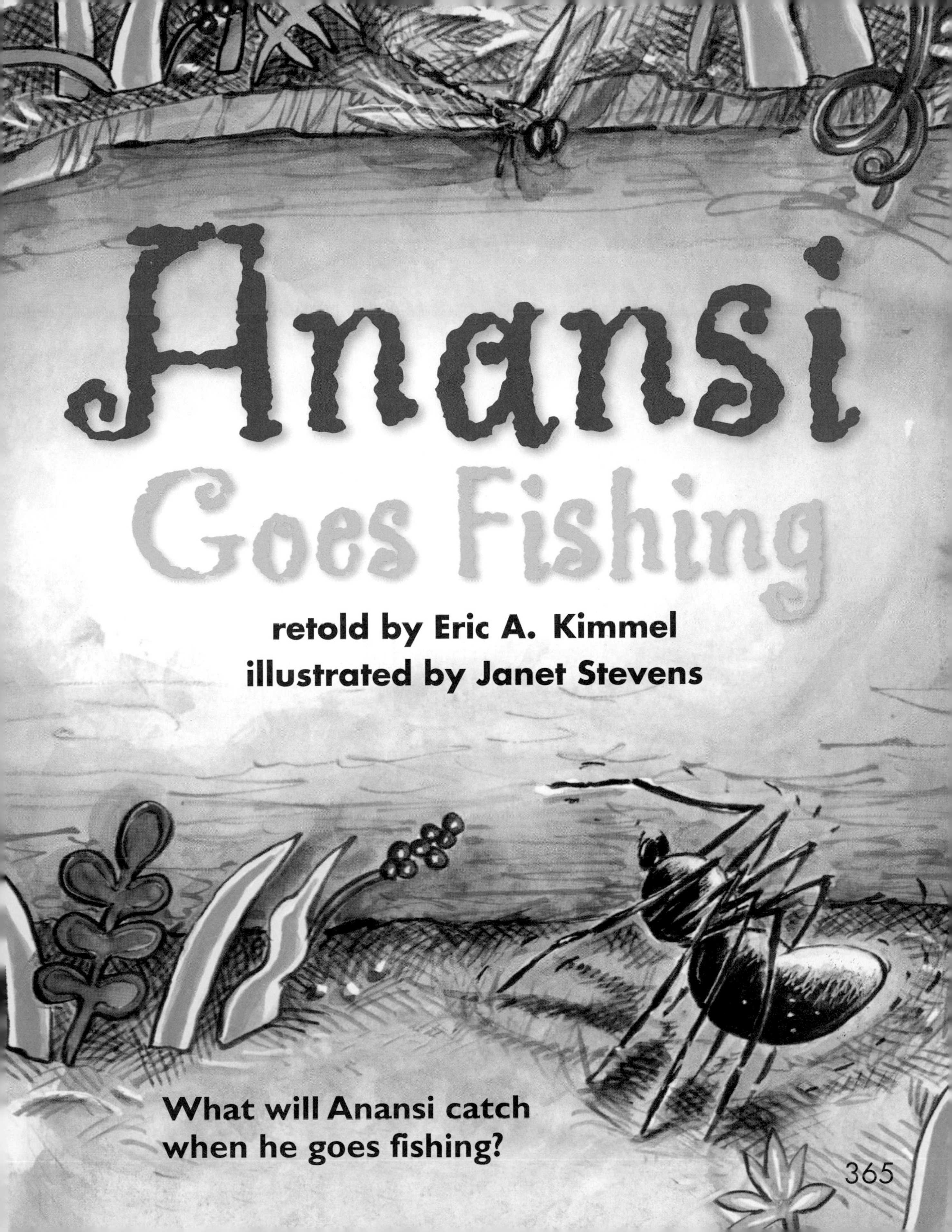

Anansi Goes Fishing

retold by Eric A. Kimmel
illustrated by Janet Stevens

What will Anansi catch when he goes fishing?

One fine afternoon Anansi the Spider was walking by the river when he saw his friend Turtle coming toward him carrying a large fish. Anansi loved to eat fish, though he was much too lazy to catch them himself.

"Where did you get that fish?" he asked Turtle.

"I caught it today when I went fishing," Turtle replied.

"I want to learn to catch fish too," Anansi said. "Will you teach me?"

"Certainly!" said Turtle. "Meet me by the river tomorrow. We will go fishing together. Two can do twice the work of one."

But Anansi did not intend to do any work at all. "Turtle is slow and stupid," he said to himself. "I will trick him into doing all the work. Then I will take the fish for myself." But Turtle was not as stupid as Anansi thought.

Early the next morning, Turtle arrived. "Are you ready to get started, Anansi?" he asked.

"Yes!" Anansi said. "I have been waiting a long time. I want to learn to catch fish as well as you do."

"First we make a net," said Turtle. "Netmaking is hard work. When I do it myself, I work and get tired. But since there are two of us, we can share the task. One of us can work while the other gets tired."

"I don't want to get tired," Anansi said. "I'll make the net. You can get tired."

"All right," said Turtle. He showed Anansi how to weave a net. Then he lay down on the riverbank.

"This is hard work," Anansi said.

"I know," said Turtle, yawning. "I'm getting very tired."

Anansi worked all day weaving the net. The harder he worked, the more tired Turtle grew. Turtle yawned and stretched, and finally he went to sleep. After many hours the net was done.

"Wake up, Turtle," Anansi said. "The net is finished."

Turtle rubbed his eyes. "This net is strong and light. You are a fine netmaker, Anansi. I know you worked hard because I am very tired. I am so tired, I have to go home and sleep. Meet me here tomorrow. We will catch fish then."

The next morning Turtle met Anansi by the river again.

"Today we are going to set the net in the river," Turtle said. "That is hard work. Yesterday you worked while I got tired, so today I'll work while you get tired."

"No, no!" said Anansi. "I would rather work than get tired."

"All right," said Turtle. So while Anansi worked hard all day setting the net in the river, Turtle lay on the riverbank, getting so tired he finally fell asleep.

"Wake up, Turtle," Anansi said, hours later. "The net is set. I'm ready to start catching fish."

Turtle yawned. "I'm too tired to do any more today, Anansi. Meet me here tomorrow morning. We'll catch fish then."

Turtle met Anansi on the riverbank the next morning.

"I can hardly wait to catch fish," Anansi said.

"That's good," Turtle replied. "Catching fish is hard work. You worked hard these past two days, Anansi. I think I should work today and let you get tired."

"Oh, no!" said Anansi. "I want to catch fish. I don't want to get tired."

"All right," said Turtle. "Whatever you wish."

Anansi worked hard all day pulling the net out of the river while Turtle lay back, getting very, very tired.

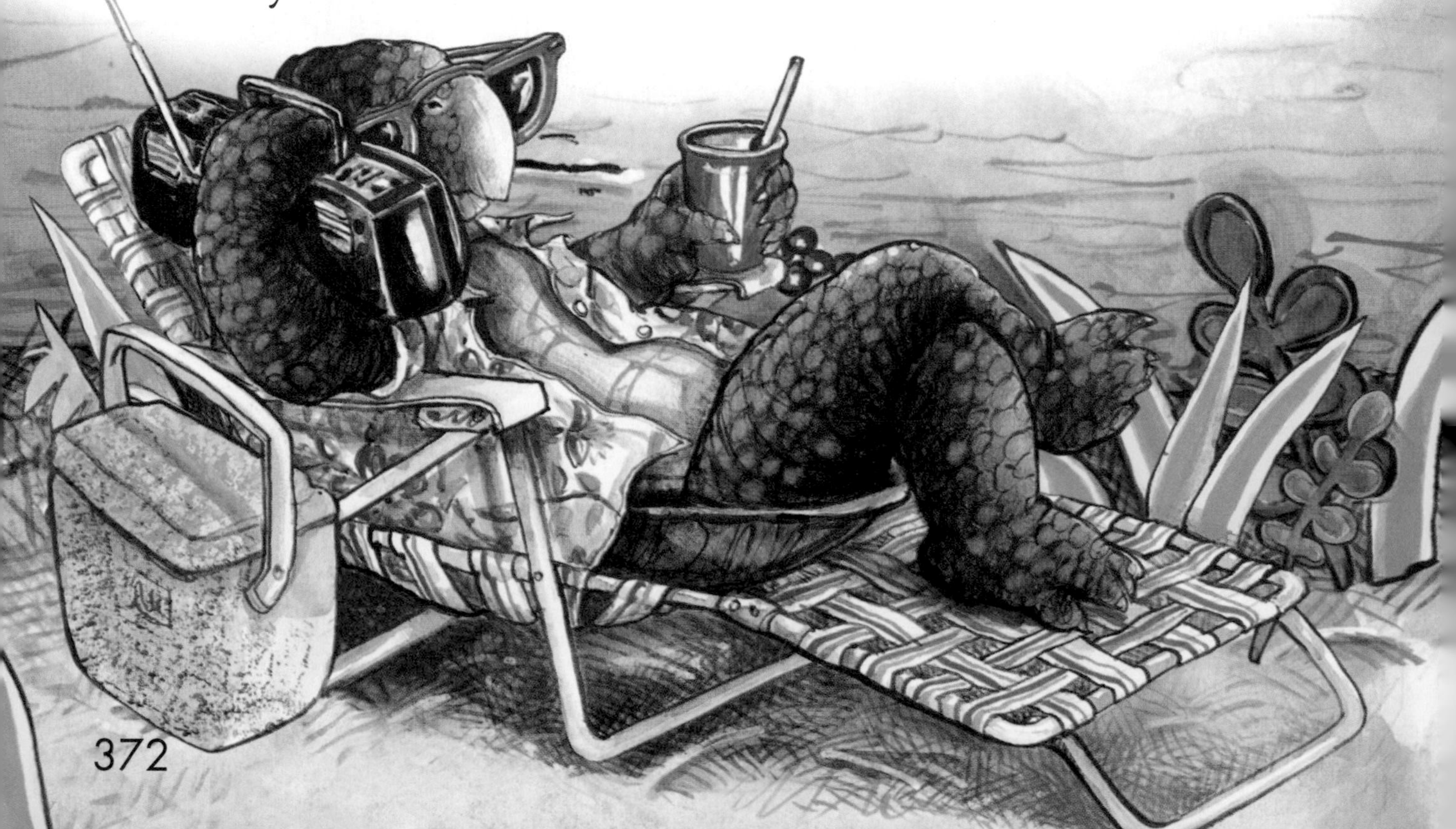

How pleased Anansi was to find a large fish caught in the net!

"What do we do now?" he asked Turtle.

Turtle yawned. "Now we cook the fish. Cooking is hard work. I think I should cook while you get tired."

"No!" cried Anansi. He did not want to share any bit of the fish. "I will cook. You get tired."

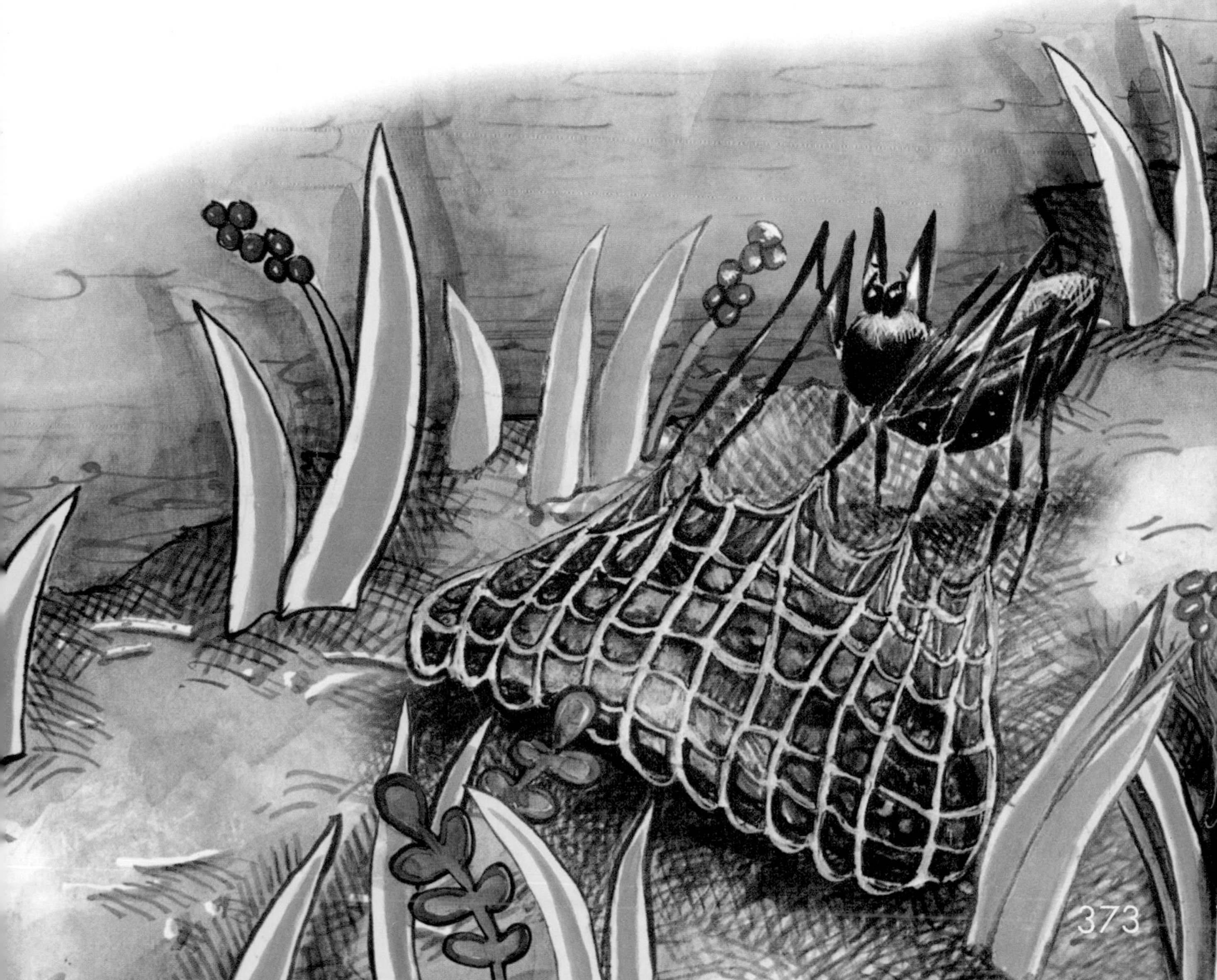

While Turtle watched, Anansi built a fire and cooked the fish from head to tail.

"That fish smells delicious," Turtle said. "You are a good cook, Anansi. And you worked hard. I know, because I am very, very tired. Now it is time to eat the fish. When I eat by myself, I eat and get full. Since there are two of us, we should share the task. One of us should eat while the other gets full. Which do you want to do?"

"I want to get full!" Anansi said, thinking only of his stomach.

"Then I will eat." Turtle began to eat while Anansi lay back and waited for his stomach to get full.

"Are you full yet?" Turtle asked Anansi.
"Not yet. Keep eating."

Turtle ate some more. "Are you full yet?"
"No. Keep eating."

Turtle ate some more. "Are you full yet?"
"Not at all," Anansi said. "I'm as empty as when you started."

"That's too bad," Turtle told him. "Because I'm full, and all the fish is gone."

"What?" Anansi cried. It was true. Turtle had eaten the whole fish. "You cheated me!" Anansi yelled when he realized what had happened.

"I did not!" Turtle replied.

"You did! You made me do all the work, then you ate the fish yourself. You won't get away with this. I am going to the Justice Tree."

Anansi ran to the Justice Tree. Warthog sat beneath its branches. Warthog was a fair and honest judge. All the animals brought their quarrels to him.

"What do you want, Anansi?" Warthog asked.

"I want justice," Anansi said. "Turtle cheated me. We went fishing together. He tricked me into doing all the work, then he ate the fish himself. Turtle deserves to be punished."

Warthog knew how lazy Anansi was. He couldn't imagine him working hard at anything. "Did you really do all the work?" he asked.

"Yes," Anansi replied.

"What did you do?"

"I wove the net.

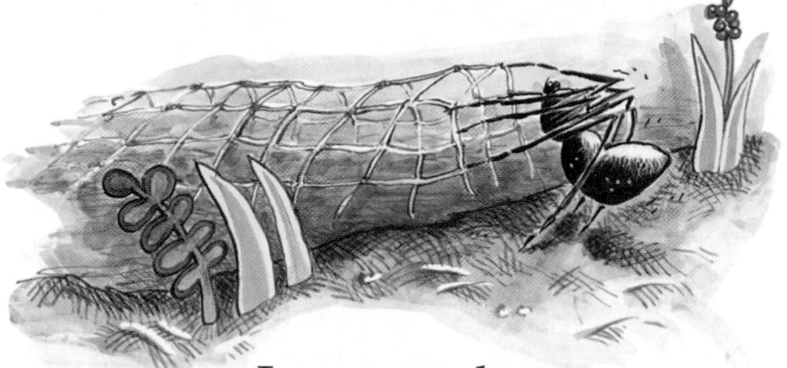

I set it in the river.

I caught the fish,

and I cooked it."

"That is a lot of work. You must have gotten very tired."

"No," said Anansi. "I didn't get tired at all. Turtle got tired, not me."

Warthog frowned. "Turtle got tired? What did he do?"

"Nothing!"

"If he did nothing, why did he get tired? Anansi, I don't believe you. No one gets tired by doing nothing. If Turtle got tired, then he must have done all the work. You are not telling the truth. Go home now and stop making trouble."

Warthog had spoken. There was nothing more to be said. Anansi went home in disgrace, and it was a long time before he spoke to Turtle again.

But some good came out of it. Anansi learned how to weave nets and how to use them to catch food. He taught his friends how to do it, and they taught their friends. Soon spiders all over the world were weaving. To this day, wherever you find spiders, you will find their nets.

They are called "spider webs."

Talk About It What three rules would you give Anansi and Turtle to follow if they go fishing again?

1. Use the pictures below to retell the story. **Retell**
2. What happens to make Anansi so angry? Look back at page 369. Read that part. **Cause and Effect**
3. Look at page 375. Read Turtle's question at the top of the page. What word does Anansi use on that page that means the opposite of *full?* **Antonyms**

TEST PRACTICE

Look Back and Write Look back at page 365. What will Anansi catch when he goes fishing? Use information from the story to support your answer.

Retell

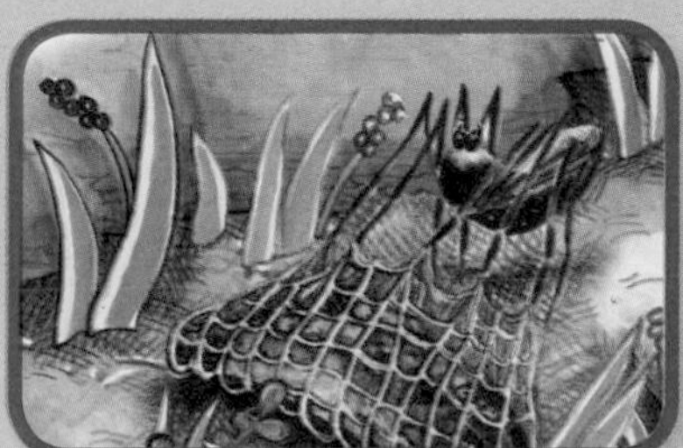

R1.7 Understand and explain common antonyms and synonyms. **R2.6** Recognize cause-and-effect relationships in a text. **LS1.8** Retell stories, including characters, setting, and plot.

Meet the Author

Eric Kimmel

Eric Kimmel first heard stories about Anansi as a child in New York City. He also heard Anansi stories from neighbors when he lived in the Virgin Islands. The stories come from Africa and are very old. "I enjoyed telling the stories so much that I tried my hand at writing them."

Mr. Kimmel says, "I like spiders. I never kill one. If I find a spider in the house, I catch it and take it outside. Spiders do us a lot of good, catching flies and other insect pests."

Read more books by Eric Kimmel about Anansi.

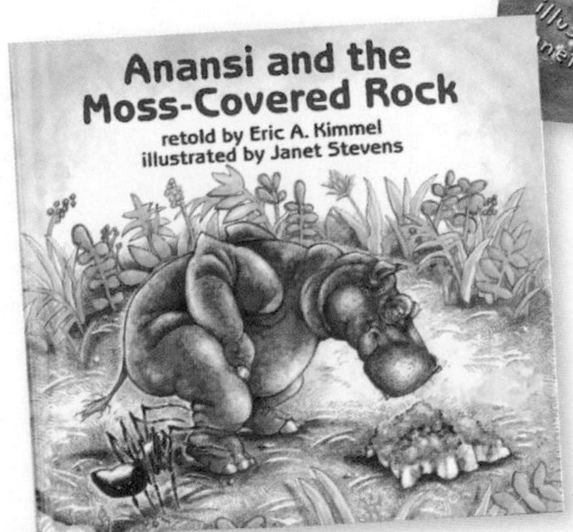

Meet the Illustrator

Janet Stevens

Before Janet Stevens drew Anansi, she read books about spiders. She thought about how to show Anansi's personality. "I mainly did it through his movement and gestures. He doesn't have a lot of face." She didn't want Anansi to look cute. "I like Anansi," she says. "He likes to get out of working."

Ms. Stevens has written and illustrated many children's books. She enjoys drawing wrinkles. "My favorite characters are rhinos, iguanas—anything with lots of wrinkles."

Janet Stevens & Susan Stevens Crummel
Jackalope
The TOWN MOUSE & the COUNTRY MOUSE
AN AESOP FABLE
ADAPTED AND ILLUSTRATED BY
JANET STEVENS

Read two more books by Janet Stevens.

Do spiders stick to their own webs?

by Amy Goldman Koss

The spider weaves a sticky web
To capture bugs to eat.
What keeps the spider's sticky web
From sticking to her feet?

Spiderwebs are very tricky
Because not all the strands are sticky.
Unlike the passing hapless fly,
The spider knows which strands are dry.

But if by accident she stands
On any of the sticky strands,
She still would not get stuck, you see–
Her oily body slides off free.

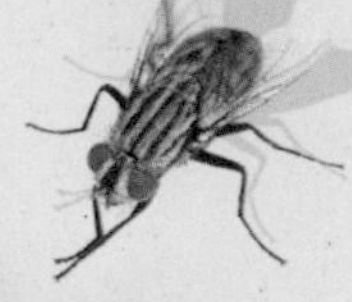

Writing Folk Tale

Prompt A spider learns from a turtle in *Anansi Goes Fishing.* Think about how creative thinking can solve a problem. Now write a folk tale in which an animal with a creative idea solves a problem.

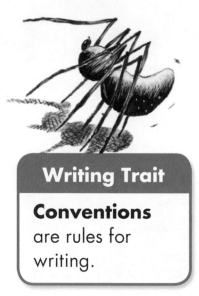

Writing Trait

Conventions are rules for writing.

Student Model

Past tense verbs may end in -ed.

A sentence begins with capital letter and ends with a period.

In a folk tale bad actions are punished.

The Top of the Tree

Mouse wanted to see the top of the tree. But he was so lazy and the tree was so tall. Then he had an idea. He climbed on Squirrel's back. He rode to the top of the tree and jumped off. But then Squirrel left. Lazy Mouse was trapped at the top of the tree.

W2.1 Write brief narratives based on their personal experience. **LC1.6** Capitalize all proper nouns, words at the beginning of sentences and greetings, months and days of the week, and titles and initials of people.

Writer's Checklist

- ✓ Did I write in the style of a folk tale?
- ✓ Did I use correct writing conventions for sentences?
- ✓ Did I use correct verb tenses?

Grammar Verbs for Present, Past, and Future

Some verbs tell about now. They may end with **–s.** Some verbs tell about the past. They may end with **–ed.** Some verbs tell about the future. They begin with **will.**

Today Anansi **waits** for Turtle.
Yesterday Anansi **waited** for Turtle.
Tomorrow Anansi **will wait** for Turtle.

Practice Look at the model. Write the past tense verbs with -ed from the sentences. Then write the same verbs in present tense.

Let's Talk About Creative Ideas

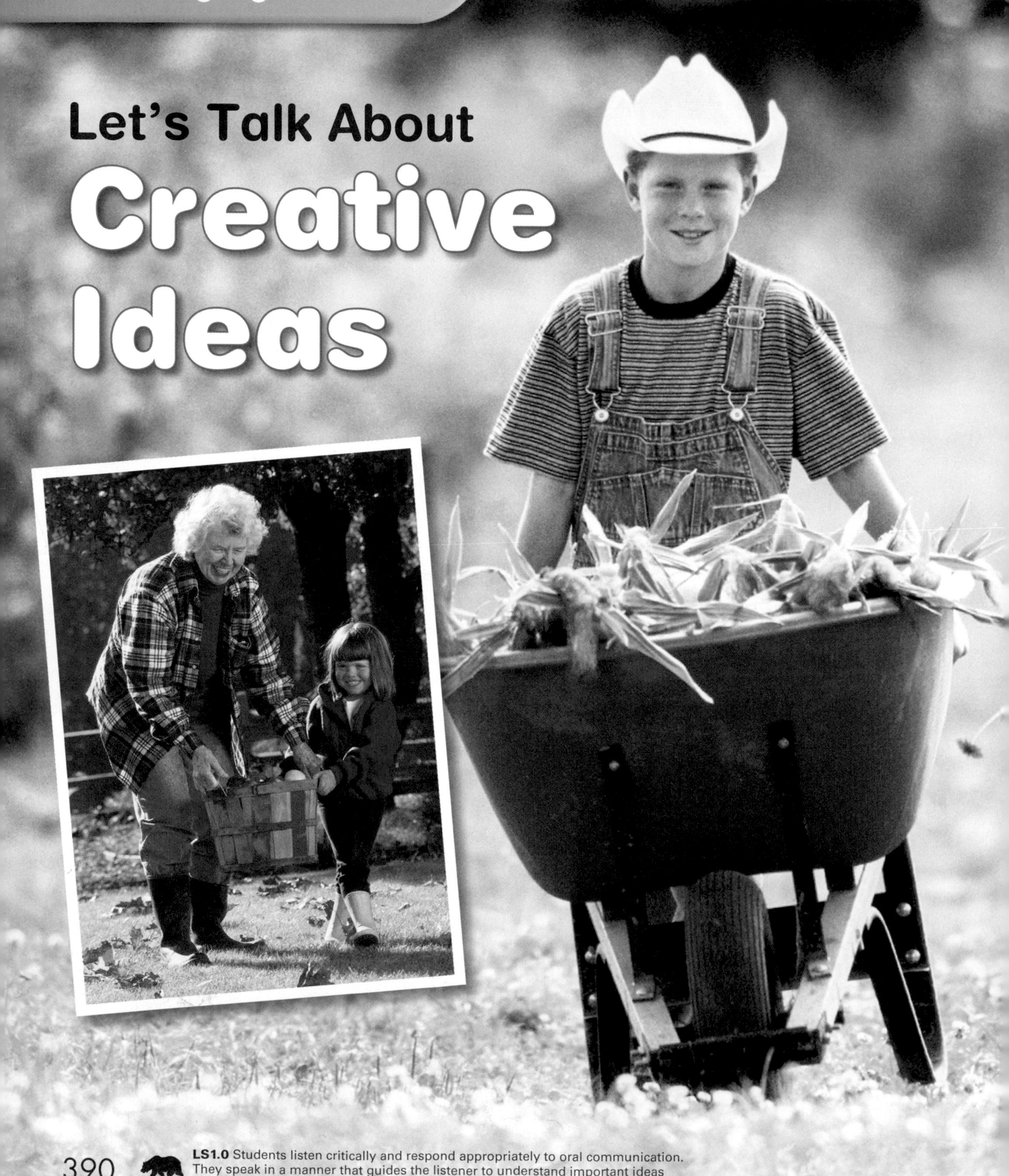

LS1.0 Students listen critically and respond appropriately to oral communication. They speak in a manner that guides the listener to understand important ideas by using proper phrasing, pitch, and modulation.

Words to Read

daughters
youngest
their
buy
many
alone
half

 G1R1.11 Read common, irregular sight words (e.g., *the, have, said, come, give, of*).

Read the Words

Rosa and Blanca are the daughters of a very loving mother. Rosa is the youngest. Their mother can't buy them many things, but she gives them lots of love. The two girls know that they will never be alone. They say that they will be happy if they can find in themselves half as much love as their mother gives.

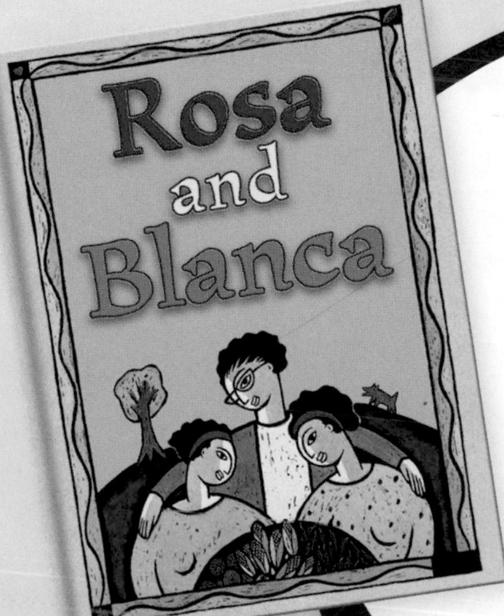

Genre: Realistic Fiction
Realistic fiction is a made-up story that could really happen. Next you will read about Rosa and Blanca, two sisters with a clever idea.

Rosa and Blanca

by Joe Hayes

illustrated by José Ortega

Who are Rosa and Blanca, and what is their creative idea?

Once there were two sisters named Rosa and Blanca. They loved each other very much. If their mother sent Rosa to the store to buy flour for tortillas, Blanca would go with her. If their mother told Blanca to sweep the sidewalk in front of their house, Rosa would help her.

Their mother would always say, "My daughters are so good to one another. They make me very happy. I think I am the luckiest mother in the town. No. I am the luckiest mother in the country. No. I am the luckiest mother in the whole world!"

When Rosa and Blanca grew up, Rosa got married. She and her husband had three children. Blanca didn't get married. She lived alone.

One year Rosa planted a garden. Blanca planted a garden too. They planted corn and tomatoes and good hot *chiles*.

When the tomatoes were round and ripe, Rosa helped Blanca pick the tomatoes in her garden. Blanca helped Rosa pick the tomatoes in her garden.

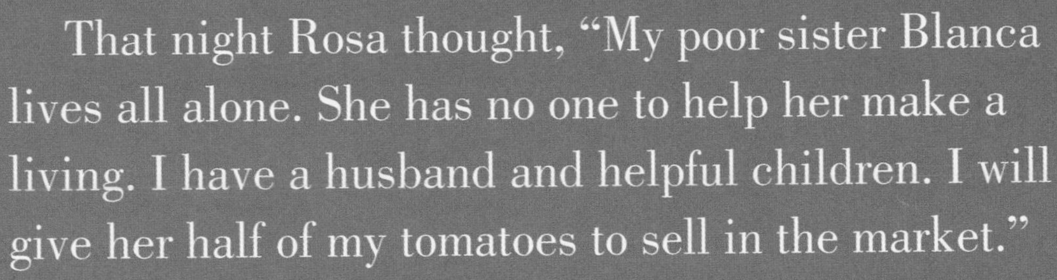

That night Rosa thought, "My poor sister Blanca lives all alone. She has no one to help her make a living. I have a husband and helpful children. I will give her half of my tomatoes to sell in the market."

Rosa filled a basket with tomatoes. She started toward Blanca's house.

That very same night Blanca thought, "My poor sister Rosa has a husband and three children. There are five to feed in her house. I only have myself. I will give her half of my tomatoes to sell in the market."

Blanca filled a basket with tomatoes. She started toward Rosa's house. The night was dark. The two sisters did not see each other when they passed.

Rosa added her tomatoes to the pile in Blanca's kitchen. Blanca added her tomatoes to the pile in Rosa's kitchen.

The next day, Rosa looked at her pile of tomatoes. "*¡Vaya!*" she said. "How can I have so many tomatoes? Did my tomatoes have babies during the night?"

The next day Blanca looked at her pile of tomatoes. "¡Vaya!" she said. "How can I have so many tomatoes? Did my tomatoes have babies during the night?"

When the corn was ripe, Rosa helped Blanca pick her corn. Blanca helped Rosa pick her corn.

That night Rosa thought, "I will give half of my corn to Blanca to sell in the market."

That night Blanca thought, "I will give half of my corn to Rosa to sell in the market."

Each sister filled a basket with corn. Rosa went to Blanca's house. Blanca went to Rosa's house. The night was dark. They did not see each other when they passed.

Rosa added her corn to the corn in Blanca's house. Blanca added her corn to the corn in Rosa's house.

The next day Rosa said, "¡Vaya! How can I have so much corn? Did each ear invite a friend to spend the night?"

The next day Blanca said, "¡Vaya! How can I have so much corn? Did each ear invite a friend to spend the night?"

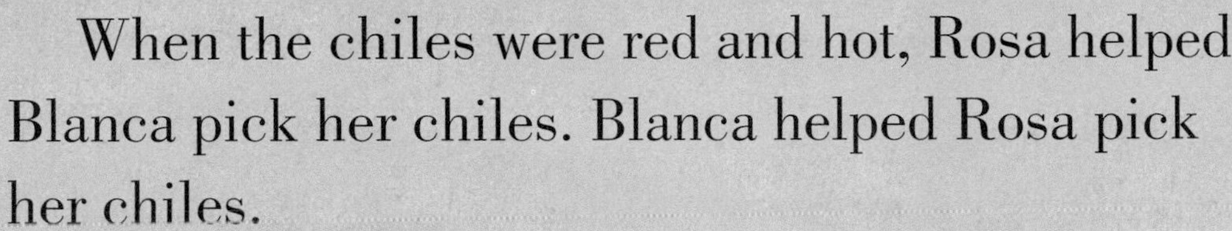

When the chiles were red and hot, Rosa helped Blanca pick her chiles. Blanca helped Rosa pick her chiles.

That night Rosa thought, "I will give Blanca half of my chiles to sell in the market."

That night Blanca thought, "I will give Rosa half of my chiles to sell in the market."

Each sister filled a basket with chiles.

Just then Rosa's youngest child started to cry. Rosa went to the child's room. She picked him up and rocked him.

Blanca was on her way to Rosa's house.

When Rosa's child went to sleep, Rosa picked up her basket of chiles. She started out the door. Blanca was coming in the door.

They both said, "¡Vaya!"

Rosa said, "Blanca, what are you doing? Why do you have that basket of chiles?"

Blanca said, "Rosa, what are you doing? Why do you have that basket of chiles?"

Rosa said, "I was going to give half of my chiles to you."

Blanca said, "But I was going to give half of my chiles to you!" Both sisters laughed.

Rosa said, "So that is why I still had so many tomatoes!"

Blanca said, "So that is why I still had so much corn!" The sisters hugged each other.

The next day Rosa and Blanca went to their mother's house. They told their mother what they had done.

Their old mother smiled and hugged her daughters. She said, "My daughters are so good to one another. They make me very happy. I think I am the luckiest mother in the town. No. I am the luckiest mother in the country. No. I am the luckiest mother in the whole world!"

Talk About It Rosa and Blanca had a clever idea that went wrong. Now they are planting again. What will you tell them so that they will not have another mix-up?

1. Use the pictures below to retell the story. **Retell**
2. What was the big idea of this story? What do you think the characters learned? **Theme and Plot**
3. What did you predict the sisters would do with their vegetables? Were you right? Tell why your prediction was correct or not. **Check Predictions**

TEST PRACTICE

Look Back and Write Look back at the story. Who are Rosa and Blanca and what are their ideas to help each other? Write your answer using information from the story.

Retell

 LS1.8 Retell stories, including characters, setting, and plot.

Meet the Author

Joe Hayes

Joe Hayes grew up listening to stories told by his father. He liked hearing stories so much that he decided he wanted to tell them too. Mr. Hayes began by telling stories to his own children. He soon realized that he liked telling stories to as many children as he could!

Mr. Hayes travels to many different places to share with children the stories he has learned. He has also published 20 books, many in English and Spanish.

Read more books by Joe Hayes.

The Crow and the Pitcher

a fable by Aesop retold by Eric Blair
illustrated by Laura Ovresat

There was once a thirsty crow. She had flown a long way looking for water.

The thirsty crow saw a pitcher of water and flew down to drink.

The pitcher had only a little water left at the bottom.

The crow put her beak into the pitcher. The water was so low she couldn't reach it.

But I must have water to drink. I can't fly any farther, thought the crow.

I know. I'll tip the pitcher over, she thought.

The thirsty crow beat the pitcher with her wings, but she wasn't strong enough to tip it.

Maybe I can break the pitcher. Then the water will flow, thought the crow.

She backed away to get a flying start. With all her might, the thirsty crow flew at the pitcher. She struck it with her pointed beak and claws, but the tired crow wasn't strong enough to break the pitcher.

Just as she was about to give up, the crow had another idea. She dropped a pebble into the pitcher. The water rose a little.

She dropped another and another. With each pebble, the water level rose more.

Soon the water reached the brim. The crow drank until she was no longer thirsty.

The crow was pleased with herself. By refusing to give up, she had solved her difficult problem.

Writing Realistic Fiction

Prompt *Rosa and Blanca* are two sisters who have creative ideas. Think about a creative idea that could lead to a surprise. Now write a realistic story about a character whose creative idea leads to a surprise.

Writing Trait

Good **word choice** makes your writing interesting.

Student Model

Word choice tells about the family.

Realistic fiction has parts that are real.

Verbs that end in -ed tell about the past.

Helping Out

Rita and Greta made dinner for their busy family. They made sandwiches. They set the table. Soon Mom walked in with two big bags.

"I picked up dinner!" Mom announced.

"We were being kind!" Rita laughed.

"You are such wonderful girls," said Mom.

W2.1 Write brief narratives based on their personal experience. **G1LC1.3** Identify and correctly use various parts of speech, including nouns and verbs, in writing and speaking.

Writer's Checklist

- ☑ Could my story really happen?
- ☑ Did I use words to make my story interesting?
- ☑ Did I use correct verb tenses?

Grammar More About Verbs

Use the correct verb in a sentence to show that something is happening now, in the past, or in the future.

Today they **plant** beans. (now)
Yesterday they **planted** corn. (past)
Tomorrow they **will plant** more. (future)

Practice Look at the model. Write the past tense verbs from the sentences. Then write the same verbs in a way that tells about the future.

Let's Talk About Creative Ideas

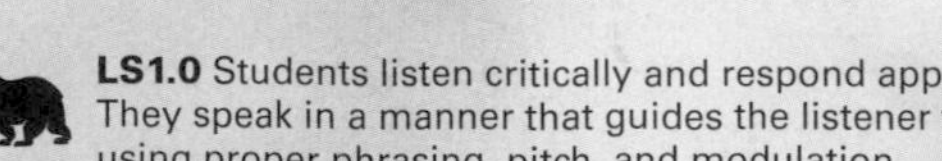

LS1.0 Students listen critically and respond appropriately to oral communication. They speak in a manner that guides the listener to understand important ideas by using proper phrasing, pitch, and modulation.

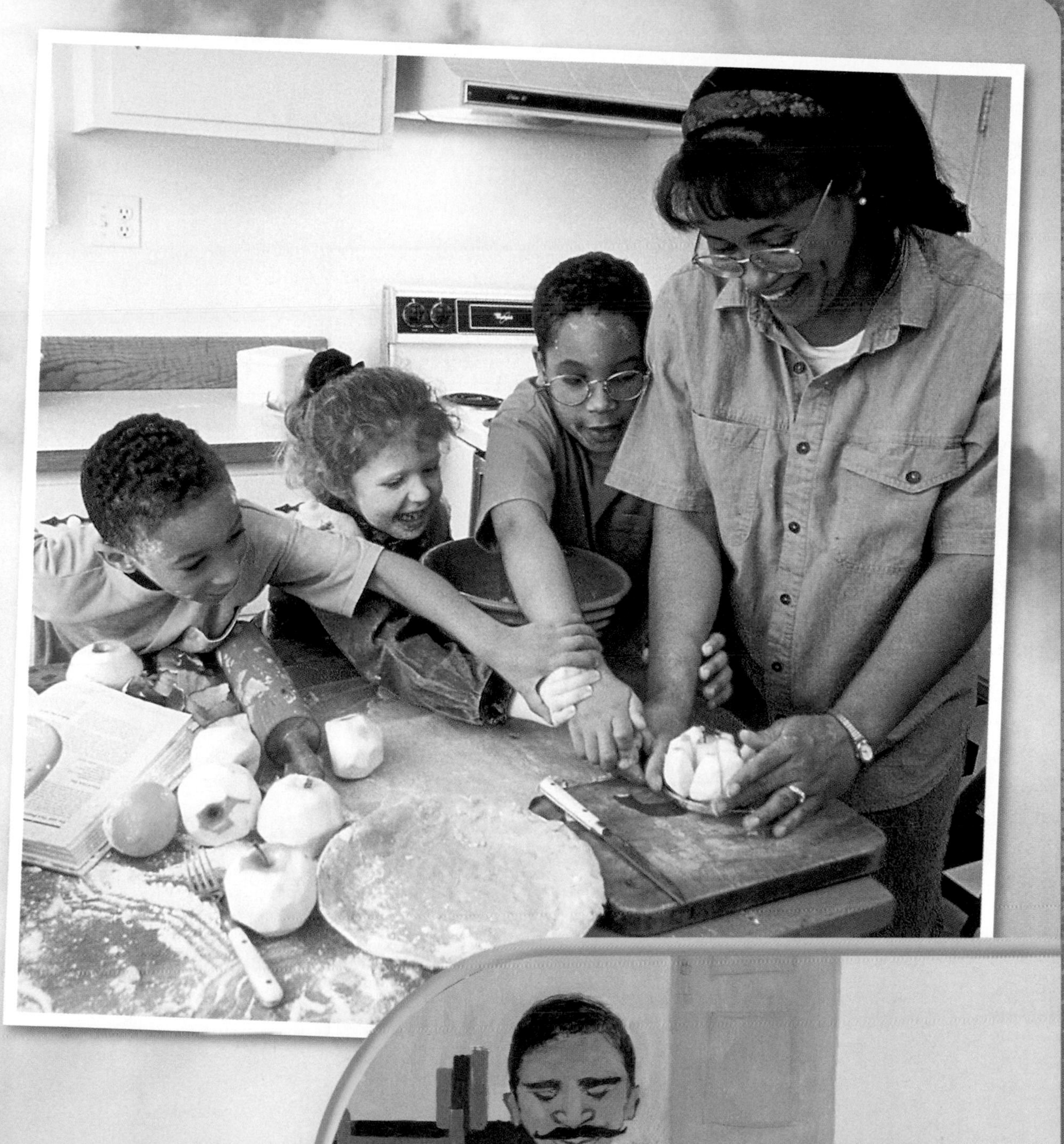

Words to Read

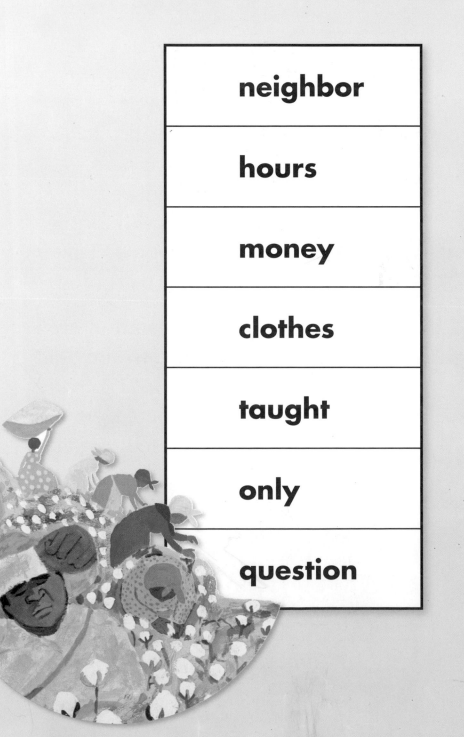

neighbor
hours
money
clothes
taught
only
question

 G1R1.11 Read common, irregular sight words (e.g., *the, have, said, come, give, of*).

Read the Words

Our neighbor spends many hours in his beautiful garden. He doesn't make a lot of money, and he wears torn clothes. However, he loves his plants and flowers. He taught himself a lot of what he knows. I have only one question for him. Can he teach me too?

Genre: Biography
A biography tells about a real person's life. It is written by another person. Next you will read the biography of George Washington Carver, a creative scientist.

A Weed Is a Flower

The Life of George Washington Carver

by Aliki

Who was George Washington Carver?

George Washington Carver was born in Missouri in 1860—more than a hundred years ago. It was a terrible time. Mean men rode silently in the night, kidnapping slaves from their owners and harming those who tried to stop them.

One night, a band of these men rode up to the farm of Moses Carver, who owned George and his mother, Mary. Everyone ran in fear. But before Mary could hide her baby, the men came and snatched them both, and rode away into the night.

Moses Carver sent a man to look for them. Mary was never found. But in a few days, the man returned with a small bundle wrapped in his coat and tied to the back of his saddle. It was the baby, George.

Moses and his wife, Susan, cared for Mary's children. George remained small and weak. But as he grew, they saw he was an unusual child. He wanted to know about everything around him. He asked about the rain, the flowers, and the insects. He asked questions the Carvers couldn't answer.

When he was very young, George kept a garden where he spent hours each day caring for his plants. If they weren't growing well, he found out why. Soon they were healthy and blooming. In winter he covered his plants to protect them. In spring he planted new seeds. George looked after each plant as though it was the only one in his garden.

Neighbors began to ask George's advice about their plants, and soon he was known as the Plant Doctor.

As time went on, George wondered about more and more things. He wanted to learn and yearned to go to school.

In the meantime, the slaves had been freed, but schools nearby were not open to blacks. So when he was ten, George left his brother, his garden, and the Carver farm and went off to find the answers to his questions.

Wherever George Washington Carver found schools, he stayed. He worked for people to earn his keep. He scrubbed their floors, washed their clothes, and baked their bread. Whatever George did, he did well. Even the smallest chore was important to him.

Some people took George in as their son. First he stayed with Mariah and Andy Watkins, who were like parents to him. Then he moved to Kansas and lived with "Aunt" Lucy and "Uncle" Seymour. They, too, loved this quiet boy who was so willing to help.

George worked hard for many years, always trying to save enough money for college. Other boys, who had parents to help them, were able to enter college much sooner than George. He was thirty before he had saved enough. Still, it was not that simple. Not all colleges would admit blacks, even if they had the money to pay.

George was not discouraged. He moved to Iowa and found a college which was glad to have a black student.

At college, George continued to work.
He opened a laundry where he washed his schoolmates' clothes.

And, he continued to learn. His teachers and friends soon realized that this earnest young man was bursting with talents. He played the piano, he sang beautifully, and he was an outstanding painter. In fact, for a time he thought of becoming an artist.

But the more George thought of what he wanted to do, the more he wanted to help his people. And he remembered that his neighbors used to call him the Plant Doctor.

He had never forgotten his love for plants. In all the years he had wandered, he always had something growing in his room.

So, George Washington Carver chose to study agriculture. He learned about plants, flowers, and soil. He learned the names of the weeds. Even they were important to him. He often said: a weed is a flower growing in the wrong place.

He still asked questions. If no person or book could answer them, he found the answers himself. He experimented with his own plants, and found secrets no one else knew.

When George finished college, he began to teach. He was asked to go to Alabama, where a college for blacks needed his talent. It was there, at Tuskegee Institute, that George Washington Carver made his life.

In Alabama, Professor Carver taught his students and the poor black farmers, who earned their livelihood from the soil. He taught them how to make their crops grow better.

Most of the farmers raised cotton. But sometimes the crops were destroyed by rain or insects, and the farmers couldn't earn enough to eat.

Professor Carver told them to plant other things as well. Sweet potatoes and peanuts were good crops. They were easy to grow. He said that raising only cotton harmed the soil. It was better if different crops were planted each year.

The farmers did not want to listen. They were afraid to plant peanuts and sweet potatoes. They were sure that no one would buy them.

But Professor Carver had experimented in his laboratory. He had found that many things could be made from the sweet potato. He made soap, coffee, and starch. He made more than a hundred things from the sweet potato.

And even though people in those days called peanuts "monkey food," Professor Carver said they were good for people, too. Besides, he found that still more things could be made from the peanut. Paper, ink, shaving cream, sauces, linoleum, shampoo, and even milk! In fact, he made three hundred different products from the peanut.

Once, when important guests were expected at Tuskegee, Dr. Carver chose the menu. The guests sat around the table and enjoyed a meal of soup, creamed mock chicken, bread, salad, coffee, candy, cake, and ice cream. Imagine their surprise when they learned that the meal was made entirely from peanuts!

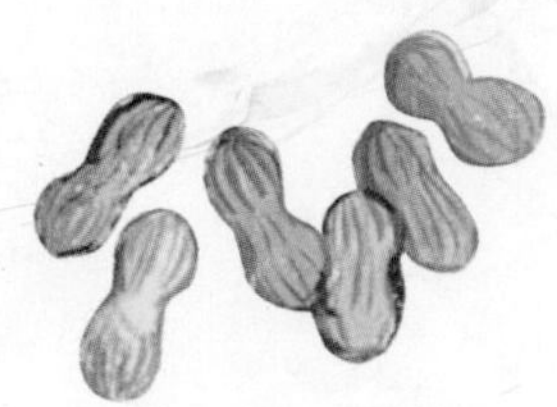

Slowly, the farmers listened to George Washington Carver. They planted peanuts and sweet potatoes. Before they knew it these became two of the most important crops in Alabama.

Soon the whole country knew about Dr. Carver and the great things he was doing. He was honored by Presidents and other important people. Every day, his mailbox bulged with letters from farmers and scientists who wanted his advice. He was offered great sums of money, which he turned down. Money was not important to him. He did not even bother to cash many of the checks he received.

Throughout his life, George Washington Carver asked nothing of others. He sought only to help. He lived alone and tended to his own needs. He washed his clothes and patched them, too. He used the soap he made and ate the food he grew.

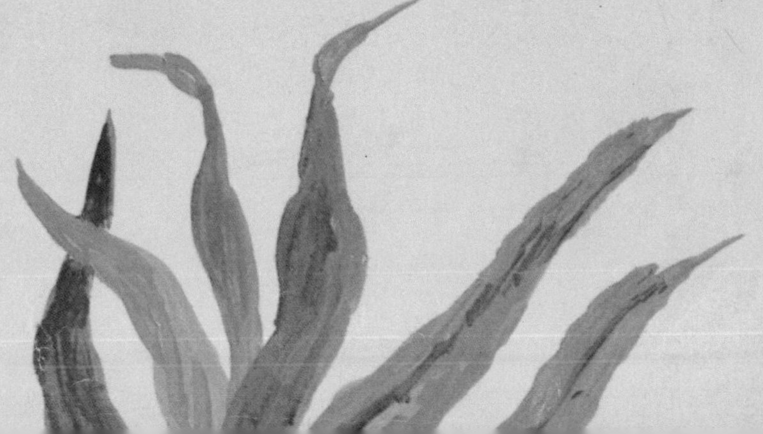

Dr. Carver was asked to speak in many parts of the world, but he did not leave Tuskegee often. He had things to do. He continued to paint. He worked in his greenhouse and in his laboratory, where he discovered many things. He discovered that dyes could be made from plants, and colors from the Alabama clay. Even when he was over eighty and close to death, Dr. Carver kept working. Night after night, while the rest of the town lay asleep, a light still shone in his window.

The baby born with no hope for the future grew into one of the great scientists of his country. George Washington Carver, with his goodness and devotion, helped not only his own people, but all peoples of the world.

Talk About It If you could visit George Washington Carver, would you visit when he was a boy, a young man, or a famous professor? Tell about your visit.

1. Use the pictures below to summarize what you learned. **Summarize**
2. Why does Professor Carver tell the farmers to plant peanuts and sweet potatoes? **Cause and Effect**
3. What do you know about flowers and weeds? How could Professor Carver's study of plants help others? **Prior Knowledge**

TEST PRACTICE **Look Back and Write** Look back at page 419. Why is George Washington Carver an important person? Use details from the selection to write your answer.

Summarize

R2.5 Restate facts and details in the text to clarify and organize ideas. **R2.6** Recognize cause-and-effect relationships in a text.

Meet the Author and Illustrator

Aliki

When Aliki writes a book, she often uses cartoons and draws funny characters talking in the margins. Her books are fun, but she does lots of research. "I spend many hours at my desk," she says. "Some books take three years to finish. That's why I call what I do hard fun."

Aliki grew up in Philadelphia, but her parents are from Greece. She speaks Greek as well as English. She prefers to use only her first name on her books.

Read two more books by Aliki.

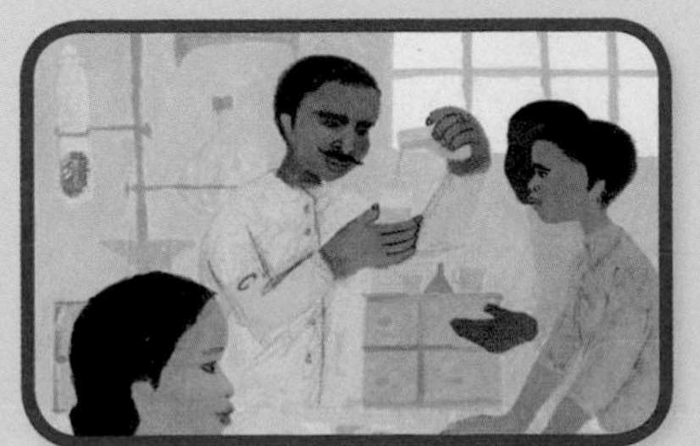

What's Made from Corn?

If you are writing a report, you can use the Internet to help find information. Maria wants to give a report on how corn is used every day. She does an Internet search using a search engine. First, Maria brainstorms a list of keywords about her topic. These can be single words or groups of words that she will type into the search window of a search engine. Maria came up with these keywords:

Corn

Uses of corn

How we use corn

She can type any of these into a search engine window and then click the Search button. After a few seconds, she gets a list of Web sites.

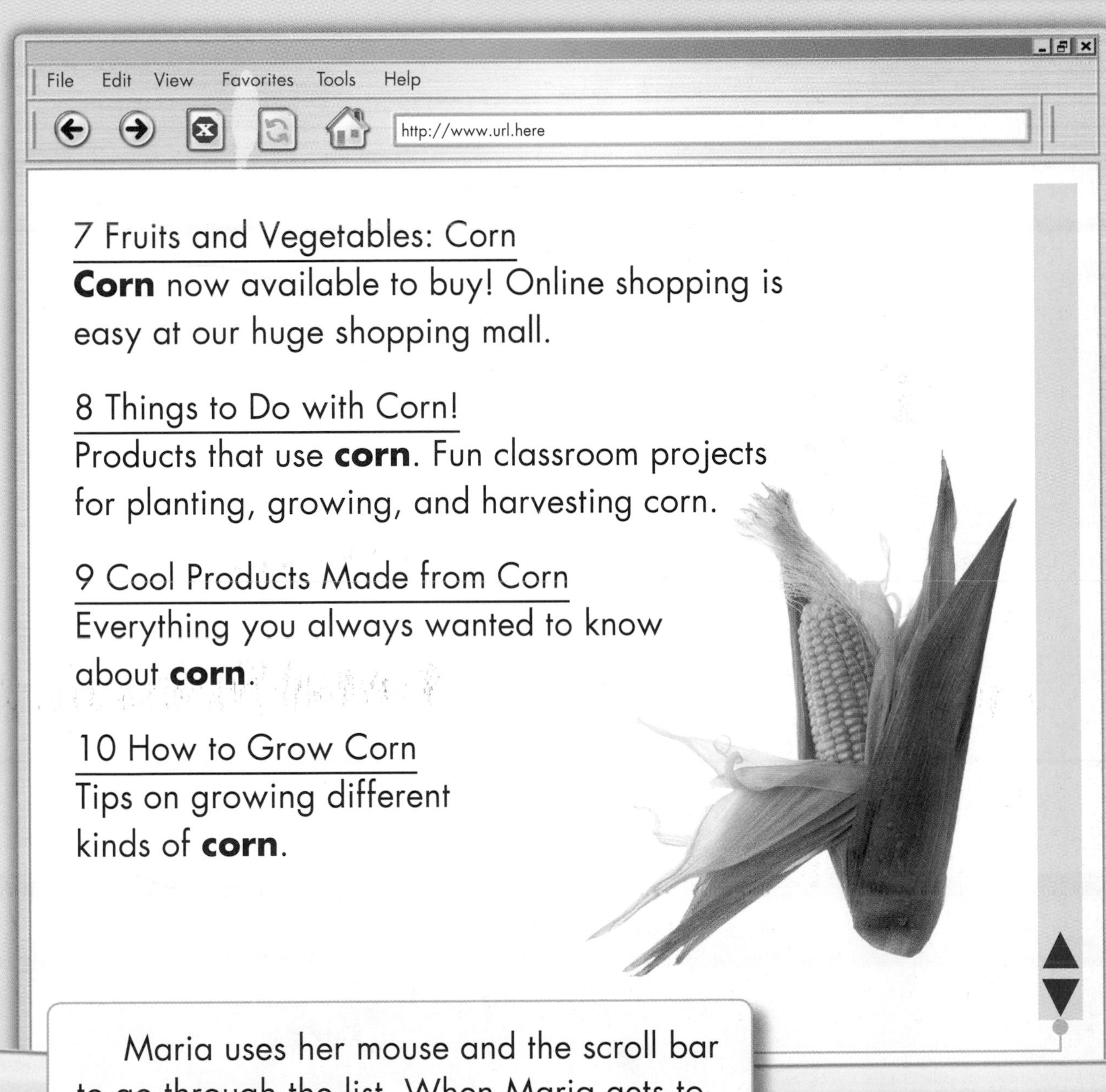

File Edit View Favorites Tools Help
http://www.url.here
7 Fruits and Vegetables: Corn
Corn now available to buy! Online shopping is easy at our huge shopping mall.
8 Things to Do with Corn!
Products that use corn. Fun classroom projects for planting, growing, and harvesting corn.
9 Cool Products Made from Corn
Everything you always wanted to know about corn.
10 How to Grow Corn
Tips on growing different kinds of corn.

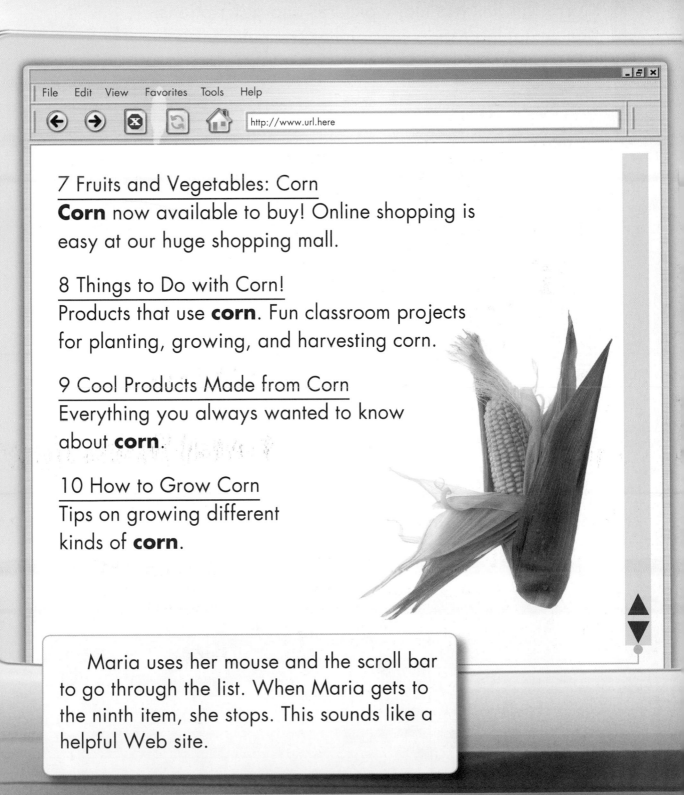

Maria uses her mouse and the scroll bar to go through the list. When Maria gets to the ninth item, she stops. This sounds like a helpful Web site.

Maria clicks on the link Cool Products Made from Corn. This link has many pictures and descriptions. The next thing Maria sees on her computer screen is:

Cool Products Made from Corn

- Corn can be used to make knives, forks, and spoons. Corn can be used to make plates, diapers, milk jugs, razors, and golf tees. All these things dissolve when put into the garbage. This helps the environment.
- Corn can be made into "packing peanuts." Packing peanuts are used to protect objects packed in boxes. These peanuts dissolve in water.

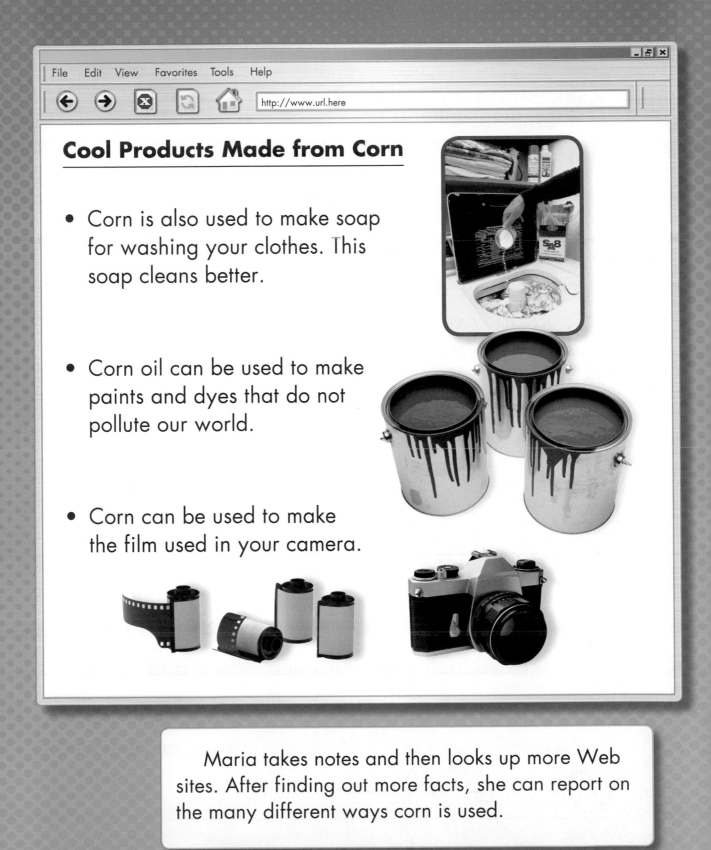

Cool Products Made from Corn

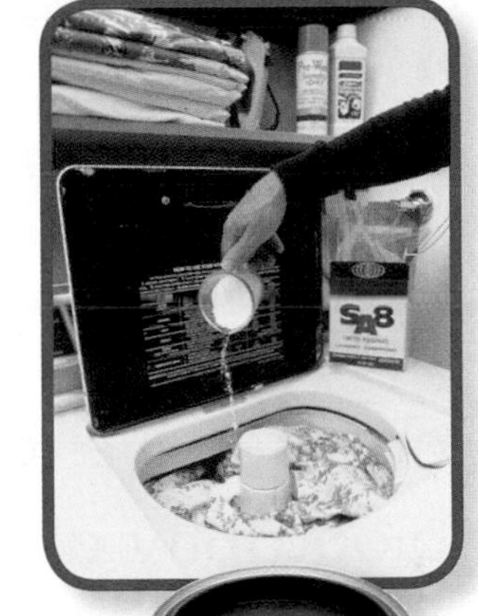

- Corn is also used to make soap for washing your clothes. This soap cleans better.

- Corn oil can be used to make paints and dyes that do not pollute our world.

- Corn can be used to make the film used in your camera.

Maria takes notes and then looks up more Web sites. After finding out more facts, she can report on the many different ways corn is used.

Writing Biography

Prompt *A Weed Is a Flower* is about the life of George Washington Carver, a creative inventor. Think about where we get our creative ideas. Now write a short biography about someone who had a creative idea.

Writing Trait

Writing **organized** in the order things happen can help a reader understand it.

Student Model

My Creative Dad

My dad was always a creative person. When he was a kid, he made toy trucks out of tin cans. Later he began to design buildings. Last week he used the parts of an old car to make a tree house. He is such a creative person. I am very proud of him.

A biography tells about a real person.

The verb *was* is a form of *to be*.

The biography is told in order.

G1LC1.2 Recognize and use the correct word order in written sentences. **G1LC1.3** Identify and correctly use various parts of speech, including nouns and verbs, in writing and speaking.

Writer's Checklist

- ☑ Is my writing about a real person?
- ☑ Is my writing in an order that makes sense?
- ☑ Did I use verbs that are a form of *to be*?

Grammar Am, Is, Are, Was, and Were

The verbs **am, is, are, was,** and **were** show what someone or something is or was. They are forms of the verb *to be.*

Am, is, and **are** tell about now. **Was** and **were** tell about the past.

Use **am, is,** and **was** to tell about one person, place, or thing. Use **are** and **were** to tell about more than one.

Practice Look at the model. Write the verbs that are forms of the verb *to be.*

Aa

astronaut

agriculture (ag ruh KUL cher) **Agriculture** is farming and growing crops. *NOUN*

armadillo (ar muh DIL oh) An **armadillo** is an animal that has a hard, bony covering. *NOUN*

astronaut (ASS truh nawt) An **astronaut** is a person who has been trained to fly in a spacecraft. While in space, **astronauts** repair space stations and do experiments. *NOUN*

Bb

brave (BRAYV) If you are **brave**, you are not afraid: The **brave** girl pulled her little brother away from the burning leaves. *ADJECTIVE*

Cc

chiles (CHIL ayz) **Chiles** are a green or red pepper with a hot taste. *NOUN*

collar (KOL er) A **collar** is a band that is put around the neck of a dog or other pet. **Collars** can be made of leather or plastic. *NOUN*

college (KOL ij) **College** is the school that you go to after high school: After I finish high school, I plan to go to **college** to become a teacher. *NOUN*

compass (KUHM puhs) A **compass** is a tool for finding directions: You can use a **compass** to help you find your way. *NOUN*

cousins (KUH zins) Your **cousins** are the children of your aunt or uncle. *NOUN*

creature (KREE chur) A **creature** is a living being: Many **creatures** live in the forest. *NOUN*

Dd

dangerous (DAYN jer uhss) Something that is **dangerous** is not safe: Skating on thin ice is **dangerous**. *ADJECTIVE*

delicious (di LISH uhss) When something is **delicious**, it tastes or smells very good: The cookies were **delicious**. *ADJECTIVE*

drooled (DROOLD) To **drool** is to let saliva run from the mouth like a baby sometimes does. The dog **drooled** when it saw the bone. *VERB*

Ee

electricity (i lek TRISS uh tee) **Electricity** is a kind of energy that makes light and heat. **Electricity** also runs motors. **Electricity** makes light bulbs shine, radios and televisions play, and cars start. *NOUN*

envelope (EN vuh lohp) An **envelope** is a folded paper cover. An **envelope** is used to mail a letter or something else that is flat. *NOUN*

excitement (ek SYT muhnt) **Excitement** happens when you have very strong, happy feelings about something that you like. *NOUN*

experiment (ek SPEER uh ment) An **experiment** is a test to find out something: We do **experiments** in science class. *NOUN*

Ff

fault (FAWLT) If something is your **fault,** you are to blame for it. *NOUN*

force (FORSS) **Force** is the energy or power to make something move: The **force** of the wind broke the tree branches. *NOUN*

Gg

gnaws (NAWZ) When an animal **gnaws**, it is biting and wearing away by biting: The brown mouse **gnaws** the cheese. *VERB*

grateful (GRAYT fuhl) If you are **grateful** for something, you are thankful for it. *ADJECTIVE*

gravity (GRAV uh tee) **Gravity** is the natural force that causes objects to move toward the center of the Earth. **Gravity** causes objects to have weight. *NOUN*

greenhouse (GREEN howss) A **greenhouse** is a building with a glass or plastic roof and sides. A **greenhouse** is kept warm and full of light for growing plants. *NOUN*

greenhouse

groaned (GROHND) To **groan** is to make a low sound showing that you are in pain or are unhappy about something: We all **groaned** when it started to rain during recess. *VERB*

Hh

honest (ON ist) Someone who is **honest** does not lie, cheat, or steal. *ADJECTIVE*

hurricanes (HUR uh kains) A **hurricane** is a violent storm with strong winds: The Florida **hurricanes** blew the roofs off many houses. *NOUN*

Jj

justice (JUHS tis) **Justice** happens when things are right and fair. *NOUN*

Ll

laboratory (LAB ruh tor ee) A **laboratory** is a room where scientists work and do experiments and tests. *NOUN*

lantern

lanterns (LAN ternz) **Lanterns** are portable lamps with coverings around them to protect them from wind and rain. *NOUN*

lawyer (LOI er) A **lawyer** is someone who is trained to give people advice about the law. A **lawyer** helps people when they go to court. *NOUN*

lazy (LAY zee) If a person is **lazy**, he or she does not want to work hard or to move fast: The **lazy** cat lay on the rug all day. *ADJECTIVE*

luckiest (LUHK ee est) The **luckiest** person is the one who has had the best fortune. *ADJECTIVE*

Mm

meadow (MED oh) A **meadow** is a piece of land where grass grows: There are sheep in the **meadow**. *NOUN*

mill (MIL) A **mill** is a building in which grain is ground into flour or meal. *NOUN*

monsters (MON sterz) **Monsters** are make-believe people or animals that are scary. In stories, some **monsters** are friendly, and others are not: Dragons are **monsters**. *NOUN*

musician (myoo ZISH uhn) A **musician** is a person who sings, plays, or writes music. *NOUN*

Nn

narrator (NAIR ayt or) A **narrator** is a person who tells a story or play. In a play, a **narrator** keeps the action moving. *NOUN*

noticed (NOH tisd) To **notice** means to see something or become aware of it: The boys **noticed** a strange smell near the cave. *VERB*

Pp

parents (PAIR ents) Your **parents** are your mother and father. *NOUN*

persimmons

persimmons (puhr SIM uhns) **Persimmons** are round, yellow and orange fruits about the size of plums. *NOUN*

photograph (FOH tuh graf) A **photograph** is a picture you make with a camera. *NOUN*

promise (PROM iss) If you make a **promise** to do something, you are giving your word that you will do it. *NOUN*

Rr

relatives (REL uh tivs) Your **relatives** are the people who belong to the same family as you do: Your mother, sister, and cousin are all your **relatives**. *NOUN*

resources (REE sor sez). Resources are things people need and use, such as food, water, and building materials. *NOUN*

robbers (ROB ers) **Robbers** are people who rob or steal: The police chased the bank **robbers**. *NOUN*

robot (ROH bot or ROH BUHT) A **robot** is a machine that is run by a computer. **Robots** help people do work. **Robots** can look like people. *NOUN*

robot

Ss

scarce (SKAIRSS) If something is **scarce,** it is hard to find because there is so little of it: Empty seats were **scarce** at the sold-out show. *ADJECTIVE*

scarcity (SKAIR suh tee) **Scarcity** happens when there is not enough of something for everyone who wants it: Dry weather damaged the farmers' crops and caused a **scarcity** of corn. *NOUN*

shivered (SHIV erd) To **shiver** is to shake with cold, fear, or excitement: I **shivered** in the cold wind. *VERB*

shuttle (SHUHT uhl) A **shuttle** is a spacecraft with wings, which can orbit the earth, land like an airplane, and be used again. *NOUN*

slipped (SLIPT) When you **slip** you slide suddenly and unexpectedly: She **slipped** on the ice. *VERB*

smudged (SMUDJD) If something is **smudged**, it is marked with a dirty streak. *ADJECTIVE*

snorted (SNOR ted) To **snort** means to breathe noisily through the nose: Her brother **snorted** when he laughed. *VERB*

snuggled (SNUHG uhld) To **snuggle** is to lie closely and comfortably together; cuddle: The kittens **snuggled** together in the basket. *VERB*

snuggled

squall (SKWAWL) A **squall** is a sudden violent wind that usually brings rain, snow, or sleet. *NOUN*

Tt

telescope (TEL uh skohp) A **telescope** is something you look through to make things far away seem nearer and larger: We looked at the moon through a **telescope**. *NOUN*

tortillas (tor TEE uhs) **Tortillas** are thin, flat, round breads usually made of cornmeal. *NOUN*

trade-off (TRAYD off) You make a **trade-off** when you give up one thing you want for something else you want even more. *NOUN*

trade winds (TRAYD winds) **Trade winds** are warm steady winds that blow across the ocean toward the equator. *NOUN*

trash (TRASH) **Trash** is anything of no use or that is worn out. **Trash** is garbage or things to be thrown away. *NOUN*

trash

Ww

wad (WOD) A **wad** is a small, soft ball or chunk of something: She threw a **wad** of paper in the wastebasket. *NOUN*

weave (WEEV) To **weave** is to form threads into cloth. *VERB*

Unit 1

The Twin Club

friend
beautiful
front
someone
somewhere
country

Exploring Space with an Astronaut

everywhere
live
work
woman
machines
move
world

Henry and Mudge and the Starry Night

couldn't
love
build
mother
bear
father
straight

Sailing in the Wind

early
warm
full
water
eyes
animals

The Strongest One

together
very
learn
often
though
gone
pieces

Unit 2

Tara and Tiree, Fearless Friends

family
once
pull
listen
heard
break

Abraham Lincoln

second
you're
either
laugh
worst
great
certainly

Scarcity

enough
word
ago
whole
above
toward

The Bremen Town Musicians

people
sign
shall
bought
pleasant
scared

One Good Turn Deserves Another

brought
door
everybody
behind
promise
sorry
minute

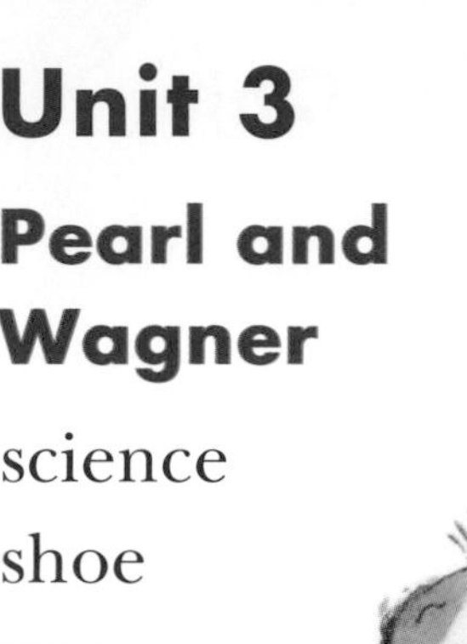

Unit 3

Pearl and Wagner

science
shoe
won
guess
village
pretty
watch

Dear Juno

picture
school
answer
wash
parents
company
faraway

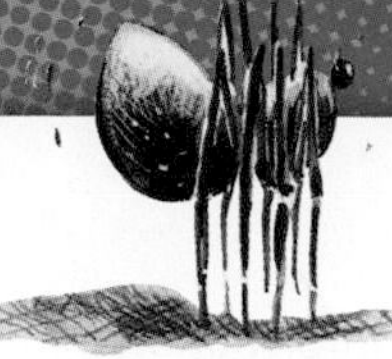

Anansi Goes Fishing

today
whatever
caught
believe
been
finally
tomorrow

Rosa and Blanca

their
many
alone
buy
half
youngest
daughters

A Weed Is a Flower

only
question
clothes
money
hours
neighbor
taught

Reading

1.0 Word Analysis, Fluency, and Systematic Vocabulary Development

Students understand the basic features of reading. They select letter patterns and know how to translate them into spoken language by using phonics, syllabication, and word parts. They apply this knowledge to achieve fluent oral and silent reading.

Decoding and Word Recognition

1.1 Recognize and use knowledge of spelling patterns (e.g., diphthongs, special vowel spellings) when reading.

1.2 Apply knowledge of basic syllabication rules when reading (e.g., vowel-consonant-vowel = *su/ per;* vowel-consonant/consonant-vowel = *sup/ per).*

1.3 Decode two-syllable nonsense words and regular multisyllable words.

1.4 Recognize common abbreviations (e.g., *Jan., Sun., Mr., St.).*

1.5 Identify and correctly use regular plurals (e.g., *-s, -es, -ies)* and irregular plurals (e.g., *fly/ flies, wife/ wives).*

1.6 Read aloud fluently and accurately and with appropriate intonation and expression.

Vocabulary and Concept Development

1.7 Understand and explain common antonyms and synonyms.

1.8 Use knowledge of individual words in unknown compound words to predict their meaning.

1.9 Know the meaning of simple prefixes and suffixes (e.g., *over-, un-, -ing, -ly).*

1.10 Identify simple multiple-meaning words.

2.0 Reading Comprehension

Students read and understand grade-level-appropriate material. They draw upon a variety of comprehension strategies as needed (e.g., generating and responding to essential questions, making predictions, comparing information from several sources). The selections in *Recommended Literature, Kindergarten Through Grade Twelve* illustrate the quality and complexity of the materials to be read by students. In addition to their regular school reading, by grade four, students read one-half million words annually, including a good representation of grade-level-appropriate narrative and expository text (e.g., classic and contemporary literature, magazines, newspapers, online information). In grade two, students continue to make progress toward this goal.

Structural Features of Informational Materials

2.1 Use titles, tables of contents, and chapter headings to locate information in expository text.

Comprehension and Analysis of Grade-Level-Appropriate Text

2.2 State the purpose in reading (i.e., tell what information is sought).

2.3 Use knowledge of the author's purpose(s) to comprehend informational text.

2.4 Ask clarifying questions about essential textual elements of exposition (e.g., *why, what if, how).*

2.5 Restate facts and details in the text to clarify and organize ideas.

2.6 Recognize cause-and-effect relationships in a text.

2.7 Interpret information from diagrams, charts, and graphs.

2.8 Follow two-step written instructions.

3.0. Literary Response and Analysis

Students read and respond to a wide variety of significant works of children's literature. They distinguish between the structural features of the text and the literary terms or elements (e.g., theme, plot, setting, characters). The selections in *Recommended Literature, Kindergarten Through Grade Twelve* illustrate the quality and complexity of the materials to be read by students.

Narrative Analysis of Grade-Level-Appropriate Text

3.1 Compare and contrast plots, settings, and characters presented by different authors.

3.2 Generate alternative endings to plots and identify the reason or reasons for, and the impact of, the alternatives.

3.3 Compare and contrast different versions of the same stories that reflect different cultures.

3.4 Identify the use of rhythm, rhyme, and alliteration in poetry.

Writing

1.0 Writing Strategies

Students write clear and coherent sentences and paragraphs that develop a central idea. Their writing shows they consider the audience and purpose. Students progress through the stages of the writing process (e.g., prewriting, drafting, revising, editing successive versions).

Organization and Focus

1.1 Group related ideas and maintain a consistent focus.

Penmanship

1.2 Create readable documents with legible handwriting.

Research

1.3 Understand the purposes of various reference materials (e.g., dictionary, thesaurus, atlas).

Evaluation and Revision

1.4 Revise original drafts to improve sequence and provide more descriptive detail.

2.0 Writing Applications (Genres and Their Characteristics)

Students write compositions that describe and explain familiar objects, events, and experiences. Student writing demonstrates a command of standard American English and the drafting, research, and organizational strategies outlined in Writing Standard 1.0.

Using the writing strategies of grade two outlined in Writing Standard 1.0, students:

2.1 Write brief narratives based on their experiences:

- **a.** Move through a logical sequence of events.
- **b.** Describe the setting, characters, objects, and events in detail.

2.2 Write a friendly letter complete with the date, salutation, body, closing, and signature.

Written and Oral English Language Conventions

The standards for written and oral English language conventions have been placed between those for writing and for listening and speaking because these conventions are essential to both sets of skills.

1.0 Written and Oral English Language Conventions

Students write and speak with a command of standard English conventions appropriate to this grade level.

Sentence Structure

1.1 Distinguish between complete and incomplete sentences.

1.2 Recognize and use the correct word order in written sentences.

Grammar

1.3 Identify and correctly use various parts of speech, including nouns and verbs, in writing and speaking.

Punctuation

1.4 Use commas in the greeting and closure of a letter and with dates and items in a series.

1.5 Use quotation marks correctly.

Capitalization

1.6 Capitalize all proper nouns, words at the beginning of sentences and greetings, months and days of the week, and titles and initials of people.

Spelling

1.7 Spell frequently used, irregular words correctly (e.g., *was, were, says, said, who, what, why).*

1.8 Spell basic short-vowel, long-vowel, *r*- controlled, and consonant-blend patterns correctly.

Listening and Speaking

1.0 Listening and Speaking Strategies

Students listen critically and respond appropriately to oral communication. They speak in a manner that guides the listener to understand important ideas by using proper phrasing, pitch, and modulation.

Comprehension

1.1 Determine the purpose or purposes of listening (e.g., to obtain information, to solve problems, for enjoyment).

1.2 Ask for clarification and explanation of stories and ideas.

1.3 Paraphrase information that has been shared orally by others.

1.4 Give and follow three- and four-step oral directions.

Organization and Delivery of Oral Communication

1.5 Organize presentations to maintain a clear focus.

1.6 Speak clearly and at an appropriate pace for the type of communication (e.g., informal discussion, report to class).

1.7 Recount experiences in a logical sequence.

1.8 Retell stories, including characters, setting, and plot.

1.9 Report on a topic with supportive facts and details.

2.0 Speaking Applications (Genres and Their Characteristics)

Students deliver brief recitations and oral presentations about familiar experiences or interests that are organized around a coherent thesis statement. Student speaking demonstrates a command of standard American English and the organizational and delivery strategies outlined in Listening and Speaking Standard 1.0.

Using the speaking strategies of grade two outlined in Listening and Speaking Standard 1.0, students:

2.1 Recount experiences or present stories:

- **a.** Move through a logical sequence of events.
- **b.** Describe story elements (e.g., characters, plot, setting).

2.2 Report on a topic with facts and details, drawing from several sources of information.

Acknowledgments

Text

Page 48: "The 1st Day of School" and "The 179th Day of School" from *Lunch Box Mail and Other Poems* by Jenny Whitehead. © 2001 by Jenny Whitehead. Reprinted by permission of Henry Holt and Company, LLC.

Page 58: From *Exploring Space with an Astronaut* by Patricia J. Murphy. Copyright © 2004 by Enslow Publishers, Inc. Published by Enslow Publishers, Inc., Berkeley Heights, NJ. All rights reserved.

Page 82: From *Henry and Mudge and the Starry Night* by Cynthia Rylant, illustrated by Sucie Stevenson. Text copyright © 1998 by Cynthia Rylant, Illustrations copyright © 1998 by Sucie Stevenson. Reprinted with permission of Simon & Schuster Books for Young Readers, an Imprint of Simon & Schuster Children's Publishing Division. All rights reserved.

Page 100: From *Geogra-Fleas! Riddles All Over the Map* by Joan Holub. Copyright © 2004 by Joan Holub. Used by permission of Albert Whitman & Company.

Page 136: "The Strongest One," from *Pushing Up the Sky* by Joseph Bruchac, copyright © 2000 by Joseph Bruchac, text. Used by permission of Dial Books for Young Readers, A Division of Penguin Young Readers Group, A Member of Penguin Group (USA) Inc., 345 Hudson Street, New York, NY 10014. All rights reserved.

Page 168: From *Tara and Tiree, Fearless Friends: A True Story* by Andrew Clements. Text copyright © 2002 by Andrew Clements. Reprinted with permission of Aladdin Paperbacks, an Imprint of Simon & Schuster Children's Publishing Division. All rights reserved.

Page 222: *Scarcity* by Janeen R. Adil, copyright © 2006 by Capstone Press. All rights reserved. Used by permission.

Page 248: From *Easy-to-Read Folk and Fairy Tale Plays* by Carol Pugliano. Scholastic Inc./Teaching Resources. Copyright © 1997 by Carol Pugliano. Reprinted by permission.

Page 278: From *Silly & Sillier: Read-Aloud Rhymes from Around the World* by Judy Sierra and illus. by Valeri Gorbachev, copyright © 2002 by Judy Sierra. Illustrations copyright © 2002 by Valerie Gorbachev. Used by permission of Alfred A. Knopf, an imprint of Random House Children's Books, a division of Random House, Inc.

Page 308: *Pearl and Wagner, Two Good Friends* by Kate McMullan, Illustrations by R.W. Alley, copyright © 2003 by Kate McMullan, text. Used by permission of Dial Books for Young Readers, A Division of Penguin Young Readers Group, A Member of Penguin Group (USA) Inc., 345 Hudson Street, New York, NY 10014. All rights reserved.

Page 328: "Robots at Home" from *Robots* by Clive Gifford. Copyright © Kingfisher Publications Plc 2003. Reproduced by permission of Kingfisher Publications Plc, an imprint of Houghton Mifflin Company. All rights reserved.

Page 336: From *Dear Juno* by Soyung Pak, text copyright © 1999 by Soyung Pak, illustrations copyright © 1999 by Susan Kathleen Hartung. Used by permission of Viking Children's Books, a division of Penguin Young Readers Group, a member of Penguin Group (USA) Inc., 345 Hudson Street, New York, NY 10014 and Dystel & Goderich Literary Management, Inc. All rights reserved.

Page 356: From *Saying It Without Words: Signs and Symbols* by Arnulf K. & Louise A. Esterer, 1980. Reprinted by permission of Pearson Education.

Page 364: *Anansi Goes Fishing.* Text copyright © 1992 by Eric A. Kimmel. Illustrations copyright © 1992 by Janet Stevens. All rights reserved. Reprinted by permission of Holiday House, Inc.

Page 386: "Do Spiders Stick to Their Own Webs?", from *Where Fish Go in Winter and Other Great Mysteries* by Amy Goldman Koss, copyright © 1987 by Amy Goldman Koss. Used by permission of Dial Books for Young Readers, A Division of Penguin Young Readers Group, A Member of Penguin Group (USA) Inc., 345 Hudson Street, New York, NY 10014. All rights reserved.

Page 394: *Rosa and Blanca* by Joe Hayes, illustrated by José Ortega, 1993. Reprinted by permission of Joe Hayes.

Page 408: *The Crow and the Pitcher* retold by Eric Blair. Copyright © 2004 by Compass Point Books. Used by permission of Picture Window Books. All rights reserved.

Page 418: From *A Weed Is a Flower* by Aliki. Text copyright © 1965, 1988 by Aliki Brandenberg. Reprinted with permission of Simon & Schuster Books For Young Readers, an Imprint of Simon & Schuster Children's Publishing Division. All rights reserved.

Page 442: "Products Made from Corn" from Ohio Corn Marketing Program Web site, www.ohiocorn.org. Reprinted by permission of Ohio Corn Marketing Program.

Illustrations

Cover: Scott Gustafson: PI1-PI13 Robert Neubecker

26-50 Jana Christy

48 Linda Bronson

100-103 Robert McClurkan

108-122 Paule Trudel

136-157 David Diaz

157 Derek Grinnell

196-208 Stephen Costanza

215 Wilson Ong

248, 253-265 Jon Goodell

276-292 Will Terry

296-299 Dan Andreasen

408-411 Laura Ovresat

W2-W15 Alessia Girasole

Photographs

Every effort has been made to secure permission and provide appropriate credit for photographic material. The publisher deeply regrets any omission and pledges to correct errors called to its attention in subsequent editions.

Unless otherwise acknowledged, all photographs are the property of Scott Foresman, a division of Pearson Education.

Photo locators denoted as follows: Top (T), Center (C), Bottom (B), Left (L), Right (R), Background (Bkgd).

24 (C) ©Powered by Light/Alan Spencer/Alamy Images, (BR) ©Tom & Dee Ann McCarthy/Corbis

25 ©Patrik Giardino/Corbis

45 Getty Images

52 (CL) ©Shilo Sports/Getty Images, (BR) ©George Hall/Corbis, (Bkgd) ©Royalty-Free/Corbis

53 (TR) ©Museum of Flight/Corbis, (BR) NASA

54 Corbis
55 (TR, CR) NASA, (B) Getty Images
56 (Bkgd, T, C) Getty Images, (BR) ©Royalty-Free/Corbis
57 NASA
58 NASA
59 (T, B) NASA
60 (L, BR) NASA
61 (TC, BR) NASA
62 ©NASA/Roger Ressmeyer/Corbis
63 NASA
64 (TR, Bkgd) NASA
66 (C, T) NASA
67 (CR, B) NASA
68 NASA
70 Getty Images
72 Getty Images
73 (T) Corbis, (CR, C) ©Richard T. Nowitz/Corbis, (BR) ©Joseph Sohm/ChromoSohm Inc./Corbis
74 (B, BR) ©Richard T. Nowitz/Corbis
75 (TR) ©Franz-Marc Frei/Corbis, (BR) ©Richard T. Nowitz/Corbis
76 NASA
77 ©Richard T. Nowitz/Corbis
78 ©Jim Ballard/Getty Images
79 (CL) ©Joe McDonald/Corbis, (CR) ©Nigel J. Dennis/Gallo Images/Corbis, (T) ©Michael & Patricia Fogden/Corbis
106 ©John Crum/Alamy Images
107 (C) ©Blend Images/Jupiter Images, (T) ©Tom Stewart/Corbis
129 ©Paul Souders/Corbis
132 ©Frans Lanting/Corbis
133 ©Martin Harvey/Peter Arnold, Inc.
156 ©Tom Brakefield/Corbis
157 ©Tom Brakefield/Corbis
158 (T) ©Roland Seitre/Peter Arnold, Inc., (Bkgd) ©Theo Allofs/Corbis, (B) ©John H. Hoffman/Bruce Coleman Inc.
164 (T) ©AFP/Getty Images, (B, Bkgd) Getty Images
165 ©Brand X Pictures/Getty Images
186 ©Tim Davis/Corbis
187 ©Bob Winsett/Index Stock Imagery, (TL) ©Andrea Comas/Corbis, ©Gambarini Mauricio/dpa/Corbis, (BL) ©Tom Nebbia/Corbis
188 (Bkgd) ©Owen Franken/Corbis, (TR) ©Vaughn Youtz/Corbis, (CR) ©Armando Arorizo/Corbis, (CL) ©Shamil Zhumatov/Corbis
189 (TL) ©Kai Pfaffenbach/Corbis, (BR) ©Ralf-Finn Hestoft/Corbis
192 ©Bernard Annebicque/Sygma/Corbis, (Bkgd) Getty Images
193 (T) ©LWA-Sharie Kennedy/Corbis, (C) ©Jennifer Brown/Star Ledger/Corbis
208 Corbis
209 (C) Corbis, (BR) ©Bettmann/Corbis
218 (CL) ©James Leynse/Corbis, (BR) ©Holger Winkler/zefa/Corbis
219 (BR) ©Owen Franken/Corbis, (C) ©Sally and Richard Greenhill/Alamy Images
220 ©Wayne Eastep/Getty Images
222 ©Chris Livingston/Getty Images
224 Jupiter Images
225 Corbis
226 ©Wayne Eastep/Getty Images
227 ©Bill Bachman/Alamy Images
229 ©David R. Frazier Photolibrary, Inc./Alamy Images
230 ©Phil Klein/Corbis
231 ©Tom McCarthy/Unicorn Stock Photos
234 ©Owen Franken/Corbis
239 (L) Index Open, (R) ©Michael Newman/PhotoEdit
240 (L) ©VStock/Index Open, (R) ©Jonathan Nourok/PhotoEdit
241 ©Felicia Martinez/PhotoEdit
243 ©David R. Frazier Photolibrary, Inc./Alamy Images
244 ©Ariel Skelley/Corbis
245 (C) ©Michael Pole/Corbis, (T) ©Paul Harris/Getty Images
268 (BR) ©Eric and David Hosking/Corbis, (B) ©Ariadne Van Zandbergen/Lonely Planet Images
269 (CL) ©Lester Lefkowitz/Getty Images, (TR) Cliff Beittel, (B) ©Peter Cade/Getty Images
270 (T) ©Ian Beames/Ardea, (B) ©Winifred Wisniewski/Frank Lane Picture Agency/Corbis, (Inset) ©Nigel J. Dennis/Gallo Images/Corbis
271 ©Darryl Torckler/Getty Images
274 (Bkgd) Getty Images, (C) ©David Katzenstein/Corbis
275 (L) Corbis, (TR) ©Design Pics Inc./Alamy
305 (T) ©Jim Cummins/Getty Images, (C) ©Mike Timo/Getty Images
306 ©imagebroker/Alamy
328 (TR) ©Koichi Kamoshida/Getty Images, (BL) ©Roger Ressmeyer/Corbis
329 ©NEC Corporation
332 (TR) ©Kitt Cooper-Smith/Alamy Images, (Bkgd) Getty Images
333 ©PhotoAlto/Getty Images
356 (BCR, BR, CR) Getty Images
357 (C) ©Ryan McVay/Getty Images, (BL, TC, TR, CC) ©Royalty-Free/Corbis, (CR) Getty Images
360 ©Masterfile Royalty-Free
361 ©Karl Ammann/Nature Picture Library, ©Robert Sabin/Animals Animals/Earth Scenes
384 ©Davies & Starr/Getty Images
386 (BL) ©PBNJ Productions/Corbis, (BL) Getty Images
387 ©Mark E. Gibson/Corbis
390 (CL) ©Royalty-Free/Corbis, (Bkgd) ©Jim Cummins/Corbis
391 ©Tom Stewart/Corbis
414 (L) ©Peter Beck/Corbis, (R) ©Royalty-Free/Corbis, (Bkgd) Getty Images
415 ©George Disario/Corbis
444 (C, B) Corbis
445 (BR, TR, BL, CR) Getty Images
448 Corbis
450 ©Jim Winkley/Corbis
451 Getty Images
453 (BR) ©Haruyoshi Yamaguchi/Corbis, (TL) Getty Images
454 ©Royalty-Free/Corbis
455 Getty Images

Reading
STREET